Jesus Crucified and Risen

Essays in Spirituality and Theology

IN HONOR OF
DOM SEBASTIAN MOORE

— *Edited by* —
William P. Loewe
Vernon J. Gregson

A Michael Glazier Book
THE LITURGICAL PRESS
Collegeville, Minnesota

The editors of this volume are grateful to *HORIZONS: The Journal of the College Theology Society,* Villanova University, Villanova, Pennsylvania 19085 for permission to reprint Stephen Duffy's essay entitled "Review Symposium: Sebastian Moore's *Jesus the Liberator of Desire"* (*HORIZONS* 18 [Spring 1991]).

The editors are grateful to the College Theology Society, The Catholic University of America, and Loyola University of the South for financial assistance provided for the publication of this book.

A Michael Glazier Book published by The Liturgical Press

Cover design by David Manahan, O.S.B. Michelangelo, The Risen Christ, 1519–20, Rome, S. M. Sopra Minerva.

1   2   3   4   5   6   7   8

Library of Congress Cataloging-in-Publication Data

Jesus crucified and risen : essays in spirituality and theology in
   honor of Dom Sebastian Moore / edited by William P. Loewe, Vernon J.
   Gregson.
         p.   cm.
      "A Michael Glazier book."
      Includes bibliographical references.
      ISBN 0-8146-5850-4 (alk. paper)
      1. Catholic Church—Doctrines. 2. Spirituality—Catholic Church.
   3. Jesus Christ Person and offices. 4. Moore, Sebastian, 1917– .
   I. Moore, Sebastian, 1917– . II. Loewe, William P., 1941– .
   III. Gregson, Vernon.
   BX1751.2.J47   1998   97-34265
   230'.2—dc21   CIP

Contents

By Way of Introduction: Sebastian Moore, Anselm, and Friends

William P. Loewe

Come now, little man,
turn aside awhile from your daily employment,
escape for a moment from the tumult of your thoughts.
Put aside your weighty cares,
let your burdensome distractions wait,
free yourself awhile for God
and rest awhile in him.
Enter the inner chamber of your soul,
shut out everything except God
and that which can help you in seeking him,
and when you have shut the door, seek him.
Now, my whole heart, say to God,
"I seek your face,
Lord it is your face I seek."[1]

Anselm, monk of Bec and later archbishop of Canterbury, penned these words around the year 1077. Almost a millennium separates Anselm from another Benedictine, Sebastian Moore, the monk of Downside, England, whom these essays honor. Yet Anselm's words evoke the heart of an unbroken tradition of contemplative prayer that binds the two monks as brothers. In addition, I would suggest, several features of Anselm's writings link him and Moore in more particular fashion.

---

[1]Anselm of Canterbury, *Proslogion* 1. 1–14, ET in B. Ward, trans., *The Prayers and Meditations of Saint Anselm* (New York: Penguin, 1973) 239.

First, within the history of Christian spirituality, Anselm is credited with inaugurating a form of prayer in which individual self-awareness came to expression in a manner hitherto unknown.[2] Prior to his day the prevailing prayer forms, dating to the Carolingian era, served as sober, laconic, and anonymous supplements to the Psalter. Anselm, however, deliberately circulated the prayers he composed under his own name, and by their length, effusiveness, and focus on the self, his prayers announce an age newly conscious of the individual.[3]

Second, Anselm's prayer gave rise quite directly to his theological reflection and in at least two ways forms a unity with it. The text we have cited opens Anselm's *Proslogion,* the work whose so-called ontological argument for the existence of God has fascinated philosophers and theologians ever since. The opening chapters of the *Proslogion* exemplify clearly, even dramatically, how theology emerges from lived piety. These pages begin with Anselm's fervent quest for the experience of union with God. Soon, however, they register a shift. First gradually, and then torrentially, prayerful recollection cedes to a different dynamic that moves Anselm out of prayer and into a quite distinct pattern of consciousness. Instead of abiding quietly in God, Anselm gives himself up to his intellect's restless desire to understand how it is that what he believes about the God whose face he seeks is true.[4] As Anselm's prayer thus gives rise to inquiry, the *Proslogion* displays the genesis of theology as lived faith seeking the intelligibility of its praxis.

Anselm was explicit on why theology must accord priority to faith. As he put it, "he who does not believe will not understand. For he who does not believe will not experience, and he who has not had experience will not know."[5] Belief opens up the world of experience within which insight into what is believed can arise. The quest for that experience moves many of Anselm's prayers in a direction opposite that of the *Proslogion.* In his prayers of this other sort, Anselm seeks in solitary meditation the grace to feel what by faith he knows to be true.[6] When that grace is granted, prayers

---

[2]Richard W. Southern, *Saint Anselm: Portrait in a Landscape* (New York: Cambridge University Press, 1990) 93ff.

[3]See Colin Morris, *The Discovery of the Individual 1050–1200* (London: SPCK, 1972) 29 and passim.

[4]Anselm, *Proslogion,* 2.

[5]*Epistola de Incarnatione Verbi,* ET in J. Hopkins and H. W. Richardson, eds., *Trinity, Incarnation, and Redemption: Theological Treatises* (New York: Harper Torchbooks, 1970) 10.

[6]See, for example, the *Meditation on Human Redemption:* "Lord, let me taste by love what I taste by knowledge." Ward, *Prayers,* 237.

of this type open a space in which faith's affirmations penetrate the imagination and shape one's affective life. Prayer then wins for Anselm the elements of experience from which theological understanding of the beliefs entertained by faith can emerge.

Third, among his theological works Anselm is best remembered for his *Cur Deus Homo,* epoch-making in the history of the theology of the atonement. So long a shadow did this work cast that nineteenth century pioneers in the history of doctrine were wont to identify it as the beginning of soteriology proper. To the liberal Protestant eyes of historians like Albrecht Ritschl and Adolf von Harnack, the millennium that preceded Anselm offered little more by way of soteriological reflection than primitive myth somewhat tutored by Hellenistic naturalism. So overstated a judgment called forth the corrective proffered in the next generation by Gustaf Aulén's *Christus Victor,* but it had a point that Aulén also recognized. Both Aulén and those he sought to correct recognized in Anselm the beginning of a new kind of mediation of the soteriological theme, the emergence of theory as a distinct mode of theology.

Of course, they also shared a quite negative view of Anselm's innovating achievement. Harnack found the substance of Anselm's satisfaction theory immoral and irreligious,[7] while Aulén took a dim view of any theory at all.[8] Yet neither of them can claim the last word. On methodological grounds, *pace* Aulén, one might wish to argue that Anselm's turn was a positive move, a turn towards the clarity and coherence of meaning[9] with which theory can discipline and enrich symbol and myth without, of course, ever displacing them or pretending to substitute for them. As for the substance of his theory, one might contend, as has Gisbert Greshake, that Anselm's satisfaction theory represents a successful transposition of the biblical theme of covenant into a medieval feudal context.[10]

In each of these respects, namely, as standing at the threshold of a new epoch in spirituality, as pursuing a theology differentiated from and yet

---

[7]A. von Harnack, *History of Dogma,* trans. N. Buchanan (New York: Dover, 1961) VI, 70–1.

[8]G. Aulén, *Christus Victor: An Historical Study of the Three Main Types of the Idea of Atonement,* trans. A. G. Hebert (New York: Macmillan, 1963).

[9]René Roques grasps this point precisely when he writes of Anselm, "Son propos est de faire autre chose que de répéter les Pères et l'Ecriture. Son exposé doit et veut répondre à d'autres besoins: des besoins d'intelligibilité." Anselme de Canterbéry, *Pourquoi Dieu S'Est Fait Homme,* Sources chrétiennes no. 91, Ed. René Roques (Paris: Les Editions du Cerf, 1963) 99.

[10]G. Greshake, "Erlösung und Freiheit. Zur Neuinterpretation der Erlösungslehre Anselms von Canterbury," *Theologische Quartalschrift* 153 (1973) 323–45.

wholly integrated with contemplative praxis, and as pursuing the theological intelligibility of Christ's cross in a culture requiring a new kind of mediation of that intelligibility, Sebastian Moore resembles his Benedictine forbear. Yet each point of similarity, because it involves an element of novelty, constitutes at the same time a measure of the difference between the two.

First, if Anselm's prayers marked an eruption of self-awareness in Christian spirituality, Moore, as we shall see, raises that self-awareness to a new art, joining with Bernard Lonergan to formalize its methodological significance. At the same time, however, Moore and his generation have witnessed—and facilitated—a massive relocation, as it were, of the practice of spirituality. It was self-evident to Anselm and, within the Catholic tradition, it remained so until quite recently, that the salvation of one's soul was pursued most securely within the cloister. Spirituality was associated chiefly with "religious life." Only very recently has this restrictive view begun yielding to the dynamics of the scriptural and liturgical renewal in Catholicism over which Moore's generation has presided.

This development among Catholics is part of a larger picture. Among Protestant Christians a classic mistrust of "mysticism" has been yielding to interest in fostering the interior life, again sometimes in tandem with an ecumenically informed liturgical renewal movement; emblematic of the latter is the work of the North American Academy of Liturgy. On a broader front, "New Age" practices, with all the ambiguity of their relation to the consumer societies in which they take rise, exercise broad appeal among both churched and unchurched people of the West. In a global context, participants in dialogue among the world religions are finding in spirituality a concrete and practical starting point for their shared journeys of exploration. Finally, the socially as well as individually transformative character of authentic spirituality comes to the fore in such expressions as the burgeoning ecological movement and the *communidades de base* of Latin America.

All this ferment signals the emergence of spiritualities that can be non-elitist and ecumenical. Such spiritualities show promise of unifying contemplation with action at the macro-level of responsibility demanded by historical consciousness. At the same time they foster the recovery, now in a differentiated manner, of the chthonic and cosmological values suppressed with modernity's anthropocentric turn.

Like spirituality, theology, too, is undergoing an axial shift. Anselm initiated a move to complement myth and symbol with a systematically coherent mediation of their cognitive dimension. That move culminated in the metaphysically-based *Summae* of the following century. As Bernard Lonergan has argued, however, theory of that sort is no longer adequate.

Founded on a paradigm of knowledge *(scientia)* as the grasp of the necessary causes of fixed truths, classical and medieval theory proves inadequate
in a culture whose science, having become empirical, embraces both classical law and statistical probability in its quest for the intelligibility of a
contingent universe still in process.[11] That same culture has become historically and globally conscious, aware on the one hand of the relative,
conditioned character of every concrete expression of meaning and value
and, on the other, of the need to assume responsibility for the course of the
history we make. In the face of these developments, the medieval achievement, for all its richness, proves obsolete.

Hence, Lonergan suggests, theology must advance to a new stage of
meaning. Theology can no longer seek its foundations in authoritative doctrines, analogous to the allegedly self-evident first principles that grounded
an objectivist metaphysics from which theology drew its systematic component. Both the meaning of those doctrines and their relationship to their
sources in Scripture and history have become not a given but a challenge
and a task. To face that challenge and perform that task, theology at this
new stage will require that one appropriate the world of human interiority, discovering there, within oneself, the dynamic sources of intelligibility,
truth, goodness, and religious love, and the immanent norms those sources
carry with them. Such a development will empower theologians to negotiate the cognitive, moral, and religious crises generated by modernity in a
way that no effort to merely repristinate the medieval synthesis can.

This transposition to what Lonergan terms a third stage of meaning,
beyond both common sense and theory, sets the context for Moore's remarkable work in soteriology over the past few decades.[12] Paradoxically,
however, the nature of this transposition at the same time highlights the
significance of the continuities that obtain between Moore and Anselm regarding the relationships of prayer to theology. As with Anselm, it is the
quest for God animating Moore's prayer that drives Moore into a process
of theological inquiry, and that process heads back to prayer as the testing-
ground for discerning the value of its results. On this score Moore strikes
one as a veritable walking contemplative laboratory. While his deep prayer
and intense, restless reflection flow in and out of one another unceasingly,

---

[11]B. Lonergan, "Revolution in Catholic Theology," *A Second Collection* (Philadelphia:
Westminster Press, 1974) 231–8.

[12]For a survey of Moore's works, see J. Daurio, "Toward a Theology of Desire: The
Existential Hermeneutic in the Soteriology of Sebastian Moore," *Downside Review* 106
(1988) 195–232.

he is eager to share the process with disarming directness, great wit, and not even a hint of the self-important posturing of many these days who hang out their shingle as experts in things spiritual.

Furthermore, if Anselm's theological achievement was to suggest a theory of redemption that was to hold the field for a millennium, Moore acknowledges, as Louis Roy reminds us in his contribution to this volume, that his own prayer and thought find their center in the spear-pierced heart of Christ crucified. From that center Moore, like Anselm, seeks the healing and creative unity of thought with feeling that the religiously transformed imagination brings about. Both these points of continuity cohere with Lonergan's insistence that at the third stage of meaning, theology's actual foundations consist, non-foundationalistically, in the intellectual, moral, and religious authenticity of the theologian.

One final point of continuity between the two Benedictines suggests itself. Anselm's contemporary and biographer, the monk Eadmer, records the eagerness with which Anselm pursued opportunities for conversation, and Anselm's numerous letters attest to the high value he placed on friendship. Sebastian Moore's robust and zestful approach to a life now in its eighth decade, his ever-youthful eagerness to share his constantly advancing questions and insights, and the ultimate simplicity of a man of polished wit and uncommonly urbane sophistication have been a gift to many. The essays that follow gather the efforts of but a small number of Sebastian Moore's friends to express their appreciation and gratitude for this monk, poet, and spiritual theologian.

Nicholas Lash honors his uncle Sebastian Moore with an art-historical detective story, "Sebastiano in Pallara, A Pilgrim's Tale." Like Moore, St. Thomas Aquinas held that it was through their awakened hearts that the disciples first saw the risen Christ, and on a recent visit to Notre Dame de Chartres Lash found the power of that kind of seeing shining forth from the Mauclerc window in the south transept. The window also poses a puzzle: what is the provenance of its image of the evangelists as pygmies seated on the shoulders of the much larger prophets? Lash's sleuthing points toward John of Salisbury, bishop of Chartres a generation before the window was finished. This John, an Englishman, was familiar with the proverb about dwarves on the shoulders of giants, and his visits to Rome likely acquainted him as well with a frieze in the church of San Sebastiano which seats the evangelists atop the prophets' shoulders.

Four contributors focus directly on Moore's work. In his boldly entitled brief reflections on "Torment as Method," David Burrell points out that whether we advert to it or not, as a matter of fact we all live our lives within a tangled thicket of conflicted emotions and desires. It is at this level that doctrines, as the expression of the meanings and values that inform a way of living as Christian, become practical and effective. Burrell finds this grasp of the practical, transformative character of doctrine operative in Moore's self-probing explorations of how contemplative encounter with the crucified and risen Jesus heals and liberates precisely at the oft-tortured level of our ambiguous, conflictive experience. To fellow teachers Burrell then offers the outline of a course in which strategic readings in figures like Ernest Becker, Freud, and Kierkegaard prepare students for the soteriology of Moore's *The Crucified Jesus Is No Stranger.*

The late Illtyd Trethowan similarly highlights Moore's characteristic emphasis on the experiential component of Christian belief. "A Christian Personalist" was the last piece in Trethowan's long and distinguished career. In it Trethowan, like Moore a monk of Downside, chose to honor his confrere with a *lectio* of an article that Moore had published in 1977 in his order's journal, the *Downside Review.* Trethowan finds it especially noteworthy that Moore, when he seeks to articulate principles for a contemporary theism, turns to the mystics and their non-conceptual awareness of God as the indispensable starting point from which to advance his project.

Stephen J. Duffy's "Ego Transcendence and Transformation: The Soteriology of Sebastian Moore" offers a substantive exposition and critique of Moore's psychological appropriation of Christian soteriology as Moore had worked it out in various publications that appeared between 1977 and 1990, notably in the series of five books from *The Crucified Jesus Is No Stranger* through *Jesus the Liberator of Desire.* Lauding both the self-appropriation on which Moore's project rests and the finesse with which he draws upon the explanatory power of contemporary psychologists to illumine the dynamics of sin and conversion, Duffy judges Moore's transposition of the intelligibility of Christian soteriology from the mode of classical theory to the realm of interiority a success. This judgment is not, however, uncritical, for Duffy also joins those who challenge Moore's claim to anchor his soteriology in a historical reconstruction of the paschal experience of Jesus' disciples.

Louis Roy offers his article on "Human Desire and Easter Faith" in defense of Moore's metapsychological theology on precisely this point. Roy begins with an explanation of how Moore appeals to psychology, epistemology, and mysticism in his account of how Easter faith first emerged. In a second step he replies to Moore's critics, including Duffy, Elisabeth Koenig, and the present writer, charging that when they fault Moore's reconstruction of the disciples' experience for exceeding what the exegetically retrieved historical data can warrant, they neglect the transcultural universality of human interiority as Moore analyzes it, and thus confuse one functional specialty, foundations, with another, history.

Joseph Flanagan offers a fuller account of the background for Roy's claim with an essay on "Transcultural Knowers and Lovers." Flanagan, now retired from a career in philosophy at Boston College, was in his student days the first to write a dissertation on Bernard Lonergan. His present piece focuses on the chapter on ethics in Lonergan's *Insight*. Flanagan offers a summary of the seventeen chapters of the book that precede it and discusses the transformation that Lonergan's thought subsequently underwent. He concludes with an example of how Lonergan's transformed ethics might function in a critique of the turn United States culture took when, in place of the sovereignty of the people, there emerged that of the individual, isolated self.

Broadening the scope of that critique, Glenn Hughes's "Reflections on the Terror of History" enlists E. Voegelin's assistance in sketching the impoverished and distorted manner in which, with modern Western culture, historical consciousness emerged from the previous cosmocentric stage of culture. Absent belief in transcendent reality, postmodernism now divinizes contingency, experience is left meaningless, and narcotics of one sort or another provide coping mechanisms in a cultural void. Traditional myth and symbol may have lost their efficacy, and yet, Hughes urges, only openness to the mystery of transcendence can render history an adventure rather than a nightmare.

In a similar vein Matthew Lamb argues that, while modern theories of space and time have played a role in the drift toward nihilism that Hughes limns, these theories are not only pernicious for Christian belief but also now outdated and inadequate to contemporary scientific cosmology. On Lamb's dialectical analysis, Newton, Descartes, and Leibniz all split time from space, absolutized the latter, and fragmented the former into a series of discrete, evanescent moments. Thus they set the stage for Spinoza's progeny of positivistically conceived modern historical critical method. Still accepting the space-time split, Hegel gave time priority over space, but on his view history became a totality inexorably dominated by the bloody logic of progress. If these developments truncate the experience of history and lead into nihilism, none of them coheres with the intelligible, if not imaginable, construct of the universe as a four dimensional unity issuing from contemporary science. Lamb suggests that the latter view allows the recovery of a fuller, premodern sense of time as a concrete totality in which the past retains its voice, and it also opens onto the classic understanding of divine eternity as the simultaneity of all creation to God's presence.

Concretely, the major bearer of transcendent meaning in Western culture has been the Christian Church. That same Church presents a thoroughly ambiguous phenomenon. Drawing upon interiority analysis of the sort sketched out in Joseph Flanagan's essay, Vernon Gregson seeks to articulate the questions, posed by the structure of our being human, to which church is the answer. By thus identifying the needs and desires of our interiority, he suggests criteria for locating where the authentic church, a church that calls together those who long for union with God, that heals our biases and releases human creativity, is to be found.

In a similar vein Carla Mae Streeter sets out from Moore's grounding of spirituality in interiority to reconstrue the categories of incarnateness, sacramentality, and expressed communality as dimensions of a spirituality capable of healing what is psychically distorted and self-isolating in the human condition. When reconstructed on a general anthropological basis, these categories transcend their original confessional context and suggest ecumenical points of contact between Christian spirituality and other traditions.

Two contributors put these methodological and heuristic considerations to work in the concrete, one focusing on a figure of the past and the other on the present. Elisabeth Koenig's "Surviving Slander With Richard Rolle" turns to the fourteenth century English mystic for insight into the dynamics of psychic healing. She follows up on a hunch, occasioned by psychological systems theory, that mystics' concern with purgation relates to the role assigned them by negative transference. Koenig finds that Rolle's consistent "sitting" in prayer led him to an emotional differentiation that, while attracting the *ressentiment* of others, at the same time freed him from its operation within himself. In tandem with that liberation, this odd and cantankerous man's relations with women underwent a notable shift away from the initial misogynism so amply documented in his writings.

No less marginal and liable to negative psychic projection than Rolle in his day are today's homosexual communities. Three years of involvement with such a community in Toronto inform Robert Doran's "AIDS Ministry as a Praxis of Hope." Starting off by reflecting on Jesus' bodily resurrection in light of Rosemary Haughton's and Sebastian Moore's insights into the sanctity of embodied love, Doran critiques the Church's official pastoral response to homosexuals as erroneous and violent. In his own ministry he encountered a community replete with fidelity, tenderness, holiness, and heroic charity amidst enormous loss and grief. Doran invites us to reverence in this community the grace of the risen Christ outpoured, a grace by which human bodies are lifted up as bearers of love both human and divine, a grace of unconditional love that evokes its like.

Such grace is of necessity cruciform, as David Tracy reminds us in his tribute to Sebastian Moore, an essay on "The Gospels as Revelation and Transformation." For all their differences, Tracy suggests that Christians nonetheless share a common belief *in* Jesus *with* the apostles. This leads to a construal of revelation: In the witness of their written Scripture, Christians encounter Jesus as the Word of God's self-manifestation, a Word of both disclosive Logos and irruptive Kerygma. Furthermore, that witness took shape first of all in the passion narratives, and it is they, Tracy urges, that lend specificity to revelation as Christian, for in them is expressed why and how Christians perceive God's Christ to be none other than Jesus. That acknowledgment requires first of all the realist, history-like texture of the Lucan narrative, but the dialectic of Word as manifestation and disruption needs the completion of the Marcan, Matthean, Johannine, and Pauline versions as well. In all of this, Tracy argues, contemporary hermeneutics and especially work in narrative vastly enriches the endeavor of Christian theology.

From Moore's own work-in-process we include a piece at once earthy and contemplative entitled "The Bedded Axle-Tree." Drawing on T. S. Eliot and Thomas Mann as witnesses to an alienated condition of men's sexuality which, Moore surmises, underlies patterns of male domination, he finds in some recent books of Jungians Eugene Monick and James Wyly a promising explanatory hypothesis for the origins of the problem in the early dynamics between sons and mother. If males compensate for the natural inferiority of their childhood by cultural domination, Moore finds this pattern rampant among celibate priests and operative in distorted forms of devotion to the Virgin Birth; hence the raw anguish he personally experienced in encountering Stephen Mitchell's proposal that historically, Mary was simply an unwed mother. Male sexuality needs to be healed by a sense of oneself as gift, a transforming grace that, Moore shows, flows from encounter with the crucified and risen Jesus.

The volume closes with a select bibliography of Sebastian Moore's writings, and thanks must be proffered to Frederick Crowe, S.J., and Robert Doran, S.J., both of the Lonergan Research Institute in Toronto, for their assistance in preparing it.

Sebastiano in Pallara:
A Pilgrim's Tale

Nicholas Lash

It is not reason that is against us, but imagination.[1]

Pilgrimage

Many roads meet at places of pilgrimage. People come from different directions, with different agendas, different dreams, different histories. And, therefore, however familiar the places that they come to, however much-visited, well-studied, and researched, not only does each traveler find something fresh there but, in their quest and their discovery, each contributes to the wealth that others, after them, will quarry.

Like all holy places, places of pilgrimage are microcosmic. What is to be found there is not less than everything: ourselves, our heart's rest, home-coming in God. But everything this side of death is found in figure, in symbol, enigmatically, and its construal needs patient, disciplined attentiveness.

---

[1]John Henry Newman, *The Letters and Diaries of John Henry Newman,* Vol. XXX, ed. Charles Stephen Dessain and Thomas Gornall (Oxford: Clarendon Press, 1976) 159. Newman was writing, on 7 December 1882, on the supposed conflict between science and theology, to W. S. Lilly (1840–1919). Lilly, a scholar of Peterhouse, Cambridge, became a Catholic in 1869, and served (from 1862 until 1872) in the Madras Civil Service as also did Sebastian Moore's father, my grandfather, who on 21 November 1897, arrived in Madras to take up the post of Assistant Collector and Magistrate.

This essay is about a window, the south transept window of Notre Dame de Chartres. For Holy Week of 1991, my wife and I made pilgrimage to Chartres. Chartres, to which, outside Jerusalem and Rome, few centers of Christian pilgrimage can stand comparison. Chartres, of which, in his fine study of Charles Peguy (whose poems we took with us at Easter), Alan Ecclestone said: "all human work ends here, so that in time to come men will no doubt do it differently but not better, will speak as clearly in their different tongues, but not say more than this."[2]

Communication

". . . but not say more than this." For nearly half a century, Sebastian Moore has *worked* a language in which to communicate, directly, straight from the heart *and* head, what he once called "the basic grammar of religion, God, you, and your neighbor."[3] I say "communicate," not popularize. Popularization is a notion to be shunned, for it too easily conjures up images of experts dispensing, with benign but condescending smile, rough crumbs from their rich table to the *populus,* the peasants at their door. But (as Sebastian and I have tried, in different ways, to say for years) in the matter of the knowledge of God, there are no experts, no privileged group of people "in the know," no Fellows of the Royal Society.

Popularization is easy; you just leave out the really interesting bits. Communication, on the other hand, the integral and complete utterance of what must be said—the preaching of the gospel—is (of ourselves) impossible; it summons all integrity and craftsmanship to fashion artifacts that echo the logic of God's incarnation; it gives God's bewildering brilliance fresh particular flesh—in just this pattern, these images, these ordered words.

Many roads meet at places of pilgrimage. In trying to "read" this window that I offer as a parable of theology well done, of good communication, I shall approach it from three different directions and with three different companions. First, with the help of St. Thomas Aquinas, I shall ask what it was they saw who saw the risen Christ. The answer that is given in the window to this question opens up a puzzle, a detective story, a search for the relationship between ideas and images or (to be more exact) between the teaching in the schools of Chartres and the frescoes in the apse

[2]Alan Ecclestone, *A Staircase for Silence* (London: Darton, Longman and Todd, 1977) 64.
[3]Sebastian Moore, *No Exit* (London: Darton, Longman and Todd, 1968) 14.

of an ancient church in Rome. Being neither an art historian nor a medievalist nor an expert on Aquinas, I shall unavoidably and unashamedly exhibit the amateurishness that is the condition of us all.

Seeing Is Believing

To preach the gospel is to proclaim Christ's resurrection. The Eastern churches' Easter greeting says it all: "Christ is risen. He is risen indeed." That is all there is to say. It can be said, completely said, in just three words (or even one: on Easter night, the first-sung "Alleluia" says it all). But, in order to help us hear the message and see the point, it also needs continual exposition and elaboration, often at great length and in great detail and in an endless variety of ways. Part of the theologian's duty is to try to spell it out. Karl Barth did this, for instance, in *Church Dogmatics*. But, as he would have been the first to acknowledge, those fat black volumes do "not say more than this": Christ is risen.

Christ is risen. Those who say this bear witness to it. "The Lord has risen indeed, and has appeared to Simon!" Simon, therefore, is an eyewitness, which is just as well because, as everybody knows, there is no testimony to touch that of the eyewitness: seeing is believing (as Thomas the apostle might have said). Luke does not tell us how Simon recognized the risen Lord when he appeared to him. On the other hand, he tells us in great detail how Cleopas and his companion at first were sad and foolish and slow of heart, but then their hearts began to burn as they listened to the Scriptures being interpreted to them, "beginning with Moses and all the prophets," until, at last, at table, with bread blessed and broken and distributed, "their eyes were opened and they recognized him." That makes them eyewitnesses, too, like Simon. The extraordinary thing is that, in the very act of recognition, Jesus disappears: "their eyes were opened and they recognized him; and he vanished out of their sight."[4] Do they, then, no longer see him? Might it not be better to say: they came to see that the understanding at which they arrived along the way, culminating in the breaking of bread, *was* what it now was to "see Jesus"?

I am trying to nudge the notion of "seeing the risen Christ" into the company of such notions as "seeing the point." To some readers this will sound suspiciously "subjective." There is, I fear, no easy exorcism of the unimaginative and destructive dualisms according to which the only options

[4]Luke 24:34, 27, 31.

open to us are either dreaming or gaping, either withdrawal into private fantasy or falling victim to brute fact. Yet, in their waking hours, sane people know that there is a difference between seeing the point and failing to do so, and that, in this difference, objectivity lies. And Christians, though not at all immune from the epistemological diseases plaguing our culture, at least have excellent medicine to hand in the endless subtlety and care with which the evangelists weave their tapestries of irony and allusion concerning faith and sight and light and darkness, sin and knowledge and unseeing.

St. Thomas was born in 1224, the same year in which (almost certainly) the finishing touches were put to our window at Chartres. In 1273, a few months before his death the following year, he constructed a Question for the Third Part of the *Summa* concerning the "manifestation" of Christ's resurrection. It is, at it were, half a diptych; an earlier Question considered the "manifestation" of Christ's birth.[5] Coming and going, Christmas and Easter: twin aspects of the single mystery we have been shown, two facets of the visibility of what faith sees in Jesus.

In each Question, the opening article considered whether his birth (or resurrection) should have been shown to all and sundry, and finds good reasons why it was not so. The second article of Question 36 then asks whether the birth of Christ should have been shown to anyone (and article 3 considers whether those to whom it was in fact shown—Mary and Joseph, shepherds and magi, Simeon and Anna—were well chosen). The reader who supposes this to be, at least in Mary's case, a silly question, has not seen the point. The point is not that Mary needed to be shown her son but that, without it being shown to her, she could not possibly, in seeing him, have seen the Lord's anointed. And, if nobody had known whose birth this was, no witness could be given and no faith born, for faith (St. Thomas reminds us, quoting Romans 10) comes by hearing.

In Question 55, the second article does not ask whether the resurrection should have been shown to anyone but, rather more pointedly, whether it would have been fitting for the disciples to see Christ rise *(utrum fuisset conveniens, quod discipuli viderent Christum resurgere).* After all, it was their duty and their destiny to bear witness to the resurrection, and the best testimony, St. Thomas agrees, is that of the eyewitness. The argument seems sound enough. How, we wonder, will Aquinas wriggle out of it since, as every schoolchild knows (and, in case we have forgotten, he himself reminds us in the *sed contra*) *nobody* saw Christ rise.

---

[5]See *Summa Theologiae*, IIIa, qq. 36, 55.

Oh, but they did! "The apostles were indeed able to bear eyewitness testimony to Christ's resurrection because with sharp-sighted faith they saw Christ risen living whom they knew dead: as we are brought through faith's hearing to what the blessed see, so those who first heard it from angels were brought to see *Christ rising*."[6] It is an astonishing passage, and the key to it, I think, is the echo, once again, of Romans 10, "faith comes by hearing." The angels proclaimed the message, broke the news, told them not to seek the living among the dead. They saw the point and, seeing it, they saw the dead one rise. The argument is so succinct that, had we not already met it, in extended narrative form in Luke 24, we might suspect some sleight of hand.

In a retreat preached to his brethren at Downside (for the text of which I am most grateful to him), Sebastian Moore insisted that Christ's resurrection is "known by the awakening of the heart alone." Only an entirely false and unsustainable dichotomy of knowledge and love can prevent us from seeing (!) that such awakening is, as the Fourth Gospel tirelessly insists, a turning from blindness to sight, from darkness to daylight. We talk, readily enough, about "blind" faith. St. Thomas was working with its contrary, with what he calls *fides oculata*. What a pity that we lost that good word "oculate," which the Oxford Dictionary has as "observant" or "sharp-sighted." There is nothing *less* blind than the awakened heart, the living faith, in the light of which the risen Christ is visible. And this transition, this awakening, this *metanoia,* this "coming to see the point about Jesus," just *is* what it is for faith's new eyes to see Christ rise.

---

[6](My emphasis) The passage is so important that, to my rough translation, I add the Latin of the Marrietti edition: "Apostoli potuerunt testificari Christi resurrectionem etiam de visu: quia Christum post resurrectionem viventem oculata fide viderunt, quem mortuum sciverant: sed sicut ad visionem beatam pervenitur per auditum fidei; ita ad visionem Christi resurgentis pervenerunt homines per ea, quae prius ab angelis audierunt." The translator in the current Dominican edition presumably saw what Aquinas had written but, failing to see the point, could not believe his eyes. That, at any rate, is one explanation of his bizarre rendering: "The Apostles were also able to offer eyewitness testimony to Christ's resurrection; for they saw with their own eyes the one in whom they believed, Christ alive whom they knew to have died. But since men attain the beatific vision through that hearing which pertains to faith, so too they ultimately attained the vision of Christ risen from the dead only through the message they had first heard from angels" (*Summa Theologiae,* vol. 55, *The Resurrection of the Lord* [IIIa, 53–9], trans. and intro. C. Thomas Moore, O.P. [London: Blackfriars and Eyre and Spottiswoode, 1976]) 43.

The Mauclerc Window

Everything, we said earlier, is found, this side of death, in figure, in symbol, enigmatically. It must be so, because to see the risen Christ is to see our unknown future, all creation's healing and fresh flourishing in God. Revelation, says Rowan Williams, is "essentially to do with what is generative in our experience—events or transactions in our language that break existing frameworks and initiate new possibilities of life."[7] But, of course, the possibilities that are thus initiated can only (being new) be indicated metaphorically, sketched in figures drawn from the familiar.

There is a helpful note inserted by some scribe into the First Book of Samuel: "Formerly in Israel, when a man went to inquire of God, he said: 'Come, let us go to the seer'; for he who is now called a prophet was formerly called a seer.'"[8] And what do seers see? They see the point, the wood for the trees, the heart of the matter; get some fresh glimpse, shaped by their particular circumstance, of where things are going, of the sense and direction of things as seen from the standpoint of God's "over-sight" or providence. In other words, to see the risen Christ is to see what seers have always seen "beginning with Moses and all the prophets," brought into sharp and final focus at the point at which, *sub Pontio Pilato,* the true light that enlightens everyone illuminates, unconquerably, all the darkness of the world.

We come, at last, to Chartres, and reach our window. Of your charity, pray for Pierre Mauclerc, Count of Dreux and Duke of Brittany, who gave this window. In case you forget him, he and his wife and children, John and Yolande, kneel, on either side of their coat of arms, at the foot of the five tall lancets set beneath the rose. In the central lancet, as in so many places in this vast building dedicated to her assumption, Mary, crowned, holds her child. Flanking them, the tall, strong figures of Jeremiah, Isaiah, Ezekiel, and Daniel, the four great seers of Israel, giants among those who proclaimed, in figure, the promise Mary bore.

The prophets are bearing on their shoulders four smaller figures, recorders of the news of Easter; Luke, Matthew, John, and Mark. All eyes turn upwards. What is the vision which, from their respective vantage points, they see? Above the lancets is the great rose itself, a shining mandala, in the center of which is "one seated on the throne. And he who sat there appeared like jasper and carnelian, and round the throne was a rain-

---

[7] Rowan Williams, "Trinity and Revelation," *Modern Theology* 2:3 (1986) 199.
[8] 1 Sam 9:9.

bow that looked like an emerald." In this case, actually, the throne is emerald and he who sits there holds one hand in blessing and, in the other, the cup of the new covenant. In the next circle, four pairs of censing angels and Ezekiel's four living creatures, symbols, now, of the evangelists. Then, in two further circles, "twenty-four elders, clad in white garments, with golden crowns upon their heads" (interspersed, it must be said, with twelve small quatrefoils bearing the arms of Dreux and Brittany).[9]

Stand beneath this south, sun-flooded window and you may see, today, as any visitor to Chartres for more than seven centuries may have seen, just what the gospel writers saw: the resolution, heart and center of the world, jewel-shining, the throne of God, the new Jerusalem, the risen one, our promised peace.

Iconographically, the rose itself, for all the splendor of its execution, is quite conventional; its theme is often found in French south-facing roses. It is the lancets, intriguingly juxtaposing prophets and evangelists, that are exceptional and that will occupy our attention for the rest of this paper. What I most want to emphasize at this point however (although it will, I hope, become even more obvious as we proceed) is the extraordinary theological richness and sophistication of this "text." This is no work of "popularization" and yet it is *accessible,* in the twentieth century as in the thirteenth, to anyone who is brought to see Christ rising, the Christ who "interpreted to them in all the scriptures the things concerning himself."[10] Faith comes by hearing: to read this window with sharp-sighted faith is to trust the awakening of the whole familiar dark world into the light of God.

Dwarfs and Giants

The puzzle or detective story that I mentioned earlier concerns the sense of a proverb and the relationship between that proverb and this window. The proverb became something of a slogan in the history of science (even Isaac Newton used it), expressing confidence in intellectual progress while yet modestly acknowledging the debt each generation owes to those who went before. "The dwarf sees further than the giant, when he has the giant's shoulders to mount on."[11] That is how Coleridge put it, and he

---

[9]See Rev 4:2-4; Ezekiel 1.

[10]Luke 24:27.

[11]Samuel Taylor Coleridge, *"The Friend* (1818). Volume II, Section the First, Essay VIII," *The Collected Works of Samuel Taylor Coleridge. The Friend I,* ed. Barbara E. Rooke

took it from Burton's *Anatomy*. Burton, in turn, had taken it from a commentary, produced in Salamanca in 1574, by the Spanish Franciscan Diego de Estella, on the verse in Luke: "I tell you that many prophets and kings desired to see what you see, and did not see it, and to hear what you hear, and did not hear it."[12]

According to Raymond Klibansky, in an article that we shall consider in more detail later on, "the painter [of our window] can hardly have intended to call St. John a dwarf in comparison to Ezekiel."[13] I have no reason to suppose that Diego de Estella had ever been to Chartres. His use of the proverb in his commentary, however, does at least suggest that Klibansky's dismissal of the possibility that it could find application in the relations between prophets and evangelists overshoots the mark.

In the window, the shock of the suggestion that, for all their privileged vantage point, the evangelists in some sense are pygmies, little people, when measured against the stature of the major prophets, is visually softened by the juxtaposition of the four pairs of seers with the mother and child in their midst. God's Word incarnate, after all, is not demeaned by resting, child-sized, in the bent arm of the tall figure of his mother, "daughter of Sion."

All this, so far, is speculation, skirmishing. The next thing we must do is try to trace the proverb to its source and ascertain its meaning. This time we start at Chartres, with John of Salisbury, who was bishop there from 1176 to 1180: "Bernard of Chartres used to say that we are like dwarfs on the shoulders of giants, so that we can see more than they, and things at greater distance, not by virtue of any sharpness of sight on our part, or any physical distinction, but because we are carried high and raised up by their giant size." That all seems clear enough, and Klibansky, in 1936, was confident that "the simile of the dwarfs is an original one and was invented by Bernard himself."[14]

(London: Routledge and Kegan Paul, 1969) 249. Newton, aged thirty-three, writing to Robert Hooke, his senior by seven years, on 5 February 1676: "If I have seen further it is by standing on the shoulders of Giants." His biographer points out that there is, in fact, an undertone of contempt in Newton's application to Hooke of what he calls a "time worn image frequently cited in the literary quarrels of the ancients and the moderns in connection with the idea of progress" (Frank E. Manuel, *A Portrait of Isaac Newton* [Cambridge, Mass.: Harvard University Press, 1968] 144–5).

[12]Luke 10:24.

[13]Raymond Klibansky, "Standing on the Shoulders of Giants," *Isis* 26 (1936) 148.

[14]"Dicebat Bernardus Carnotensis nos esse quasi nanos, gigantium humeris insidentes, ut possimus plura eis et remotiora videre, non utique proprii visus acumine, aut eminentia

We might have left it there, but for the fact (one of the fascinations of this story is the number of different threads that need to be connected) that, according to one commentator on medieval Jewish science, "The simile of the pigmy apparently was first employed by Zedekiah Anav, citing an ancient sage." According to the French translation from the Hebrew, which Jeauneau helpfully provides, Zedekiah Ben Abraham Anav, a thirteenth-century Italian talmudist who lived in Rome, attributed the saying to Isaiah of Trani. Confusingly, there seem to have been two "ancient sages" of this name, but this need not disturb us, since the elder of the two was only born in the late twelfth century.[15] So we are back to Chartres, where Bernard was chancellor of the schools from 1119 to 1126. The proverb may, in fact, antedate Bernard himself by a few years if, as has recently been suggested, it can now be traced to Ivo of Chartres, who was bishop there from 1090 to 1116, from whom it was mediated to the painters of the window by Gilbert de la Porrée (1076–1154), colleague of Bernard and teacher of John of Salisbury.

Whatever the exact date of the proverb's first expression, it was undoubtedly in use in the schools of Chartres in the twelfth century. Unless we have some idea of its likely meaning in that place, at that time, we cannot estimate the ease or difficulty of its application, in the early thirteenth century, to the relations between prophets and evangelists.

According to Foster Guyer (who made no mention of the window) the proverb expresses "a belief in the general advance of humanity accompanied by a feeling of natural inferiority." This is in keeping with what seems to have been the accepted view of historians of ideas in the 1930s: namely, that the notion of intellectual "progress" (Klibansky uses the word) first found expression, however tentatively, in the schools of Chartres. Recent studies have been more cautious. Brian Stock, for example, says that Bernard of Chartres' own age "was a continuation of the classical world in

---

corporis, sed quia in altum subvehimur et extollimur magnitudine gigantea" (John of Salisbury, *Metalogicus,* Book III, Chapter 4 [Migne, *PL* 199, col. 900]); Klibansky, art. cit., 148. In this same passage, however, Klibansky disputed Delaporte's claim that the window is connected with Bernard's saying on the grounds that "Bernard dies before the actual building of the cathedral began, and . . . the window in question belongs to a relatively late stage of the construction." See Yves Delaporte, *Les Vitraux de la Cathédrale de Chartres* (Paris, 1926) 432.

[15]S. W. Baron, *Social and Religious History of the Jews,* Vol. VIII (New York: Columbia University Press, 1958) 347. Baron cites the full proverb in his text (140). See E. Jeauneau, "'Nani gigantum humeris insidentes.' Essai d'interprétation de Bernard de Chartres," *Vivarium* 5 (1967) 79–99.

faithfully reproducing its concepts, styles, and cultural ideals. But Bernard was prepared to grant that in other respects it had perhaps surpassed even the ancients." Within the framework suggested by the metaphor of dwarf and giant, "the classical debate on myth and science, which had really begun with Aristotle's critique of Plato's *Timaeus,* was reopened in a new context."[16] But Stock, it must be noticed, still assumes that the proverb gives lapidary expression to a *Weltanschauung,* a general understanding of the philosophy of history.

It was precisely this reading of the proverb that Jeauneau, with daunting erudition, contested, insisting that what was at issue, in the debates of the period, was solely the sense in which it is possible, in the world of "arts" or "letters," to "do better" than those who had gone before. It was, from first to last, a matter of what counted as good speech, good writing: of striving to *say it better.*[17] What none of the commentators seem to have observed is that, seen in this light, the proverb is admirably fitted to express the reciprocal relationship between the Testaments.

Thus, on the one hand, there is that which, from the standpoint of Christian belief, was unseen by the prophets but which the apostles saw. And if "the answer given in revelation clarifies the question a man asks,"[18] might we not construe the history of witness borne by prophet and evangelist in terms of the attempt to "say it better" in response to God's ever more exactly uttered Word? On the other hand, we forget at our peril that the Gospels are, from first to last, interpretations of the Jewish Scriptures. To read them otherwise (and it matters not whether the style of our forgetfulness is "liberal" or "literalist" in character) is, in effect, to clamber down from the shoulders of the prophets. But, if we do climb down, one thing is certain: the risen Christ will disappear from view.

My first conclusion, then, is that, so far as the sense of the saying is concerned, there is no good reason to suppose that it did not serve as inspiration for our window. There is, however, another ground on which this claim has been contested.

---

[16]Foster E. Guyer, "Dwarf on Giant's Shoulders," *Modern Language Notes,* XLV (June 1930) 399; Klibansky, art. cit., 148; Brian Stock, *Myth and Science in the Twelfth Century; A Study of Bernard Silvester* (Princeton, 1972) 6–7.

[17]See Jeauneau, art. cit., 98.

[18]Karl Rahner, "The Foundations of Belief Today," *Theological Investigations* XVI, trans. David Morland (London: Darton, Longman and Todd, 1979) 9.

The Road from Rome

According to no less an authority than Emile Mâle, the inspiration for the window is not to be sought, as people once supposed, in the schools of Chartres, but further back in time and far away: in the Rome of the late tenth century. It is here, therefore, that our pilgrimage to Chartres begins again. In the apse of the church of San Sebastiano in Pallara, on the Palatine, there is a double frieze. In the upper part, the elders of the Book of Revelation, on bended knee, offer to God their golden crowns. Beneath, a line of vigorous old bearded men bear on their shoulders younger men, with haloes, who hold up their hands to heaven.[19] There seem to be very few extant instances of prophets bearing apostles or evangelists on their shoulders, and at least one of these is thought to have been influenced by the Chartres window.[20] When, therefore, the scarcity of the motif is taken together with the fact that, in San Sebastiano as at Chartres, it appears together with the elders of the Apocalypse, the dependence of the window on the fresco is surely incontestable. How did the idea get from Rome to Chartres? Mâle speculated that a canon of the cathedral may have visited Rome in the early thirteenth century, but he knew no evidence of pilgrimages from Chartres to Rome.

The final step in Jeauneau's argument in favor of the view that the proverb and the window belong to two different traditions is the claim that, in the window, "the apostles are not pygmies, nor are the prophets giants."[21] It is exactly here, however, that the visual evidence from San Sebastiano is most telling. The apostles in the Roman painting are every bit as large as the prophets who support them, whereas the evangelists in Chartres are noticeably smaller. It beggars the imagination to suppose that

---

[19]See Emile Mâle, "Etudes sur les Eglises Romaines. L'Empereur Otto III à Rome et les Eglises du Xe Siècle," *Revue des Deux Mondes* XLI (1937) 70–1. The passage is repeated in Mâle, *Rome et Ses Vieilles Eglises* (Paris, 1942) and can be found on pp. 109–10 of the English translation: *The Early Churches of Rome*, trans. D. Buxton (London, 1960), in which a seventeenth-century copy of the fresco is reproduced as Plate 69 on p. 209. Mâle dates the painting around 970. The Church has been called many things—SS. Sebastiano e Zotico, Santa Maria in Palladio, and so on—but its best known title is also by far the best suited to this occasion!

[20]This is the Princes' Gate at Bamberg cathedral, where the twelve lesser prophets carry the twelve apostles: see Mâle, art. cit.; Louis Réau, *Iconographie de l'Art Chrétien. Tome I. Introduction Générale* (Paris: Presses Universitaires de France, 1955) 197; *Tome II. Iconographie de la Bible* (1956) 324. Klibansky (art. cit.) also mentions a Saxon font at Merseberg, dating from around 1175.

[21]See Jeauneau, art. cit., 93.

this is *simply* due to the "pressure" of the proximity of mother and child in the central light, and is not also an indication that those who designed the window had the saying in mind.

Let us review the evidence. The three principal grounds on which the indebtedness of the window to the proverb are disputed are: the date of the window, the meaning of the saying, and the iconographic evidence that the inspiration for the window is to be sought not in Chartres itself but in Rome.

I have argued that, so far as the sense of the saying is concerned, there is no good reason to suppose that it did not serve as inspiration for the window. The objection on the ground of date is very unconvincing; there was a continual stream of teachers in the schools of Chartres to keep a memorable saying alive from Bernard's death (before 1130; or Ivo's in 1116) to the construction of the window in the 1220s. That the window draws, iconographically, upon the painting in San Sebastiano seems certain but, far from this standing as an objection against the claim that it was also inspired by the proverb, I have suggested that the visual evidence is in its favor.

In order to draw the threads a little closer together, it would be helpful to find someone who may well have known the Roman painting, who remembered and thought highly of the proverb, and who was in a position of influence in Chartres not long before the cathedral was built (work began almost immediately after the disastrous fire of 10 June 1194, which severely damaged the previous cathedral and destroyed most of the city).

There is one quite good candidate; an Englishman, born in Ivo's lifetime, who was taught by pupils of Bernard of Chartres, who served in the Roman Curia between (approximately) 1149 and 1153, and who may thus well have known the fresco in San Sebastiano; a man of vast learning and considerable public influence who was present at Becket's assassination in Canterbury in 1170 and who, from 1176 until his death in 1180, was bishop of Chartres; the man through whose writing we came to know of Bernard's saying in the first place: John of Salisbury.

The experts will, I am sure, find good reason to contest this suggestion. While awaiting their verdict, however, I remain astonished that none of the authorities to whom I have referred appears to have considered the possibility that John is a key figure in the interweaving of the two images that find such powerful expression in that transept window. It gives me great pleasure, therefore, to propose that we owe this masterpiece of theological communication, in part, to an English theologian and an ancient church dedicated to Sebastian.

― 2 ―

Torment as Method

David B. Burrell, C.S.C.

The word of God is something alive and active:
it cuts like any double-edged sword but more finely;
it can slip through the place where the soul is divided
*   from the spirit, or joints from the marrow;*
it can judge the secret emotions and thoughts (Heb 4:12).

I first read *The Crucified Jesus Is No Stranger* on the bus from Tel Aviv to Jerusalem on Holy Thursday of 1978. Using it to block out the pop music that often invades Israeli buses only heightened the clash of sacred times. For it was one of those infrequent years when Passover fell outside of Holy Week. Something clicked for me in that reading; the doctrine of atonement was rescued from Anselmian calculations to express a *fact* about our attempt to live with ourselves *before God* (as S. K. liked to put it). I wrote Sebastian en route: "By jove, I think you've done it!" and on the plane home I sketched out a course—Psychology and Religion—to help students capture the dynamic of his development. For that's what it was: development of doctrine. Not in Newman's sense, to be sure, of progressive ecclesial formulation, but in the existential sense of showing how doctrines inform the life of those who would be faithful to their teaching.

That has been, I take it, Sebastian's vocation and his correlative contribution to us all: to insinuate ways for us to respond faithfully to what we have received, by intimating to us how those realities do, in fact, inform our inquiring selves at the critical junctures of our quest. In that sense, his written work resonates with inner work carried out with directed re-treatants, thus displaying what it is to do theology in an Ignatian mode. Yet that same inner work responds to an anxious query in himself:

> Only suspicion can pick up the sense
> Of the official narratives we have:
> Cover-up or a mystery's defense?
>
> And with suspicion born, doubt forms a wave
> Suddenly floods the garden of the soul:
> Could you really have risen from the grave?[1]

Yet here the suspicion spawns more than a hermeneutic; it breeds torment. Torment is Sebastian's "method," and we are beholden to his refusing to let go of it. In my letter to him extolling *Crucified Jesus* I remarked on his device of using short chapters of two to three pages to elucidate one facet after another of sin, recognition, and forgiveness. He later explained to me that this was no device: Marquette University policy permitted free duplication of single dittos, so he would fill them single-space for circulation among his colleagues. What resulted, after much outworking, was a concatenation of pithy expositions, each bringing a new perspective to bear. (A wonderful corroboration of Stephen Toulmin's reminder that "methodology" usually doubles as a retrospective description of one's graduate training; most of us write chapters of term-paper length.) What Sebastian had done here, as elsewhere, was to bring Lonergan's reflections about *method* to life: beyond the grammar of such matters lies their appropriation by the spirit, and for human beings, that demands corroboration. Theology is at once an interior and a communal affair. Yet grammar, in the sense of a struggle for appropriate formulation, remains crucial to both concerns: interior and communal. For we need clarity to breathe, and especially to unscramble our conflicted emotions and desires.

It is into that tangle that Sebastian ventures; or perhaps better, it is out of that tangle that he keeps trying to find his way. And his inestimable worth as a guide turns on the fact that we all live enmeshed in that tangle, yet few of us are able or willing to acknowledge it. Perhaps it was Ignatius's grasp of the power of images to illuminate the twists and turns of desire that lured Sebastian along the paths he has taken, but there is no doubt that his experience with the *Exercises* has shaped his theological explorations. For that is precisely what his writings amount to: decidedly *not* a

---

[1]"Dolores," by Sebastian Moore (Christmas 1991).

revisionist theological program, but, rather, a continuing struggle to find the formulations that will release the dynamism hidden in revelation to unleash the spirit to "truly live."

There is a palpable urgency about this, as though failure to find these formulations will condemn this generation, which thinks it has already heard the message, to miss the life-giving power of Jesus. The title of Sebastian's first book, *God Is a New Language,* sounded the tocsin, for it was written in the flush of attention to language in theology after Wittgenstein's aphorism "Theology *as* grammar." This book argued that the revelation of God in Jesus was not to be adjudicated according to procrustean verificationist schemes, but itself pointed to fresh and refreshing uses of the language we have come to know. That language has to try to express rather than to suppress our longings. Once we begin to sensitize ourselves to the new rhetoric of the Gospels, we ourselves can also imagine new uses of language: "the question about Jesus challenges the mind of the questioner."[2]

And frees the heart as well, for Sebastian's struggle led him ineluctably towards the gospel as "the story of the liberation of desire from its crippling and inwoven companion," guilt (xii). This could happen only when the formula of Nicaea was "rediscovered as the truth that frees the heart for God" (xiv). In the sequel to *Crucified Jesus, The Fire and the Rose Are One,* he described this inquiry as the "mutual invigoration of speculative intelligence and the heart," remarking how it "is fundamental to the Catholic theological tradition" (xiv). Such is indeed the witness of Sebastian's writings: "the opposite of reductionist . . . ; the recovery of the belief in the divinity of Jesus *as* the Holy Spirit's principal therapy of our spirit" (xiii). I have described this strategy as bringing Bernard Lonergan's reflections on method to life, for it focuses on the point where authentically theological method, as Lonergan elaborates it, must outreach the demands of logic. While always presupposing and exploiting those demands, our inquiring spirit is nonetheless impelled by a primordial "desire to be desired by the one we desire" (xii), so that to recognize that One in the crucified Jesus, the sinless one, is to set the "heart [and the mind] at peace with God's truth" (xiv).

Allow me to show how a course designed to bring students to appreciate the richness of Sebastian's pathway can spell out for us as well the possibilities of Lonergan's theological method. While acutely conscious of the limitations of Ernest Becker's *Denial of Death* (see *The Fire and the Rose,*

[2]Sebastian Moore, *The Fire and the Rose Are One* (New York: Seabury, 1980) 132.

xiii, 32–4), Sebastian shows how that seminal study nonetheless helps us articulate that "one universal human desire without some satisfaction of which our life would be unendurable" (xii).[3] What Becker must tentatively reconstruct from the impasses of depth psychology, Sebastian is able to name as our "pre-religious love-affair with God" (32). Yet people of faith must apprentice themselves to Becker's re-appropriation of the psychological tradition, lest they succumb to "the human proclivity to think one is reporting experience when in reality one is merely importing an idea from memory" (132).

The teacher is advised to let Becker set the stage, and then to follow the contours of his book, using it as a "threading-text." One is also counseled to read Aristotle's *Ethics* to appropriate the traditional language of *character*, as well as Freud's *Civilization and Its Discontents*, Kierkegaard's *Sickness unto Death*, and Jung's *Psychology of the Transference*, for these are the thinkers who showed Becker how the questions of psychology eventually flowered into theological queries. (Becker himself was most moved by Otto Rank, yet trying to use Rank's writings in class only confirmed the source of Becker's joy at having finally penetrated their meaning!) After students assimilate this language for their journey, through writings difficult yet engaging, they will find that *The Crucified Jesus Is No Stranger* emerges as a lucid reprise of the "depth-structure" or plot of the drama.

The advantage of such a strategy is twofold. First, it is doubtful that students would appreciate Sebastian's approach without such prior apprenticeship; secondly, the works chosen, with Becker's guidance, approximate Sebastian's own *prise de conscience* of Christology as the heart of God's new language. Yet the course is not yet completed, for the *dénouement* comes in their reading Etty Hillesum's *An Interrupted Life*, where a young Jewish woman's diaries in Nazi-occupied Holland offer a window into a soul that has been brought to recognize the One whom she desires.[4] And the fact that this transformation happens through a relationship as tormented as human relationships can be serves only to accentuate Sebastian's articulation of the tangle of desire, while its culmination in a life of service unto death etches the visage of the crucified. Moreover, it is fitting that the theological method of *The Crucified Jesus*, itself forged in and through the tangled experience of desire, be exemplified through an extraordinarily lucid account of a personal transformation, in which desire

[3]Ernest Becker, *The Denial of Death* (New York: Free Press, 1973).
[4]Etty Hillesum, *An Interrupted Life* (New York: Pantheon, 1983; Washington Square Press, 1985).

is transmuted into sacrificial love. The journey to discovering "the crucified" is brought home to the very locus of discovery that Sebastian has staked out in his works: the follower of Jesus. That Etty Hillesum is Jewish makes the story that much more poignant, for her appropriation of the gospel has a purity about it that carries one back to Jesus' initial followers, the *anawim* (or "little people") of Galilee; that she is a quintessentially contemporary person gives life to Sebastian's thesis much the way his strategy brought Lonergan's reflections on method to life.

Finally, the entire exercise reminds us that theology is less written than *done,* so that teaching a course approximates more to that doing than to composing a book, but only because the primary locus for method in theology is, as Lonergan reminds us again and again, not a scheme but a person. As Sebastian completes his Christmas 1991 poem, cited at the outset:

> But here I know you as myself, a whole
> Cannot go back to being half-alive
> As Adam hearing God out for a stroll.

> She who had you outside what laws contrive
> Lost all protection, and I too must dive.

Etty Hillesum's diaries display that "dive" better than any narrative I know, for the immediacy of the diary genre allows one to capture the moments of transformation with a transparency otherwise inaccessible. And her subsequent death in Auschwitz forbade her any *arrière pensées* that might have tailored the experience to conceptual expectations. Her presentiment of her own death as a sacrifice, and hence of the transforming power of the resurrection, corroborates Sebastian's insight into the mystery of "the crucified" as only a completed human life can; her testimony in the form of disingenuous diary entries makes that mystery exceptionally accessible to us. Torment we can feel, and transformation through it. Yet it is Sebastian's work that allows us to identify this torment as the "method" involved in understanding what following Jesus comes to in each of us.

A Contemporary Personalist

Dom Illtyd Trethowan, O.S.B.

God is the person in obedience to whom I am fully a person. God is the person who persons me.   —Sebastian Moore

The person cannot exist without communion . . . The demand of the person for absolute freedom involves a new birth . . . a baptism.
                                        —John Zizioulas

"Personalist" is a label attached from time to time to Christian thinkers who assign a special importance to what we ought to mean by "person." The one whose achievements in this area I shall try to indicate seems to me peculiarly useful in our present needs.

An article by Dom Sebastian Moore, "Some Principles for an Adequate Theism," was contributed to the *Downside Review* for July 1977. It has not appeared in any other form and is therefore relatively unknown. It seems to me most valuable. Here we have in a dozen pages a wide-ranging, closely-packed statement of a point of view, expressed in an idiosyncratic style at the furthest remove from artifice, which demands one's closest attention. I have read it several times with both profit and entertainment. (It is pervaded by a characteristic wit, sometimes at the expense of undiscriminating theologians.)

The article opens with a demand that must come as a shock to anyone expecting to read an academic piece on the philosophy of religion: "The implication of Abbot Chapman's description of contemplative prayer must be attended to." How violent such a shock can be was made clear to me many years ago when, as Dom David Knowles's secretary, I was sent to collect a subscription to the *Downside Review* from an aged subscriber. *"Downside Review!"* said the ancient. "It has nothing about Downside in it—it is all about things like [here he paused to select something sufficiently horrifying] . . . like *mysticism!"* Things have changed much in this regard since Vatican II. Yet in many quarters the idea of a direct contact of the human mind with God is still looked upon with horror.

God's accessibility proves to be at the heart of Dom Sebastian's theology, which is addressed in particular to young people, whose needs he knows so well, but also to anyone to whom human existence is a puzzle. He proceeds at once to make clear that he is concerned, not with mere speculations, but with vital matters of human experience. Their resolution, he tells us, requires, in Chapman's words, "an act of inattention to everything else" so that "the intellect faces a blank wall and the will follows it." We have to empty our minds and wait obediently to hear what God wants of us, that is, if God proves to be real and not a figment of our imaginations. So far as I know, Chapman had never even heard of Maurice Blondel, but what he is saying here is what Blondel says at the end of his now famous *L'Action* of 1893. Normally, it is pointed out, our concepts are based on experiences and we refer back, return, to these experiences in our use of the concepts. (One of my nephews had the experience of being introduced to religion by listening to what his mother told him about God. "When will God land?" he asked. He had a concept of a super-aeronaut.) Our passage continues:

> The only return to experience that is comparable, in the case of God, with that return to experience which is available for other concepts is the experience of the mystic. The mystic is conscious of being touched by that reality to which the concept of God as the ultimate, all-containing mystery is pointing. . . . The shift from the *concept of* the infinite to the experienced and verbally-suggested *touch of* the infinite is the most devastating mindshift conceivable.

Dom Sebastian may appear at first to be telling us that in order to become a genuine believer in God it is necessary to achieve a state of perfection, a sanctity commonly supposed a great rarity in human living—and all this on the first page of the article.

In fact, as we shall see, he holds that religious conversion can be prepared for through a gradual development, although it must come to a point at which a definite recognition and acceptance of God occurs, obviously a unique experience. Of course, as we shall also see, *Christian* conversion has its own requirements. And, in any case, conversion is the beginning of a further development which must run its full course, if not in this world, then in the next (purgatory is coming to be recognized not as a punishment, but as the closing of a gap). This further development is not mentioned in the article, but it is in harmony with it.

The central point is that, if God is to be genuinely known, there must be a non-conceptual awareness of God. In that form the thesis is more widely supported than might be supposed from a survey of the relevant literature. It is more often implied, taken for granted, than explicitly stated. "Mystic" and "mysticism" are still very off-putting words for most people in our post-Christian society. They suggest oddities of a distinctly disagreeable kind. But in an older culture they were used to refer simply to proper Christians and their life of prayer. Literate Christians could be known as "theologians" and what is called "mystical theology" today was just "theology." The effect of this non-conceptual awareness is finely evoked if one turns to the next page of the article:

> So my life, which is a complex built-up system of habits, of arrangements, of blind-spots, of complacency, of "resentment," is, in principle, shielded from God by the concept that encloses him. With the birth of contemplative prayer, this peace-treaty between God and my life is broken and I come to sense that *any* point in my world may be suddenly touched and brought newly to my attention as a new territory for his gracious occupation.

Then the point is well made that the talk which we so often hear about "encountering God" is inappropriate. It seems to suggest running into a friend in the street. It suggests that for the (professional) theologian who informed Dom Sebastian, "over a cocktail," God has to change too, "for do not friends change each other?" There follows a splendid outburst of Sebastianic indignation and metaphysical *brio* that eventually fades out into this lament: "Who or what could this character possibly be who is called God, said to be not myself, and who will change in getting to know me just as I will change in getting to know him?"

We have now reached another page, which raises the questions: "What is the relation in which the concept of the infinite stands to the experience of the infinite, what does it mean to say that the one is 'pointing' to the other?" We are told:

> There is a knowledge of God without a concept, that, far from rendering the concept of God otiose and far from giving us permission for a concept—spurning fideism—gives to that concept a peculiar validity. . . .

Conversely, the concept of God gives something to the direct knowledge. For it spells out the absolute and all-conditioning quality that the mystic obscurely knows to be his who is embracing him. . . . It does not amplify the direct knowledge. It does not clarify it. It does not give it content. Rather it affirms, at the undeniable level of rational philosophic wonder and discovery, that total mystery of God which the mystic obscurely knows at first hand. . . . There is an organic relationship, a play, a balancing about-a-pivot between them.

What does the concept, any concept, do for us? It tells us how certain expressions in our language are to be understood. "God" *means* the Creator, and this normally carries with it the notion of infinite power, glory, and beneficence. But just understanding what "God" means cannot convince us that there is a creator. The "ontological argument," insofar as it tries to do this, is clearly fallacious. The fact that we can talk about centaurs does not of itself prove that there actually are any. The fact of the concept of God and the importance attached to it certainly shows that there is *plausibility* in the proposal that God is real. But even conventional Thomists do not go further nowadays than saying that this is the obvious inference to draw from the facts of the world around us. There is no solid logical proof of God. And then the fact of evil in the world is enough to settle the matter for an honest agnostic who knows of no other Christian approach to the great question. Talk of an awareness of God such a person has never heard of. And the same is true for many doubtful people, not excluding apparently untroubled Christians. But innumerable people, knowing nothing of philosophy or theology, have this awareness and are content with it. It is at the heart of their faith.

Let us pause for a moment to remember that a "concept," in the strict sense, is a universal idea, one, that is, which has particular instances. In that sense there is no concept of God. A well-known philosopher-theologian wrote a book some years ago called *The Concept of God*, which, for several excellent reasons, he disavowed not long afterwards. This was a sign of the times. We are gradually coming to realize that the so-called "Enlightenment" in fact darkened counsel on many issues. We have to form and organize concepts because we have to sort out the world in which we live. We form what is perhaps best called a "notion" of God. It was once at the root of our culture and normally taken for granted. It therefore tended to be ignored and forgotten. It is a necessary preliminary to the discovery of God, even when its content is a super-aeronaut. But, however refined and imposing it may come to be, it can never, if what I am saying makes sense, "spell out," of itself, as Dom Sebastian put it, the "absolute and all-conditioning quality" or convincingly "affirm," of itself, "at the undeniable level of rational philosophic wonder and discourse that total mastery of God. . . ." Nothing can *show* us God, except God. We have been also told that there are two "levels" of our knowledge of God, the "conceptual" one and the "direct" one, and that there is "an organic relationship, a play" between them. This suggests to me that before the direct knowledge has fully declared itself, it may alternate with the conceptual one, even from moment to moment and that this might remove, at least in principle, my difficulties about the two levels. I fully agree that mystics ought not to regard rational coherence as superfluous—in its proper place.

The next two pages emphasize the culminating point now reached in this discussion:

> It is, that the direct knowledge of God is the *reception* of an *initiative* that is God's, that is God. That is the necessary condition of its directness. There is simply no direct knowledge of God that would consist in somehow happening upon him, intuiting him as the source of all reality, in the manner of some deep and genial insight . . . it is to the stern injunction of the mystic to suspend, at the appropriate moment, all thought, that we must attend.

The relationship between the direct knowledge of God and the concept is now further explored. The direct knowledge means

> experiencing the initiative which is implied above all in the concept of God . . . a realization of the reign of God such that he who experiences it feels compelled to say: we acknowledge this reign in our liturgy and in our theology, but we do not there know what we are talking about; nor can we describe a reign that is so radical that its subjects have no experience apart from it. But there too the liturgical image acquires for the contemplative a deeper resonance.

That puts it perhaps too mildly. A little later we find: "The direct knowledge of God is the making of a saint, the building of the kingdom . . . it is not the lonely intuition of a genius."

This last point is of a special importance. It reminds us that the approach to Christianity and the development of Christian faith are not normally the affairs of isolated individuals. When religion is really alive it is infectious. Being alive, in this context, is not a matter of heartiness, hugs all round, continuous noise and sermons which seldom suggest that it is possible or desirable to get beyond information about God, to discover God at first hand. The next page tells us, admirably, that "contemplation does *validate* the concept of God for a person" although it does not "change" it, and adds: "It does, however, critique it in a peculiar way, in that it justifies the outburst, 'We don't know what we are saying when we say that God is the absolute and all-conditioning.'" This means, I take it, that people can use such formulas without realizing that these can refer to an experience about which they themselves know nothing.

At this point difficulties are thought to arise from the fact of Christian revelation: "We have to say of God *as we can conceive of him* that he is coming to be in us, and indeed that he became man." And this leads to the question whether "the Gospel radically alters the concept of God." Dom Sebastian tells us that at one time he thought that it does this and that he no longer thinks so. What the gospel does is "so to call us into the direct intimacy of God that we realize with a qualitatively new intensity the inadequacy . . . of the concept of God." I suggest that we become aware of God in Jesus or of Jesus in God according as we start with the gospel or start as just theists. When a latent awareness of God is aroused by considering Jesus, in reading the gospel or other Christian literature, God's offer of himself may be recognized. Then it can be as though the Father were saying to us: "This is my beloved Son." Alternatively we may have answered the question of the Father already and later find him witnessing to his Son.

Dom Sebastian goes on to say that he is made uneasy by the way in which "the Will of God" is talked about by theologians in regard to God's revelation of self to us: "I want another word, suggesting the wanting-to-be of God in our lives. A word, in other words, that comes closer to that obscure *pressure* which is the experience of the contemplative." I want to suggest that this can be put into a form about which no question arises of God's *needing* us.

Textbooks still in use say that God did not need to create the world. God could have abstained from doing so. Whether the world was there or not could make no difference to God. There were innumerable possible worlds which God could have created and God picked on one of them. It is absurd to suggest that God chose the best of all possible worlds because any created world could always be improved on. It seems to me that this picture of an arbitrary God is unacceptable. The notion of possible worlds presenting themselves for creation surely involves a notion of God as being *acted upon.* It destroys God's "absoluteness." What we must say, it seems to me, is that God is absolute love. In other words, he is the Trinity. To call the Trinity "he" is absurd, but unavoidable. We just have to remember what we mean by it. God is absolute generosity. There can be no question of his ever being other than he is. The Father cannot be who he is without the Son and the Spirit. They are interdependent, the activity, the life of changeless, absolute love. Absolute freedom and absolute necessity coincide in them. They just "do their thing." It is meaningless to suggest that they should do anything else. And "their thing," because here we are, includes ourselves and our world. God loves what he has made and he has his place for it. It is the place where the divine Son, in the power of the Spirit, is to live a perfect human life with which, if we will, we are all to be united. Nothing could be better.

Objections, no doubt, will be raised. It will be said that, in this account of the world's creation, God will create necessarily, and not freely. The world itself will be necessary and become part of God. But the fact that no question arises about whether God creates or not, that things are just *so,* has no such implication. The world remains wholly dependent on God. To object that we are restricting God's powers by saying that there is no question of God *not* creating the world is surely to claim for God a very odd sort of privilege. And it exposes one to the objection made against textbook theology by the veteran process-theologian, Charles Hartshorne, that, if God had not created, he would be a different person. God would not be the Creator and would have no world to love. So far I have seen no satisfactory reply to Hartshorne. Or rather, none is possible until people stop talking about a God to whom it is a matter of indifference whether there is a world for God to love or not. Here we have to remember that God's love is simply a *giving.* For us it is what we *get,* and our love for God is adoration. Dom Sebastian is very helpful here in his insistence on God's absolute initiative.

Nothing of this can be properly understood unless it is clearly understood that God is *beyond time.* (On this Brian Leftow's article, "Time, Actuality and Omniscience" in *Religious Studies,* September 1990, seems to me excellent.) Only "mysticism" can make this clear to one. God knows time timelessly. Time began with creation. We cannot help having a picture of God as enclosed by eternity because we are ourselves in space-time. But we can acquire a conviction that there is more beyond our world. We can get in touch with it. In talk about this "beyond," which it is so difficult to contrive and so easy to misconstrue, it can be helpful to compare one topic with another. So, to return now to the Trinity, the three persons cannot be said, intelligibly, to share a divine nature. That would produce three gods. They depend on one another, lose themselves in one another, in a life of endless ecstasy. They are perfectly united. It is this notion of union that now needs to be explored. It provides the clearest clue to the meaning of human existence.

It is to be found in any act of basic human knowledge, which I call "awareness." Something requires attention, has to be attended to. It may prove to be trivial, but we may have to open our minds to it. This is the necessary preliminary for what most of us regard as most important for our lives, our response, our love. Love and knowledge go together, to misquote, like a horse and carriage. Neither comes into its own without the other. Knowing, in this fundamental sense of mental, spiritual *contact,* is given to us to become part of ourselves, yet it has not been lost to the giver. Someone explains to us, say, how to listen to music. We learn this and we share the enjoyment (up to a point). This ought to be perfectly obvious, but such ancient themes of Christian mysticism are out of fashion. The "soul" is suspect, not without reason, but the mind, the point of contact with God, can become suspect too.

To complete this general clearing of the ground that seems necessary if one is to get a hearing for mysticism today, something must be said about the world's destiny. It reaches its climax or turning-point in the life, death, and resurrection of Jesus Christ. It was not the fact that there was sin in the world that brought Jesus into it. God did not think that up to deal with an unexpected emergency. It was to happen in any case. (It is said that this view is accepted today by most working Catholic theologians—those, that is, who did not lose touch with theological goings-on once they had gained their degrees.) But what is sin? How did it happen? It happened because humans succumbed to an inevitable risk. It is always possible for humans to refuse God's offer. God is ultimate love, and since, being love, God creates humanity *for* love; we must be ready to accept it. God cannot create another God. There must be some disadvantage in not being God. Man, not God, runs a risk. "God doesn't care, I suppose," someone will say, sarcastically. If a person has destroyed self, *as a person,* there is nothing left to care about. Finally, in this area, something must be said about the doctrine of redemption. Theologians have so often taught in the past that Jesus satisfied an angry God, saved us from punishments by dying on a cross. Nowadays it is generally recognized that Jesus came to show us the Father by living a perfect human life among us with the predictable result that he was put to death. Thus he achieved his destiny as the risen Christ whose new life is shared by his followers.

"Do you really think," the sarcastic one may ask, "that you will get us to take a lively interest in Christianity by handing out this wide-ranging sort of religious metaphysics?" I have been trying only to suggest that there may be more in religion, in particular the Christian religion, than meets the eye. Anyone ready to read something about Christianity itself and its relevance to human problems should read Dom Sebastian's recent book, *Jesus the Liberator of Desire*.

In the second half of his "Principles for an Adequate Theism," to which I now return, the most important conclusions of the first half are expounded in a way the reader of the first half should find clear and helpful:

> The very principle that declares the concept of God inadequate but indispensable insists that for serious Christianity we must seek the grace of contemplative prayer. In other words a serious Christian must let himself be taught why the concept of God is not what we are to know God by. His commentary for the wonderful statements of the New Testament about God—that he so loved the world, etc.—is his fruitful and loving affair with "the blank," with "the cloud."

It is encouraging to realize that this reference to *The Cloud of Unknowing* will be meaningful to far more people today than it was forty or fifty years ago. The only danger, as I see it, is that the unknown author's contrast between knowledge and love may be misinterpreted. The "dark nights" are the effects of *contact* with God unless we can discover other reasons for them.

Dom Sebastian then shows how this point of view safeguards one from a "fundamentalist" tendency in expounding the New Testament ("a God out there who entered history") and from a "modernizing" tendency ("to change the absolute God into some sort of immanent love-force"). He goes on to illustrate what happens if one assumes that "the concept of God is what we are to know God by," taking as an example "the way people handle the dual commandment of love of God and love of neighbor." On that assumption, "we . . . derive the love of neighbor from the love of God by way of extrinsic command" (the fundamentalist approach) or "we make of our neighbor . . . and his demand on us the only way in which God is known to us, which is the modernizing approach." We reach the impressive conclusion: "The truth is that a growing intimacy with God in contemplative prayer is a radical changing of the heart which alters, as nothing else can, those relationships without which a person is not human at all. In the light of contemplative prayer we can understand that the love of God *is* the love of our neighbor."

A few paragraphs back I remarked that talk of God's "pressure" upon us must not be interpreted to mean that God "needs" us. That makes it necessary that I should now quote the following passage:

> Further, God as pressure, God as presence, God as incomprehensible immediacy, is God as love. And as the pressure is only known in so far as it is

received, accepted, the pray-er's active receptivity is the fullness of the immediacy of God's love to him. While being his, the pray-er's, love, and so a finite act, it stands in a unique relationship to God's love, a relationship which cannot be understood outside the context of contemplative prayer. In that context, we can say that God is extending himself, or that he is achieving that want-to-be-in-us which, I have argued, is the contemplative core of "God's will." Outside that context this language becomes vague and pantheistic.

This passage deserves to be read, it seems to me, over and over again. It releases the full significance of that relationship of intelligent and loving *union* which is so little understood among us and so urgently required.

Next we are shown how it was that Anders Nygren's *Agape und Eros* received such an acclaim. Nygren was well aware that the Christian love of God

is not the human eros at its full stretch but is a love that originates in God and is bestowed by him on man. But confined to the conceptual order . . . he was deprived of that type of discourse in which this divinely initiated love could be at least dimly understood as becoming love *in* man and man's finite act. He had to say that it was by faith *and not by love* that man received God's love . . . that this conceptually known God loved man could only be an awesome *fact,* to be humbly believed, instead of being . . . *pressure* to be *received* in the act of love that is the fulfillment of man's being. So he regarded the Christian mystical tradition as a perversion of agape.

I hardly need to say that this is followed by another splendid outburst of Sebastianic indignation. This attitude to mysticism is deeply rooted not only in various forms of Protestantism but also in traditional Thomism insofar as that retains an appeal to love as *going beyond* the intellect in the act of faith. I agree with those who think that the one great mistake of St. Thomas Aquinas was to regard knowledge of God as a matter for logical argument and to reject, at least in principle, a natural awareness of God.

The next point is that

contemplative experience . . . makes us aware, at a depth that no other experience can touch, of sin. The contemplative becomes conscious of a resistance to the unimaginable takeover hinted at . . . that is more radical than bad will and that is somehow constitutional, woven into the human condition. This sense of sin as constitutional is being corroborated in our time by the brilliant meta-anthropological work of Ernest Becker, not himself a believer in God but at the end of his short life close to being one.

One of the strengths of Dom Sebastian's writing is his familiarity with these thinkers of our time who grapple with fundamental human problems. His own experience has taught him to discuss their work with a rare sympathy and understanding that must have led many to become acquainted with Christian points of view which might otherwise have remained unknown to them. Becker, we are told, "found at the heart of all human culture a desire, and for all practical purposes a need, of man to think of himself as *causa sui,*" utterly his own master. "Thus the biblical statement that at the origin of human life as we know it there is a sin, a mythic expression of what might be called the birth-trauma of human consciousness. . . ." This leads to the suggestion that "the human alienation pointed to by Becker (and, incidentally, by Marx) is not simply and only constitutional, but is some radical refusal, not reversible by us yet located in the free spirit and so remediable by God, and by him alone." Finally Becker is quoted as producing "a daring, if gimmicky formula"; he said that "our only possible release would be an absolution by the absolute."

On the next page Dom Sebastian enlarges his proposal:

> The experience of contemplative prayer and the change of life that it initiates comes up against the intractable fact of sin and finds resolution only in the contemplation of the man without sin, Jesus Christ. . . . Contemplative experience gives the meaning of "incarnation." The contemplative's sense of sin looks to the man in whom this meaning is realized in a way that reckons with sin. . . . Thus we shall have to think of God as "doing the theologian's thinking for him." This crude phrase attempts to represent what must be the nerve of theology, that thinking about God which is responsive to God's action on the thinker. There is given, in contemplation, an understanding of the connectedness of infinite with finite reality which does not depend on the concepts with which that connectedness is necessarily expressed. The change of heart that God effects suffuses with a divinely unitary understanding the connections that the theologian makes. Hence Lonergan's insistence on conversion as the essential meaning-giver for the theologian.

In the last of these peculiarly valuable lines, there is an unfortunate tendency to regard Lonergan's most important work as philosophical, with the result that his more recent theological writings are less well-known than they should be. Also, Dom Sebastian's style tends to be discursive— but in a way entirely suitable for his lecturing. I hope to have presented a condensation of his article, putting together those sentences that I judge to be forceful summarizations of the text, which will, I hope, in this form, give the reader their full impact. Lastly, the influence of God on our thinking is something which is written about a good deal more in the Continent of Europe, and especially in France, than it is elsewhere. In the English-speaking countries, mine particularly, it tends to be regarded with suspicion. We still suffer from the crushing effects of the Enlightenment. But anti-Enlightenment writers such as Andrew Louth and Alisdair MacIntyre are making headway among us.

The final section of the article, on the importance of "the sense of obligation," remains to be discussed. It quickly disposes of a popular objection: "To argue, as many have done, that because 'ought' cannot be deduced from 'is,' it must be irrational and simply a matter of conditioning, is simply a failure in introspection—and a very common one." There must be many people tempted to decide that the world makes no sense, and that one must just fend for oneself according to one's tastes, who have drawn back from the brink by realizing that there are vital differences between truth and falsehood and between savagery and kindness which they will disregard only on pain of some mysterious and fundamental loss to themselves. The topic is further pursued: "It is God that is here revealed, because only a mysterious ultimate authority can obligate one's freedom without destroying it. If my freedom is the essence, the coming-to-a-head, of my personhood, the ultimate authority must be some sort of super-essence of personhood." We are warned, finally, lest we should be excessively impressed by the "piece of reasoning" just quoted, that its major premise is "an *experience* of moral self-awareness as responsible. . . . The prime *argument* for God is to point to the fact that to become more self-aware is to become obligating-other-aware."

It may seem that I have taken the easy way of keeping a promise by quoting Dom Sebastian's article at such length. My excuse, to repeat, is that otherwise, apparently, it would remain so little known. I look forward to hearing from the editor of the *Downside Review* that he is inundated with requests for copies of the July 1977 issue.

～ 4 ～

Ego Transcendence
and Transformation:
The Soteriology of Sebastian Moore

Stephen J. Duffy

For some time now Sebastian Moore has been hard at work in a field that for too long has lain fallow: soteriology.[1] He has labored long and fruitfully on an axial problem: How are we to understand the relationship between Jesus and his crucifiers? How are we to understand the dynamics of healing and transformation in the person who admits the crucified into his or her life? How does the crucified help us to become whole human persons? In the first part of this essay I shall expose what I take to be the salient points of Moore's soteriology. In the second part I shall offer a critical theological reflection on Moore's position and on some of the basic questions it compels us to re-examine.

---

[1] S. Moore, *The Crucified Jesus Is No Stranger* (New York: Seabury, 1977); *The Fire and the Rose Are One* (New York: Seabury, 1980); *The Inner Loneliness* (New York: Crossroad, 1982); *Let This Mind Be in You* (New York: Harper & Row, 1985); *Jesus the Liberator of Desire* (New York: Crossroad, 1989). See also "The Language of Love," in F. Lawrence, ed. *Lonergan Workshop,* III (Chico: Scholars Press, 1982) 83–106; "Original Sin, Sex, Resurrection and Trinity," *Lonergan Workshop,* IV (1983) 85–98; "The New Life," *Lonergan Workshop,* V (1985) 145–62; "The Communication of a Dangerous Memory," in F. Lawrence, ed., *Communicating a Dangerous Memory: Soundings in Political Theology* (Atlanta: Scholars Press, 1987) 55–61; "The Forming and Transforming of Ego: An Explanatory Psychology of Soteriology," in F. Lawrence, ed., *Lonergan Workshop,* VIII (1990) 165–90. For an excellent early analysis of Moore's soteriology see W. Loewe, "Encountering the Crucified God: The Soteriology of Sebastian Moore," *Horizons* 9 (1982) 216–36.

I

The leitmotif of Moore's ongoing probing of the above questions is this: humanity crucifies God and itself but by the cross "the banality of evil" is embraced in the mystery of unconditional love, transformed into sin, and sin into healing and re-creating grace. Moore's soteriological project situates the intelligibility of the cross within the sphere of human interiority. Crucified innocence unmasks the inauthenticity of my self-pity and reluctant resignation as I play the role of one fallen victim to an evil world. But the sinlessness of Christ, so central to Moore's project, proves my innocence a charade and triggers the transfiguring dynamic of encounter with the crucified. Redemptive transformation cannot commence until by contemplating the suffering of the sinless Jesus I become aware of my sinfulness. Only then can I see myself as crucifier and crucified; only then does evil become sin; only then do I see the canyon yawning between what I am and what I am called to, the authentic humanity embodied in the crucified Jesus; only then do I see the multi-shaped alienation of my conscious ego from my total self. When that happens victim becomes culprit; lament and complaint, repentance, as I open myself to receive forgiveness, healing, reconciliation, and resources to begin the long journey toward my true self.

Only in recognizing the world's evil and my own sin do I recognize Christ and his God for what they are, and myself for who I am, one who is accepted even in my worst, loved, forgiven, redeemed. Any piety not rooted in such recognition of the world's evil and our sin is pseudo-piety, works-righteousness. As we journey toward our true selves, such recognition is never complete. We are masters of illusion and the lie and all our actions are marked by a coefficient of ambiguity, for the best heart's love falls short. As a favorite text of Luther starkly puts it: "All our righteousnesses are filthy rags" (Isa 64:6).

In the crucifixion, Moore asserts, we catch the historic drama that each of us plays out, the killing of our self-transcendence, the attempt to annihilate the intentionality of our "selves" by the ego's preference for its own self-importance. In contemplating the cross, it comes home to me that life's crucifixion of me is really my crucifixion of life and of myself. I crucify the possibilities of life not only for myself but for others. In the cross we see the contrariety of human nature, the psyche at cross-purposes with itself. This tension between ego and self, between crucifier and crucified is never definitively resolved in human history. We move in rhythm between polarities of sin and grace; each one is *simul iustus et peccator.* Paradoxically sin's essential effect, the crucified, is its undoing. The defenses mounted to conceal my mediocrity having been dismantled by the cross, sin is forgiven, undone, as it succumbs to divine love.

The cross is not just a reason to trust in God's love so that this trust may then vanquish my self-hatred. Rather, the cross is a *real symbol*. The events of the crucifixion are reenacted in the consciousness of the sinner and have psychological power to transform human subjectivity. In contemplation of the cross, the process whereby my self-hatred reaches realization, confession, and surrender is made visible and set in motion.[2] Self-hatred is obstacle to acceptance of divine love; but it can also be the medium in which God's love is revealed in the very moment that that love transforms self-hatred. I meet God's love not by denial of my self-hatred, not by turning away from it to some other motif, but as climax of my self-hatred, its crisis and resolution. "God transforms my self-hatred into love. That is the meaning of the cross."[3] Mysteriously our evil, our bias against wholeness, exposes us to God's love in a way and at a depth that even our desire for wholeness cannot. Jung is right. One must befriend one's shadow. Evil must enter into our integration. But it does so only through the crucified. With the crucifixion our hearts of darkness are made manifest. The worst has happened, the ultimate sin. And we await retribution; we await the iron law of divine justice to come down upon our heads. But it does not. The illusion that God is bound by such a law is now seen to be the projection of our own narrow ego's petty vindictiveness.

The true self, according to Moore, is relationship to and natural desire for the incomprehensible mystery, desire to be for another. In this, Moore echoes the Platonic-Augustinian anthropology, and Rahnerian variations on that theme.[4] The presence of the transcendent, the why of all whys, is a mediated immediacy; it is encountered only in the categorical reality of other selves and events. I seek the mystery; it clasps me. Desire is self-love

---

[2]While Moore works out his soteriology in terms of modern psychology, his theological underpinnings are Lonerganian. Lonergan's soteriology, "the just and mysterious law of the cross," can be found in the last three theses of his *De Verbo Incarnato* 3rd ed. (Roma: Universitá Gregoriana, 1964). W. Loewe contextualizes Lonergan's soteriology within his overall scheme and his approach to the problem of integration and shows his elucidation of the special theological categories of "sin" and "redemption" through the general categories used to articulate his analysis of transcendental method in "Lonergan and the Law of the Cross: A Universalist View of Salvation," *Anglican Theological Review* 59 (1977) 162–74.

[3]S. Moore, *The Crucified Jesus,* 37.

[4]This is especially so in *The Inner Loneliness.*

trusting in the mystery embracing and drawing me. It stretches the being I am. One desires because one is hopeful, hopeful because trusting; hope, trust, and desire make for self-love. For too long the Catholic tradition has repressed desire, Moore thinks. Jesus is presented as a model of mortified desire when in fact he is the liberator of desire. Desire for the absolute draws with it and orders *all* the appetites of our being, physical and spiritual. The concupiscence that leads to evil is the same erotic drive that leads to passionate love of God. Bank the fires of passion and you extinguish the lights of civilization and the fervor of religion. For too long Catholic concern with the failure of the "lower" appetites to obey the "higher" has overlooked the failure of the "higher" to befriend the "lower." The result is pious men and women who are half-persons.

Yet, becoming one's self is like hand-to-hand struggle in spiritual combat, for radical desire meets with radical impotence. In a way that Rahner never did, Moore charts in psychological terms the dark underside of our humanity that impedes our intentionality's thrust to the infinite. What is truly tragic is not so much our inclination to evil but our inability to pursue the great good that lures us. Moore puts us in mind of Augustine's "cruel necessity of sinning" because "our hearts are not in our power."[5] We have free will but our freedom is fettered. We experience a kind of will not to love the good, a dark involuntary within the voluntary, as Ricoeur has it; we experience the undertow of an evil that is our own and not our own.[6] Thus Moore's desire for the absolute is countered by a "will not to be," by a "desire to undo the order of being," by the sin of the world of parents and institutions that shapes our hearts and all too frequently conduces to ego-arrest, as object-relations theorists like D. W. Winnicott and Alice Miller make clear.[7] Sin for Moore is "the inescapable narcissism of our consciousness," a failure of self-transcendence.[8] Standing with the tradition since Augustine, Moore affirms that sin has no being; the only kind of being it can have is the sight of itself in its ultimate effect, the crucified. Moore's perspective is similar to Lonergan's on "basic sin." In Lonergan's words: "Basic sin is not an event . . . it consists of failure of occurrence,

[5] *De Perfectione Iustitiae Hominis* 9; *De Dono Perseverantiae* 13.

[6] Cf. P. Ricoeur, "Original Sin: A Study in Meaning," in D. Ihde, ed., *The Conflict of Interpretations: Essays in Hermeneutics* (Evanston: Northwestern University, 1974) 269–86, and "The Unity of the Voluntary and the Involuntary as a Limiting Idea," in C. Reagan and D. Stewart, eds., *The Philosophy of Paul Ricoeur: An Anthology of His Work* (Boston: Beacon Press, 1978) 3–19.

[7] S. Moore, *The Crucified Jesus,* 13, and *Jesus the Liberator,* 25–30.

[8] S. Moore, *The Crucified Jesus,* 35.

in the absence in the will of reasonable response to an obligatory motive."[9] Even so, that "which could and ought to be but is not" has devastating effects, as we see in the cross of Jesus, which confronts us with our own basic sin, our suicidal and murderous renouncement of ego-transcendence for ourselves and others.

In other words, the alternative to the torturous process of becoming one's self is to remain unconscious, to atrophy in egoism. Thus evil appears as failure, want, privation, not as the symmetric, active opposite of the good. And while intelligibility demands sufficient reasons, the evil that is ego-attachment can claim none. Yet the mind clamors for reasons but finds only rationalization piled upon rationalization, creating a wall of deceit and illusion. Reasons are self-supporting; rationalizations demand unending reinforcement. Especially in the case of group-egoism the deceit becomes aggressive. In every case it is illusory for the deceivers must believe the rationalization themselves.

Moore finds the ego caught in a tension between separateness and wholeness. Authentic humanity requires the reconciliation of these polarities: being oneself yet one with the pervading mystery. Creative tension between the oceanic and the finite, between separateness and wholeness or oneness occurs at crisis points in human growth from infancy to death (and perhaps beyond?) when a new me is struggling to emerge. Growth is overcoming the cleavage in us, an ever-deepening liberation of desire, and discovery of the self. Desire's full liberation comes only in oneness with God. Beyond transcendence of the ego into the self lies transcendence of both in encounter with the holy mystery. In this, Moore is reminiscent of the Greek tradition's concern with *theopoiesis*. The God-image comes more into focus the more the ego dies into fuller selfhood. Mark well, however; liberation is not "getting what I want," as modern self-fulfillment peddlers insist, but coming to want as ultimately the relatedness I am to everything and everyone in the mystery. Gratification is not necessarily growth. For desire is not an emptiness waiting to be filled; it is a fullness needing relationship, love trying to happen. Desire is not just fastening onto a new object; it is finding a new subject, a new "me."

True growth is stunted because desire is shackled, because in our moral ineptitude we dread giving up the present ego to become a self we do not know. The uncharted sea unnerves us. Ego-fixation has its comforts and securities, though they are masked-death. The bias that is sin idolizes the

---

[9]Ibid., 8, and B. Lonergan, *Insight: A Study of Human Understanding* (New York: Harper & Row, 1978) 667.

individual or group ego at its present stage of development and snuffs out the desire to be more. The anxiety-driven tenacity with which we cling to illusion can never be underestimated. Only the love that comes with liberated desire casts out anxiety and hence the bias that distorts our knowing and numbs desire. The rebirth that is growth requires change, suffering, dying in installments, the trajectory of a thousand ego deaths, negation of the biased, warped ego that must be transcended. It requires the suffering that comes with dying to sin but also the distinctly other suffering that accompanies all transformation.

We customarily connect the death-requirement of personal growth with sin so that dying to ego means dying to sin. But how then, asks Moore, can we speak of the sinless Jesus as having to undergo this kind of death? His answer: dying to ego and dying to sin are not identical. Dying to ego is the dying of present ego-consciousness, which is indispensable, yet must be transcended if growth is to occur. Sin may try to hold fast to it. Hence dying to ego may involve dying to sin's holding action, its pretexts and rationalizations. However, the sinless, fully liberated person is one in whom ego-dying, undeterred by sin, occurs with greater frequency and intensity. As sinners we flee from self by a thousand strategies of inauthenticity; we cannot let go of our gods—success, fame, security, self-justification. The sinless one recognizes that our deepest yearnings for wholeness are grounded in reality and so lets go into that final reality, the pure, unbounded love that is God.

Thus dying to ego is not completely the same as dying to sin. The distinction is important to Moore. The stronger the weddedness to present ego, the less I experience the real fear of what draws me beyond ego. We cannot define our basic posture vis-à-vis the infinite in terms of our attachment to the ego-phase, i.e., by sin. We see this basic attitude in its pure state in the sinless Jesus. That attitude is to be ours. Finitude, creaturehood is not sin. The dread that grips the creature at the call to transformation is not sin. Sin is its absence. There is a resistance to the call that is appropriate to the finite when the infinite impels it to liberated desire. It is the natural pain of being human and must not be confused with sin. Being human exposed Jesus to this suffering, and with a unique intensity. To link all suffering to sin is, therefore, to muddle things. Suffering inheres in finitude in presence of the infinite. Jesus takes on *this* suffering that we, because of our sinful ego-fixation, are not able to take on until we recognize our true self and its proper suffering in his cross. Empathetically he suffers with that in us which due to sin makes us unable to suffer. Consciousness of being suffered with where sin impedes our acceptance of the suffering that in the nature of things must be gone through to transcend ego to a new "me" causes sin to fall away.

Summarily, sin deadens the nerve of creaturehood; the empathetic suffering of the crucified resurrects it. Conversion occurs in the moment I discover that I am suffered within the deepest core of me that suffers from not being able to suffer.[10] We need to be carried beyond the suffering we inflict on ourselves and others through sinful clinging to the present ego to the suffering that leads to liberated desire. The sinless Jesus is the human who suffers only God. He suffers the pain our sinful ego-clutching obstructs. From his baptism to Golgotha and Easter he shed the ego of a good Jew for a world-embracing self. He is the paradigm of conversion, not from sin, but from innocence. In him we grasp the conversion we are called to, beyond ego, which is not sin, to a Spirit-filled and directed existence. There is no reason to mistake that in us which has to die for sin, for we have seen it die in the sinless Jesus. The creature's sluggishness and reluctance for transformation must not be confused with sin, for we have seen that reluctance wear the face of agonized dismay in the garden. In Jesus death to ego is unobstructed by sin; it is not, however, unattended by dread.

Thus Moore gives us "an inverse soteriology," as he calls it.[11] Soteriology is inverted by starting not with him who suffers for us but with us who have to be suffered for. What is it we are not able to suffer because of our sinfulness? Simply, God. The inherited, universal illusion that ego is for keeps stands in the way of suffering the transformation of ourselves. The deadened heart of creaturehood revives when we recognize that we are suffered for where we most need and desire to suffer by one who suffers always and only what it is to be human and never from his own struggle to preserve and absolutize ego at any cost. This willed, redemptive suffering that is at the heart of creaturehood counterpoints all the detestable suffering we heap upon ourselves and others in our struggle to maintain and deify ego and breathes life into that in our humanity which needs, wants, and fears to suffer.

Willingness to suffer and die changes everything. Insofar as one does not reach that point the world is wicked and I its victim. To the extent one

---

[10]Moore finds a poignant analogy in Dostoevsky's Raskolnikov, who experienced in the love of Sonya not opposition to his sin but its undermining when she takes on in Christlike fashion the suffering he rendered himself incapable of so as to murder an old woman. His rebirth is in the moment when, having confessed to Sonya, he hears her say: "What have you done to yourself?" The ego sufficiently absolutized (to commit murder in this case) puts the self beyond the possibility of the suffering that transforms. It is frozen there until we see another suffer this forgotten pain of ourselves. Cf. *Jesus the Liberator*, 36.

[11]"The Forming and Transforming of Ego," 182.

does reach that point (and here, I think, Moore meets Ricoeur), the self-perceived victim becomes culprit; but even more, suffering as penalty or affliction becomes suffering as action and the world ceases to be too wicked for God to be good. Suffering as action is suffering offered in creative transformation of self and therefore of others. Only when we are willing to suffer the ever-demanding lure of God, to embody the demands of full humanity, to court suffering and rejection at the hands of the unliberated, only when we have moved from suffering as just punishment or undeserved affliction to offered suffering as redemptive transformation does theodicy move to another register. A way out of the blind alley that all speculative theodicies end in is found. The terminal aporia that argument inexorably leads to now becomes fruitful. For the dialectical movement is resolved as one moves from Adam to Job to Christ, from culprit and victim to servant, from evil as retributive penalty and surd affliction to evil redeemed, from God as just judge and God as tyrant to God as fellow-sufferer.[12] Sin is the refusal to move forward in this dialectic. It is the strangulation of desire and hope. It is the fear that will not let us "hope that we could actually encounter either all the forgiveness we need or all the love we long for."[13] In the cross we see vividly portrayed the tragic consequences of our action and non-action. But we also see that it does not incur wrath and retribution but mercy and prodigal forgiveness. The *lex talionis* is replaced by the law of the cross. A hyper-ethical God beyond accusation and consolation is encountered. But resistance sets in. To entertain transcending the *lex talionis* is to entertain two threatening possibilities: that justice does not rule the cosmos but something less, chaos, or something more, mercy. Hence we are summoned to go beyond vindictiveness and a penal vision of the universe, beyond justice to costly merciful love. Only the willingness for voluntary, offered suffering affords wisdom enough to affirm that God is not wickedly chaotic. Only suffering servants drive out the demonic deity. The priority is praxis, not argument, nor even the conviction that God is good; the priority is being a redeeming person. Only then can one see the goodness of a God beyond justice and caprice and believe in redemption. Hermeneutics is more than a cognitive process, more than an intellectual or theoretical task. It is an ethical task as well.

[12]Cf. P. Ricoeur, *The Symbolism of Evil* (New York: Harper & Row, 1967) 306–46. Here, admittedly, I read Moore through Ricoeurian lenses, but I think it enhances our perception of Moore's position.

[13]V. Gregson, "The Faces of Evil and Our Response: Ricoeur, Lonergan, Moore," in T. Fallon and P. Riley, eds., *Religion in Context* (Lanham: University Press of America, 1988) 139. See also S. Moore, *The Crucified Jesus*, 107; *The Fire and the Rose*, 13–4, 91.

But how is one to come to the intellectual, religious, and moral conversion needed? For Moore, human impotence for the absolute finds empowerment in encounter with the figure of the crucified and risen Christ. To avoid reducing the Jesus story to myth, Moore attempts a historical reconstruction of the Easter experience of the disciples, which, for him, is the foundational experience of Christianity. The story of Jesus does not exist without the disciples.[14] His question now becomes: What was it like to meet the risen Jesus? Thus his focus is on the inner, subjective change experienced by the disciples without denying, as some have erroneously thought, that something also happened to Jesus.[15] Moore's historical reconstruction is as well a psychological appropriation of the Jesus story, for it centers on the struggle to liberate desire, to overcome ego-arrest, and to move toward the true self.

Before the crucifixion, the disciples' horizons had been exploded. Their hearts stirred, desire awakened, a new and dangerous hope arose as the gaze of their eyes and the touch of their hands came upon a man whose own desire was wholly liberated, a man who moved inexorably toward the mystery that was his life. The kingdom, wholeness was here, now, in this marginal Jew living in a marginal province of the Roman Empire. He was the new being, a man totally free of sin's captivity and consumed with hunger for a God whose love he was convinced of, a man unimpaired by self-hatred and guilt, a man who embraced suffering as an action, laying down his life of his own accord in constant ego-dissolution in its divine ground which culminated in the cross, the work of the fearful and unliberated. What brought about the crucifixion was the crucifiers' rejection of the oneness and personal transcendence to which they were summoned by the life and teaching of Jesus. No masochist, Jesus was not attracted to the cross; the cross was attracted to him, as consummation of all his deaths to ego. To suffer God, to live finite exposed to infinite is to court suffering at

---

[14]For Moore's reconstruction of the Easter experience, cf. e.g., *The Fire and the Rose,* 80–91; *The Inner Loneliness,* 88–93; *Let This Mind Be in You,* 117–45; *Jesus the Liberator,* 41–76. See also his summation of his views in "Experiencing the Resurrection," *Commonweal* 109 (1982) 47–51, and his response to critics, 220–2.

[15]"To say that the real evidence of the resurrection is in the sense the community has . . . of being 'in' the leader recently done to death is to say that this new sense of relatedness to and in Jesus had *to have a start.* Thus 'something is the case' brings in its train 'something happened' . . . That shortly after his death he became known as the body to which they belonged—*that* is the resurrection . . . Leaving the tomb is probably involved. But to speak of that as the resurrection is totally to miss the point . . . (He) became in their midst a life-giving Spirit. To explain this as simply a post-bereavement adjustment seems to me the quintessence of reductionism." "The Forming and Transforming of Ego," 180–1.

the hands of those reluctant to leave the ego's citadels. The cross, however, in its harsh negativity shattered the dream; the disciples plummeted into the darkest abyss of separateness, despair, and desolation. Jesus and his God were dead. All he had said, done, and been was now in question. They had caught the contagion of his defamiliarizing, life-transcending desire that led beyond this world's horizons. But now his life had been brutally ended. Where was he now? And where were they? The death of Jesus, paradigm of desire, brought their desire into crisis. Their loneliness and confusion were aggravated by their feelings of guilt. They had left him in the lurch. Conversely, he had left them in the lurch. With his death they really died and with him they and their newly awakened desires and hopes were buried. They had lost everything. They entered the void that is death, a void that only the Spirit of God can fill with a new creation. But it was all to prove a traumatic gestation.

For then the risen Christ appeared. He empowered them with the Spirit and rekindled the fires of liberated desire. The disciples experienced conversion, a dissolution of guilt, a superabundance of new life, fullness of joy and peace, all of which could only be the presence of God. Only *because* they had lost everything could they receive everything. Their desires and hopes were resurrected; the resurrection of Jesus was yes to all that. For it affirmed that Jesus is where all his life, teaching, and intentionality had been headed—with God. His Spirit-giving life lifted the burden of their guilt and unleashed their true selves. If the crucified Jesus had led them to experience the dark abyss that is death, somehow the risen Christ had taken them experientially beyond earth. In the death/resurrection of Christ the death of meaning exploded into the meaning of death. In him they now met the God they hungered for. But this God was a crucified God and in Jesus would draw those who would be disciples to the *via crucis.* To fear the suffering of the cross as the enemy of desire is the false consciousness that equates desire with the egoism that is given to ego-satisfaction and arrest, never to know the true self. Small wonder, then, that Paul sees Christians dying and rising with Christ. Christianity, for Moore, is thus a story of bereavement, of moving through desolation to the awareness that the world is God's, not death's.

II

What are we to think of Moore's fascinating and enlightening soteriology? What Moore has attempted is to unlock the intelligibility of the

Jesus story by way of a psychological mediation. His concern, which the literal-minded cannot fathom, is less with what is objectively involved in the life-death/resurrection of Jesus ("Oh, I see, the tomb's empty; he's alive again!") than with its bearing upon the disciples' subjective transformation and my emergence as a self. Human interiority has for Moore an invariant set of psychic structures and operations that govern the dynamics of self-emergence. Within the world of interiority his focus is on the affective as it orients or impedes the cognitive and moral life in their thrusting toward the absolute mystery that is the horizon grounding desire and the possibility of all personal activity, especially our valuing. In his exploration of this psychic structure Moore enlists especially Carl Jung, Ernest Becker, and the object relations theorists. In a kind of Tillichian correlation they lay bare for Moore the sinful human predicament to which the sinless and risen Christ offers hope, and they map the affective dynamics for understanding how that is so. Articulated in light of Moore's analysis of human subjectivity, the Christian mystery of redemption is disclosed to symbolize a dynamic that can be empirically verified in human interiority.

Moore's appropriation of the intrinsic intelligibility of the Christian story of redemption by way of an intentionality-shaped psychology is most appealing. His is a praying, self-involving, dare I say, monastic theology with roots deep in the Catholic tradition and ethos, a theology concerned with conversion. It is a theology that, while sacrificing none of its requisite critical rigor, will preach in Peoria. Moore's genre is the exercise; his language, often phatic. Reading Moore involves far more than gathering information or even arriving at a bloodless theoretical understanding. It is an exercise in self-appropriation. This is why reading him is a workout. It involves more than keenness. It demands self-awareness, and a level of it that is not for some easy to sustain. One has not only to read Moore but to discover oneself in oneself. His work has an Augustinian-Lutheran ring in that he too writes in the blood of his experience. Moore's workbooks challenge the reader to taste and see, for only by sounding one's own experience can one grasp the liberating, transforming power of the crucified. Ultimately Moore's own experience and his critical appropriation of it are the validation of his soteriology. In this, Moore's work clearly reflects modern theology's experiential starting point following Schleiermacher.[16]

---

[16]Moore's soteriology bears some affinity to Schleiermacher's. Schleiermacher too focuses on the sinlessness of Jesus awakening in us consciousness of sin and views redemption as the transformation of the believer's interiority. Cf. *The Christian Faith,* Vol. 2 (New York: Harper & Row, 1963) 427–8.

Moore thus makes a valuable contribution to post-conciliar theology's effort to exorcise the demons of extrinsicism, juridicism, and subject/object bifurcation that haunt the Catholic house, for he gives full play to subjectivity. One truly knows the Christ not by entering the world of theoretical theology but by asking: what does the Jesus story mean for me? As for Luther, so for Moore. Salvific knowledge of Christ is had not by analyzing the Nicene *homoousios* doctrine or the Chalcedonian two nature model, but by experiencing in one's interiority what the crucified is doing for one as he transforms evil into sin and guilt and them in turn into grace.[17] There is no naive neo-Pelagianism in Moore. The attainment of the self is not a human achievement. If ego is the me I sometimes have a hand in making, the self is what I am invited to discover. I am more narrator of my story than author. All is grace. "Where sin abounded, grace abounded all the more" (Rom 5:20). The mystery of iniquity yields to the anomaly of the good. History is perdition but more so salvation. And here Moore invokes the soteriological corollary of Athanasius at Nicaea. Since saving grace is mediated through the risen Christ, and God alone can re-create us whole, there is divinity in God's Christ, who must be *homoousion tō Patri.* Moore's soteriology retrieves for him belief in the divinity of Jesus as the Spirit's therapy for the human spirit.

It is not clear to me whether Moore's high christology (he laments the ante- and anti-Nicene bias of so much contemporary christology) ties the divine enabling love exclusively to the Easter experience. Are there paradigmatic persons and events in all the world's high religions? Or is Christianity to be absolutized? Can the Buddhist not find in and through Buddhism the mystery beneficent that offers the salvation that is ego-transcendence? Jesus is unique, but is he the absolutely normative savior of all?[18] Perhaps Moore's christology needs fuller explicitation and his critical soteriology tempering by intercourse with the soteriologies of the great world religions, which Moore considers "sub-Christian." One must acknowledge, following Moore's own heuristic, that religious conversion can be mediated by the symbol systems of the world religions. Insofar as their

---

[17]S. Moore, *The Crucified Jesus,* 4–5. To see Moore's affinity to Luther one need but read part of the latter's 1535 *Lectures on Galatians* in J. Pelikan, ed. *Luther's Works* (St. Louis: Concordia, 1963) 26:276–91. See on this W. Loewe, "Encountering the Crucified God," 225–30. Lonergan, and no doubt Moore, would remind us that Abelard, writing before the theorem of the supernatural had been developed, seems to omit the fact that justification is not won by human effort but is the work of God.

[18]See my own attempt to come to grips with this question in "The Galilean Christ: Particularity and Universality," *Journal of Ecumenical Studies* 26 (1989) 154–74.

symbols empower ego-transcendence they too incarnate the dynamic of the divine redemptive process that Christianity finds embodied in the cross. May not that dynamic also be at work in those who live out their lives within a horizon that is not explicitly religious, indeed, even anti-religious? Where the law of the cross is operative, where ego-transcendence and the active sacrificial love it entails are realized, there the divine redemptive process is at work. Thus Moore's heuristic of redemption should, it seems, be verifiable in other religions and in persons not explicitly religious. The specificity of Christianity may be said to reside in its originating redemptive event and the symbols that re-present it. But may not the dynamic of the cross and its transformative power, as least as articulated by Moore, come alive in diverse religious symbol systems? Dialogue, encounter with the stranger, and the stranger's symbols, should conduce to a deeper, broader, more nuanced understanding of human interiority and the redemptive process struggling to be released within it.

Moore's psychological categories certainly render intelligible the phenomenon of redemption and conversion within Christianity. He has provided a soteriological heuristic of human redemption by an analysis of sin based on an anthropology of self-transcendence. Perhaps his categories also provide a basis for cross-cultural interreligious dialogue in that they expose psychic dimensions common to all religious conversions, a dynamic thought to be empirically verifiable in the arena of interiority. On the other hand, the possible fruitfulness of this horizon may demand greater clarity, if indeed that is possible, concerning Moore's understanding of the elusive "self" over against the ego as conscious personality. What is the "self"? One has access to the self only by becoming oneself. The self I would be I am not yet. Thus the elusive self is more aspiration than fact, an objective rather than an object of inquiry. We catch glimpses of the self only by reflecting on our efforts to attain it. Success is gradual and limited, as successive images of the self prove hollow. "Death" is the exposure of a particular self image as an ego-protection, an idol. And can there be transcultural agreement about a transcendent selfhood that is protean in its cultural forms? Talk of universal, invariant, anthropological structures that norm authenticity always makes skittish those who consider the quest for such structures a perennial Catholic idiosyncrasy. Moreover, at a time when political and liberation theologies are the order of the day, some will find Moore's soteriology highly individualistic and too removed from the public arena. But certainly Moore's approach is patient of a socio-political exponent, basically because by dying to ego a person becomes progressively more solidary with others, shatters the defensive barriers between people, and

challenges all the role-defined relationships that institutionalize the nor-
mativity and perdurability of individual and group ego as a way of being.

Moore's highly creative psycho-historical reconstruction of the Paschal
experience of Jesus and his disciples is a narrative we can resonate to. However, it drops us smack into a thicket of questions. Aware of the uniqueness of historical events, the historian cannot rule out *a priori* an event's
possibility. Where an event or its evidence are not publicly accessible, the
best we can do is to precariously reconstruct the most consistent narrative
account of the event that we can, given the materials accessible to us. This
Moore has quite legitimately attempted, much as Rudolph Pesch and
Edward Schillebeeckx have.[19] Moore has tried to get behind the appearance sightings and the empty tomb accounts with his psycho-religious
horizon and creatively fill in gaping holes in the data. His reconstruction,
while appealing, even ingenious, appears a conjectural and skewed extrap-
olation of his second order psychological appropriation of the Easter story.
Pesch and Schillebeeckx appear closer to the mark. Moore knows too
much about the consciousness (and unconscious?) and self-understanding
of Jesus and his disciples.

The obscure seems to be explained by the more obscure. There is an
exegesis of the self by an exegesis of the notoriously difficult resurrection
narratives, an exegesis of the transforming journey from ego to self by an
exegesis of the elusive appearance stories and accounts of the empty tomb,
both essential to Moore's reconstruction of the disciples' Easter conversion.[20]
More than that, ego-transcendence and resurrection are dialectically inter-
locked much as though Rahner's transcendental method were at work. The
transcendental desire for the real self and historic proclamation of and testimonies to the resurrection ground and reveal one another. The resurrection

---

[19]See R. Pesch, "Zur Enstehung des Glaubens an die *Auferstehung* Jesu: Ein Vorschlag
zur Diskussion," *Theologische Quartalschrift* 153 (1973) 201–8 and 270–83; "Das
Messiasbekenntnis des Petrus: Neuverhandlung einer alten Frage," *Biblische Zeitschrift* 17
(1973) 178–95, and 18 (1974) 20–31; "Die Passion des Menschensohnes. Eine Studie zu
den Menschensohnworten der vormarkinischen Passionsgeschichte," in R. Pesch and R.
Schnackenburg, eds., *Jesus und der Menschensohn* (Freiburg: Herder, 1975); *Das Abendmahl
und Jesu Todesverständnis* (Freiburg: Herder, 1979). E. Schillebeeckx, *Jesus: An Experiment
in Christology* (New York: Crossroad, 1979) 320–97 and 516–45; *Interim Report on the
Books Jesus and Christ* (New York: Crossroad, 1981) 74–93. For a sympathetic exposition
of Pesch's views within current options see J. Galvin, "Resurrection as Theologia Crucis
Jesu: The Foundational Christology of Rudolf Pesch," *Theological Studies* 38 (1977)
513–25, and "Jesus' Approach to Death: An Examination of Some Recent Studies,"
Theological Studies 41 (1980) 713–44.

[20]See especially *Jesus the Liberator*, 51–76.

for Moore is object and ground of Christian faith and hope because the transcendental hope for a self that is whole finds expression in the Christian historical hope in Jesus' resurrection. For Moore the appearances and the empty tomb, the "historical trace" of the mystery of the resurrection, are not merely secondary literary embellishments of a primal experience, as they are for Rahner and others.[21] The ground of faith for Moore is in the life of Jesus and in the appearances of the risen Christ, which effected a conversion in the disciples, a conversion confirmed by the empty tomb, which is historical and a necessary though insufficient condition for Easter faith.

However attractive it may be, Moore's reconstruction is not problem-free.[22] An experience cannot be disjoined and isolated from its interpretation, as if the former were prior to the latter. The interpretation is integral to the experience, somehow constitutive of it. The early Christian resurrection experiences cannot be siphoned off and viewed independently of the interpretation of these experiences. Hence the diverse testimonies in the oral tradition and in their very diverse literary forms *are* in part the experience itself. They are not a secondary phenomenon. This is sobering. It moves us to ask whether attempts to get behind these testimonies may lead us to reducing the revelation to one mode of religious discourse and to saying not more but less about the meaning of the resurrection. Hymnic language, creedal formulas, apocalyptic, androcentric theophanies are the diverse literary forms that articulate the meaning and significance of Jesus' resurrection. The form determines how the event and experience of the resurrection are to be expressed. Attempts to go behind them to some conversion experience are fascinating but may be misleading because they inadequately weigh the tight correspondence between literary forms and their revelatory content and because they inadequately consider how the interpretation of the resurrection in these forms constitutes the experience of the meaning of the resurrection.

Experience occurs within interpretation and meaning is voiced in and through literary forms. The hymnic and creedal testimonies disclose the meaning of the resurrection to be the manifestation of God's power over life and death, of God's covenant fidelity, of God's vindication of injustice

---

[21]K. Rahner, *Foundations of Christian Faith: An Introduction to the Idea of Christianity* (New York: Seabury, 1978) 276.

[22]For what follows I am indebted to the insights of F. Schüssler Fiorenza, *Foundational Theology: Jesus and the Church* (New York: Crossroad, 1984) 39–46, and P. Ricoeur, *Essays on Biblical Interpretation,* ed. L. Mudge (Philadelphia: Fortress, 1980) 73–154. See also Ricoeur's *Hermeneutics and the Human Sciences,* ed. J. Thompson (New York: Cambridge University Press, 1981) 274–96.

against the righteous, of the establishment of God's kingdom, and of the resurrection of the dead. Paul interpreted this resurrection power as ground of the consoling hope of life after death, a hope probably not widespread at that time. The gospel narratives link this hope with the historical Jesus as they attest to the vibrant reality of the risen Christ who is identified with the earthly, crucified Jesus. They also link this hope with the emerging church insofar as they tie together the crucified and risen one and the commissioning of disciples. Cumulatively these forms are more than assertion of an isolated datum within history. They bespeak a vision of all reality, which now, by reason of Jesus' resurrection, is believed to be meaningful and gracious because we live in the presence of a loving God and because in the end goodness and life, not injustice and death, will have the final word since love is the final power. Thus history and its struggle can be trusted. But it is also a vision linked to the life-praxis of Jesus and to the genesis and mission of the church. The resurrection inaugurates the eschatological vindication of God. In a word, what we find in these forms is the rooting of individual and eschatological hopes in the historical and risen Jesus, the commissioning of the community, and the bonding of the community with the life-praxis of Jesus, who had been vindicated by God's raising him. Belief in the resurrection led the disciples to focus on the meaning of Jesus' life and praxis, on their own roots in that life, and on its community building power.

Perhaps this reading of the resurrection experience, modest by comparison with second order readings, marks the boundary of our exegesis. Beyond that, we are brought to a *docta ignorantia,* to making do with life as best we can, holding fast to the hope-full belief that ours is a God of life, and quite legitimately, even necessarily, reading our belief, as Moore does, in light drawn from the insights of contemporary disciplines. Thus are the criteria of appropriateness and intelligibility satisfied.[23]

---

[23]Using Lonergan's differentiation of stages of meaning—common sense, theory, interiority—we may locate the New Testament in the stage of common sense. Cf. *Method in Theology* (New York: Herder & Herder, 1972) 85–100. The gospel message of redemption cannot adequately speak to our condition as it stands. It needs mediation. An analysis of the New Testament's concepts of salvation can inspire and enlighten today only when combined with insight into the historical conditions of New Testament times and our own. Thus are born second order interpretations. Cf. E. Schillebeeckx, *Interim Report,* 13–19. But all second order interpretations christologically grounding programs of social reform, models of psychological development, calls to authentic existence, etc., necessary as they are, must be subjected to criticism. For "the historical Jesus" forever eludes our programs, subverts our ideologies, and escapes our neat categories. With reason did Schweitzer contend that he will always be "strange and puzzling" for our age.

Moore's entire corpus is studded with gems of wisdom and subtle humor, lined with pathos, and of late punctuated by telling poetry. But one eccentricity in *Jesus the Liberator* I must note. Moore defends the priority of Matthew's Gospel over Mark's, asserts the non-existence of Q, and holds to the historicity of the witness of Matthew to the resurrection because he is in fact Matthew the apostle. All this seems eccentric in light of current scholarly consensus and irrelevant to the thrust of Moore's work, which does not require Matthew as the proto-gospel.[24]

At the end of the day, however, Moore surfaces again a nagging foundational question. He compels us to reconsider it. Need we, can we, tie existential psychologies, programs of liberation, and political theologies to "the historical Jesus" and the historical experience of the disciples? Are "the historical Jesus" and the disciples' Easter experience too elusive to serve as moorings? Like the great myths, the Jesus story developed by Christians over centuries offers an enabling hope of salvation as it tells us who we are and who we are meant to be and how we are to make the journey from here to there. But Moore's easy access to "the historical Jesus" must give us pause. It compels us to look again at the modern abstraction and hypothetical construct (not to be equated with the real Jesus) that Jesus research has come to call "the historical Jesus" or "the Jesus of history." Such research can at best retrieve only pieces of a lost mosaic, faint traces of a faded fresco that invite a variety of interpretations and projections. The Gospels provide glimpses of the real Jesus. They do not portray "the historical Jesus," though they are the sources of reconstructions of "the historical Jesus." To think otherwise is anachronistic.[25]

The tradition is the chief mediation of the event of Jesus Christ. Jesus is the man remembered from the earliest apostolic tradition to the present. "Christians believe *in* Jesus Christ *with* the apostles as witnesses and thereby in the tradition which mediates that belief *with* and through the apostles."[26]

---

[24]In a presentation at the annual meeting of the College Theology Society in New Orleans in June 1990, Moore quipped that the monks of Downside are said to take a fourth vow, to defend the priority of Matthew over Mark. *Se non e vero, e ben trovato.*

[25]On this problem see J. Meier, "The Historical Jesus: Rethinking Some Concepts," *Theological Studies* 51 (1990) 3–24. In this lucid essay Meier shows the difficulties surrounding the distinction introduced by Martin Kähler between the historical *(historisch)* Jesus and the historic *(geschichtlich)* Christ and suggests an alternative terminology. While he succeeds in clearly synthesizing the ambiguities known to becloud "the speech habits of close-to-a-century of scholars," he does not, I think, succeed in minting an alternative terminology.

[26]D. Tracy, *The Analogical Imagination: Christian Theology and the Culture of Pluralism* (New York: Crossroad, 1981) 227. I have found Tracy's approach to this entire problem

The witnesses witness to their faith and they assume, as generally Christians do, that their understanding of Jesus is substantially true to the actual Jesus who lived among them. The only Jesus we know is the Jesus remembered by the whole tradition and experienced by ourselves individually and communally. The tradition's yardstick of authenticity is its fidelity to the original apostolic witness to the event, which stands as a corrective for discerning developments and deviations. One moves to personal response to the Christ event through personal recognition of the mediating role of the tradition, which, in its myriad of expressions, remembers Jesus as the Christ present here and now in word, sacrament, and action. A converse movement closes the dialectic. Experience and response are thus channeled through the whole Church as a living tradition. While one comes to trust the tradition, one also senses its ambiguity and ongoing need of self-correction, lest it betray the event entrusted to it. Experiences in the present can provide further resources for understanding the event and the tradition for our own time and culture. As the tradition runs its course, new second order interpretations emerge seeking to reappropriate the event.

Most theologians have abandoned the earlier liberal quest for "the historical Jesus" and, above all, the search for the "religious consciousness" and "psychology" of Jesus. Most now concede that the "psychology" of Jesus is inaccessible to critical study. The primary question of christology is not whether Jesus actualized in his own consciousness the genuine possibility for cruciform, agapic existence that he symbolizes. It is the question of apprehending the meaning and truth of the confession that Jesus is the Christ, that in proclaiming him the truth of human existence is re-presented with finality. What critical study can and must retrieve is the substance of the apostolic witness to Jesus. Historical-critical recovery of that witness and of the memory images of later New Testament communities adjudicates all later formulations and practices claiming continuity with the Jesus living in the memory of the apostolic witnesses.

It seems misguided, then, to construct a christology or a soteriology on the wobbly foundations of a historical-critical unraveling of the faith or consciousness of Jesus. The existential significance of the re-presentative words, deeds, and destiny of Jesus does not stand or fall on that. Such efforts seem more preoccupied with the intelligibility of the Christ event for modern, historically conscious persons than with problems of appropri-

---

most helpful. See 231–338. See also his *Blessed Rage for Order: The New Pluralism in Theology* (New York: Seabury, 1975) 204–36.

ateness to the Scriptures.[27] Aside from the extreme hazards in reconstructing the psychological state of any historical figure, those seeking to unlock the consciousness of Jesus seem to overlook the fact that what Christianity calls for is faith *in* Jesus, not faith in the scholarly reconstructed faith of Jesus. If "the historical Jesus" were the object of faith, whose "historical Jesus" would it be? And would faith be possible for the unscholarly? Faith clings to the person of Christ and only secondarily to ideas about him. To critically test the reliability of the apostolic memory against "the historical Jesus" is legitimate though difficult, but not *theologically* required. Though scholarly study may enrich understanding, and faith is interested in what scientific history can know of Jesus, research does not ground faith. The tradition stretching from the earliest witness to the present community's memory does that. Perhaps the same reservations can be registered concerning philosophical reconstructions of Jesus' consciousness that psychologize the tradition's high christology, as does Rahner.[28] The assumption at work in some historical reconstructions reappears, viz., that the establishment of Jesus' actualization of the possibility he embodied as the Christ is a theological requisite, that the only way to arrive at the "fact" of Jesus is to establish (historically or philosophically) his own realization of a genuine possibility for existence rather than to concern oneself with the fact of Jesus the Christ as the re-presentation of that possibility.

In other words, the Christian claim for the existential significance of Jesus' words, deeds, and destiny does not depend on our historically laying bare the faith and deepest levels of Jesus' consciousness. When such a precarious critical (though all too often uncritical) endeavor is undertaken, it can result only in low degrees of probability. What scholarly historical reconstructions of Jesus' life and message can and must do is provide the content of the community's proclamation of the manifestation of God's unconditional love in the Christ who is its incarnation, Jesus of Nazareth.

[27]As Tracy points out, in questions concerning "the historical Jesus" these two problems are often confused. For some the problem of "the historical Jesus" is more a problem of intelligibility than of appropriateness. For others, myself included, who do not consider "the historical Jesus" (a construct of research), as distinct from the Jesus witnessed to by the apostolic witness, to be the norm of tradition (the norm is the apostolic witness), the relevance of "the historical Jesus" issue is something else: viz., to retain the vitality of the "dangerous memory" of Jesus in fidelity to the original kerygma. Cf. D. Tracy, *The Analogical Imagination,* 238ff.; *Blessed Rage for Order,* 217.

[28]See e.g., Rahner's, "Current Problems in Christology," *Theological Investigations,* I (Baltimore: Helicon, 1961) 149–200, and "On the Theology of the Incarnation," *Theological Investigations,* IV (Baltimore: Helicon, 1966) 105–20. Similar moves were made by Schleiermacher, Ritschl, and Tillich.

Otherwise, faith becomes a contentless cipher and the Christ an eternal ar-
chetype, a mythic figure bereft of historical specificity. Historical study
throws into relief faith's specific content and its focus on a specific person.
Moreover, critical scholarship wards off the docetic and monophysitic ten-
dencies that have always bedeviled Catholicism. In addition, critical study
prevents facile bourgeois and liberal political co-options of Jesus by an exegesis that amounts to special pleading. However, "the historical Jesus remains at best a relatively external, secondary criterion of appropriateness
for certain necessary assumptions or presuppositions of that witness to
Jesus."[29] Historical-critical methods, along with other critical tools, must
be employed to authenticate, explicate, nuance, and correct all christological formulas by critically taking their measure against the community's
earliest memory images. Similarly, social-scientific methods that provide
ideology critique also afford a safeguard against distortions of the tradition's memory. This is exemplified in the praxis-oriented christologies of
Metz, Moltmann, Ruether, and Sobrino.

If we approach the gospel narratives using historical-critical methods,
we can know with varying degrees of historical probability some facts
about "the historical Jesus." We can also know the substance and forms of
his teaching as proclamation of God's reign. And in the memory-images of
the earliest communities we can perceive how Jesus' actions were seen as
symbolic embodiments of his teaching about the kingdom, indeed of the
kingdom already present. His authority came through as demanding a decision of faith in his God and in the kingdom. And yet, while we can to
some degree gain access to "the historical Jesus" through historical-critical
methods, the theological grounding we seek is found not in the reconstructed historical Jesus but in "the dangerous and subversive memory" of
Jesus treasured by the community and confessed in the gospel narratives.
The Jesus we know is the Jesus remembered and confessed by the original
witnesses in proclamation, symbol, and narrative, and much later in reflective thought. One need not search out "a canon within the canon" and
rest everything solely on that; rather, the Jesus-kerygma is the primary constitutive witness within the whole, long tradition of witnesses.

It has been customary to level the charge of "docetism" against the
stance taken here. However, this position does not negate the historical reality of Jesus or its relevance to faith.[30] What is negated is the presupposi-

---

[29]D. Tracy, *The Analogical Imagination,* 238.

[30]"The historical Jesus" is the *real* Jesus who lived but *only insofar as he is knowable today
in a construct produced by historical-critical method.* This is not identical with the real or ac-

tion that faith and theology must be adjudicated by and grounded in historical-critical investigation of "the historical Jesus." The fundamental material criterion remains the historically reconstructed apostolic witness and its unfolding in the plurality of explicit christologies of later witnesses that in fidelity to the original witnesses came to enrich Christianity. Though some primary control is attributed to the Jesus kerygma of the original apostolic witness, the entire tradition is the starting point of christology. Thus while the claim of some christologies to be grounded in "the historical Jesus" may not be wholly warranted, nonetheless their extrapolations may offer disclosive theological interpretations of the Jesus kerygma. This is the case, e.g., with Sobrino's liberation theology, Cobb's process tradition, and Moore's psychological appropriation. In such christologies one encounters the challenging memory of Jesus anew as a transforming word in the present. Herein resides the significance of these new christologies and soteriologies, not in their claims concerning "the historical Jesus." The disclosive power of these christologies is that they return us to the "everyday" reoriented to life's forgotten or undreamt of possible modes-of-being in the world.

Despite these reservations one must concede that Moore's reconstruction is heuristically valuable, perhaps more so than other second order appropriations, e.g., some liberationist appropriations,[31] or the existential appropriation of Bultmannians, or the psychologizing appropriations of the nineteenth-century "liberal lives." Large hermeneutical issues, however, must be engaged: whether the interpreter must get behind the text and into the mind of the authors or whether the interpreter finds a surplus of meaning in front of the text, which by a process of distanciation has taken on a life and meanings of its own, and what criteria determine that one second order appropriation is more adequate than another.[32] In any case, it is the second order appropriations that bring the Jesus story to life and fire imaginations and hearts. If war is too important to be left to generals, the Jesus story is too important to be left to some neo-gnostic

---

tual Jesus who lived, which all christologies acknowledge. The issue is not *whether* the real Jesus is to be affirmed, but *how.* Through critical historical reconstruction or through the memory of the tradition? I have opted for the latter, though without denying the tradition's foibles and the ongoing need of correction by a variety of methods.

[31]For a critical reflection on some Third World liberation theologians' reflections on "the historical Jesus" see J. Meier, "The Bible as a Source for Theology," *Proceedings of the Catholic Theological Society of America* 43 (1988) 1–14.

[32]For an introduction to these questions see e.g., P. Ricoeur, *Hermeneutics and the Human Sciences.*

Scripture scholars who view it as a private reserve closed to non-scholarly poachers. Faith in the resurrection requires that this faith not only be linked to the intellectual horizons of the first disciples but also with our intellectual horizons. And that linking, Moore, to his credit, has labored long and fruitfully to forge. We must be grateful.

— 5 —

Human Desire and Easter Faith

Louis Roy, O.P.

Sebastian Moore's theology is both contemplative and discursive. His is a synthetic mind, which sees at one glance the numerous components of the Christian mystery: "There, born fully grown like Minerva, was my christology."[1] He tells us that in 1959 a unifying insight, emerging from his psychic life, occurred to him in an Italian church as he heard the familiar words of John 19:34: "One of the soldiers opened his side with a spear, and immediately there came out blood and water." His commentary is so personal and eloquent that it is worth quoting entirely:

> Quietly I knew that the whole thing was there; that everything I would ever want to say, in the meandering but persistent prosecution of an interest that has been mine for thirty years, would stem from that image. It is extraordinary how one's psychic life, on the rare occasions that it gets our ear, can programmatize decades of persistent and curious inquiry. For in that image I experienced the vital conjunction, the vital meet-up, of our bitter and desperate aggression with the grace and love that embraces it and reveals itself in, and only in, that embrace. That vital conjunction is what nearly two millennia of soteriology have sought, with widely varying success, to explain. The psyche knows nothing of all this necessary intellectual fussing. It draws on a privileged source of meaning, the heart. Something got to my heart, in that moment in the musty church, as surely as the soldier's spear found its mark.[2]

[1] *The Fire and the Rose Are One* (New York: Seabury Press, 1980) xiii.
[2] "Christian Self-Discovery," *Lonergan Workshop,* I, ed. Fred Lawrence (Missoula, Mont.: Scholars Press, 1978) 218–9.

Moore is aware of the psychic-affective source of his vision. Such vision had been prepared, and it subsequently unfolded, thanks to the daily *lectio divina* of the Benedictine monk. There is no linear progression in his thinking, but rather a continual deepening and re-expressing of a whole. Many of the threads that are woven into his theological tapestry were already present in his early writings.[3] It is only in the mid-1970s, however, that he found his own, unique style.[4]

Besides being contemplative, Moore is discursive. His ideas have been tested with friends in conversations, with students in the classroom, and with colleagues in conferences. When he reads books, he perceptively spots the often underdeveloped intuition that can play a role in his own system. He thus borrows elements from poets, psychologists, mystics, exegetes, theologians. Sometimes his dissatisfaction with fashionable ideas—regardless of whether they come from conservative or liberal circles—makes him react and rephrase his thought in sharp contrast to alternative views. We then witness the dialectician at work.

This essay attempts to show both how and why Moore draws on the resources of psychology, epistemology, and mysticism in order to account for the emergence of Easter faith. The first part presents the *how,* or the way he actually implements his project. It is subdivided into two sections. The first section introduces the resources later to be used in christology. The second section highlights the experience of the disciples of Jesus, from the Galilee period, through his passion and death, until the moment their experience culminated in the Easter faith. The second part deals with the *why.* It discusses the feasibility of the project, in dialogue with those who have responded to Moore's writings and criticized some of his ideas, and in light of the several passages in which he has explained his intention.

The Vision—Desire and Refusal

Humans experience desire in two ways. First, since they have basic animal necessities, they feel in themselves deficiencies that make them reach out for known objects. Desire that is simply a felt need ceases once the need is satisfied. When people only want what they know, they have not discovered the specifically human side of desire.

[3]See Janice Daurio, "Toward a Theology of Desire: The Existential Hermeneutic in the Soteriology of Sebastian Moore," *Downside Review* 106 (1988) 195–232. This article is a masterly survey of Moore's writings up to 1988.

[4]With *The Crucified Jesus Is No Stranger* (New York: Seabury Press, 1977).

Second, the typically human form of desire does not cease but rather increases with satisfaction. In contrast to the former, which directly aims at the release of tension, the latter even desires its own increase. Because it is not restricted to particular objects, it acquires fuller meaning from being situated in interpersonal contexts.

Such relatedness can be experienced both horizontally and vertically. We are related to other human beings and we are related to the transcendent mystery. We are awakened to our own worth either from outside—by people who value us—or from within—by the Creator who has made us valuable in the first place. When we are awakened from outside, we know happiness; when we are awakened from within, we know joy and we experience grace.

To explore the horizontal side of this phenomenon, Moore focuses on sex as the locus where the issue of self-esteem is most striking. The pleasure of sex is much more than getting physical satisfaction. It consists in mutual arousing. There is nothing more rewarding than to feel the desire of the person I desire. Of course, that person must be genuinely and happily interested in me. Moore extends this paradigm to all affirming interpersonal situations. When a person feels desired, she feels her own desirability. As she feels significant, she comes alive. She becomes aware of her own goodness and beauty, as they are noticed by the other. From now on, she is someone for someone else, and this mutual reality is made visible in a special manner. Furthermore, the multiplicity of human relationships makes for the rich variety of ways in which people enhance one another. Personal fulfillment and other-centeredness go hand in hand. The "I am" that exists, *thanks* to those who appreciate me, is the same as the "I am" that exists *for* them.

In addition to their horizontal relationships, humans are vertically related. To account for this vertical relatedness, Moore offers two approaches: a discursive one, and a mystical one.

Discursively, the question of God germinates within the experience of desire. For Moore the question of God, instead of being simply theoretical (that is, restricted to cosmological, metaphysical, or epistemological considerations), is both intellectual and affective. Such a move is possible because he views human desiring as shot through with meaning. In relationality he sees intentionality at work. "The intentionality of the primal zest to feel myself alive is to enhance with itself the zest for life in another."[5] Relationality is a self-transcending thrust toward the other. At its best, it intends a love for the beloved, which is based not on projection but on true knowledge.

[5] *The Fire and the Rose*, 9.

Moore does not try to prove the existence of God, but rather the existence of a human desire for there to be God. He sees this desire for God as springing not from self-disbelief but from a passionate sense of our worth. Having been valued by other people, we realize that we all come from and return to an unknown mystery. Clouded in unknowability, our origin and our destination give rise to wonder. For all their attentiveness and care, other finite loves cannot provide any final answer. The desire to be significant for another thus becomes the desire to be significant for the unknown mystery that is my beginning and my end. And since to be significant is "to be," I can get a glimpse of what creation means: to be willed into existence. Those who have experienced being in the eyes of the persons who love them, advance in the same direction when they perceive their own being as efficaciously wished by their Creator.

Thus what differentiates the love of God (or love with God) from all other loves is that the love of God *is* love as the place of reception of the creative act. The love of God is differentiated from all other loves *not* by having a different object (God) but by the fact that while other loves are specified by the object, the love of God is specified by the condition of the subject.[6]

The mystical approach to the same vertical relatedness also unifies the intellectual and the affective. Intellectually, we realize that our mind is open to more than discrete objects. We can access a kind of consciousness that goes beyond images and concepts. Moore refers to Abbot Chapman, who talks of "an idiotic state"; he gives an illuminating twist to Chapman's phrase, "wanting nothing but God," which becomes the more directly conscious experience of "just wanting."[7] He also refers to Jacob Needleman, who, at the age of fourteen, had the astonishing experience of discovering, "I exist."[8] Affectively, the same kind of experience is reported by C. S. Lewis. Moore sees in it a peculiar longing, "a yearning for we know not what . . . a strange, poignant, bittersweet desire for we know not what."[9] And he comments: "the one thing one longs for once the desire has gone is to have it again, to be once again aching with it."[10]

[6]"The New Life," *The Way* 24 (1984) 45.

[7]John Chapman, *Spiritual Letters* (London: Sheed & Ward, 1989) 119–20, referred to in *Let This Mind Be in You* (Minneapolis: Winston Press, 1985) 5–6. Chapman's name is not mentioned here, but Moore mentions it several times in other writings.

[8]Jacob Needleman, *The Heart of Philosophy* (New York: Knopf, 1982) 64, quoted in *Let This Mind*, 37.

[9]*Let This Mind*, 36 and 45, referring to C. S. Lewis, *Surprised by Joy* (San Diego: Harcourt Brace Jovanovich, 1955) 16–8 and 72–3.

[10]*Jesus the Liberator of Desire* (New York: Crossroad, 1989) 11.

To describe the interaction between the horizontal and the vertical, Moore talks of the ego and the self. They are not two entities, but two ways in which I feel myself. "I am using the word ego much more loosely than Freud, to mean any sense of myself as individual."[11] The ego wants to keep a balance between oneness and separateness by equally attending to one's depths and to practical needs. In contrast to ego, the self does not rest content with such a compromise: its being drawn by the oceanic (or mystical) pull makes possible the existence of a fully responsible individual. The self is the locus in a person where oneness and separateness come together. It is the source of ego, at any stage of their restive development. Thus the self experiences at the same time "being one with the pervading mystery" and "being myself and no one else."[12]

To grow into an ever greater self constitutes the normal human adventure. The dramatic character of individuation, however, hampers such growth. The accession to individual freedom brings about a guilt feeling. Instead of remaining one with the parents, the child becomes separate. Such an experience can be lived with a pleasant thrill—as when the parents approve and encourage the awkward efforts of the child to become an individual. But it can also be seen as a dangerous deviation—as when the parental message is: "Either you are a part of me, or you are totally on your own!"

This abrupt pair of alternatives has the effect of inducing children to begrudge the desire that led them into bitter disappointments. Such mistrust of one's desire entails a rejection of a part of oneself—the best one. Desire becomes an object of suspicion. The result is what Moore calls "erosthenia," weakness in desire. It is the same phenomenon as sin-inflicted death, which is totally different from ego-death. The former is the resistance to growth, whereas the latter is the condition for growth. When it is embodied in an action that harms someone else, this refusal to trust one's desire and to love is sin. The happiness of one's desirability is replaced with the pleasures of power and possessions.

For Moore, guilt and sin are different. Guilt accompanies an individual's claim to independence. It creates the atmosphere in which sin is likely to happen. Sin is the acting out of one's sense of isolation and forlornness, and such acting out results in failing the other. Moore also calls guilt "infant guilt," and sin "adult guilt," for which the appropriate feeling is sorrow. Sin is the awkward self-asserting that cuts us off horizontally from

---

[11]Ibid., 15.
[12]Ibid., 16.

other human beings, and vertically from the source of our desirability. It consists in failing and wounding oneself, the other, and God at the same time. It is an attack against desire, both in ourselves and in those we harm. We then succumb to fear of what may be involved in following our basic Godward orientation. Fear is the motive for sinning, although not its reason. In the last analysis, there is no reason for sinning. Like Aquinas and Lonergan, Moore thinks that sin is a surd, a choice for the unintelligible.

The Disciples and Jesus

As he proceeds to retrieve the experience of the first Christians, Moore introduces a threefold schema that sums up the successive phases in their relationship with Jesus. This sequence is based on a parallel between the three mystical phases and Christian discipleship. The analogy drawn from classical mysticism is meant to be an analogy, that is, to indicate similarity and difference between the mystical journey and the experience of the disciples of Jesus (both first- and twentieth-century disciples). It does not assume that they were or are mystics in the strict sense.

The first phase is consolation without a cause, as reported by Ignatius of Loyola. Horizontal and vertical arousal of desire is what the disciples experienced in Galilee. The spiritual strength of the one who was proclaiming the reign of God, in the midst of the crowds' enthusiasm, had an enormous impact on the disciples. The integrity of the sinless Jesus stirred up the sense of their own beauty. They were thus awakened by Jesus from outside, and such an awakening triggered an awakening by God from within. Moreover, a phenomenon of addiction occurred: a dependency, as they hung all their hopes upon their charismatic leader.

The stage was thus set for the second phase—the collapse of their dream. They fought to the last moment Jesus' disconcerting acceptance of forthcoming defeat. They did not understand that he could not give up the very authenticity that had become a threat to the unauthentic guardians of the religious and political status quo. As he proved to be a loser by suffering humiliation and death, they felt being let down. They were cut off from their beloved friend. He had passed into the realm of the dead. Therefore, no relationship was any longer extant between their deceased master and them. They were alienated from their dream, and from the two sources of their dream: Jesus and his God.

They were deprived of life because they had ignored its condition: the ego-death to which Jesus had consented. Clinging to their ego, they remained prisoners of socially imposed roles and they denied their openness to the self. Refusing ego-death entailed recoiling from their basic desire, from communion with God. In the case of Jesus, on the contrary, ego-death coincided with his acceptance of the death inflicted by sinners. Since they had not been in solidarity with him, they found themselves on the side of the betrayers. They were in need of forgiveness.

They had yet to come to grips with their recent first-hand contact with violence. That violence had crushed their leader. They realized that pervasive violence must find its victims. They discovered in Jesus the victim par excellence, because he was the only one to be totally innocent and utterly open to the divine. Jesus had to be a victim. For one thing, he was the charismatic, "larger-than-life" person, who had promised nothing less than the Kingdom of God; second, within the severe limits of space-time, he could not deliver the total presence of the Infinite, for which people hunger and thirst. Furthermore, Jesus and the other victims of history, from whom the disciples had distanced themselves, represented the true self that they wanted to ignore, in order to get on with life.

In this reconstruction of the disciples' odyssey, the experience of death is envisaged as preparatory to Easter faith. The death was twofold: Jesus' and theirs. Bereavement placed them on the side of death. The loss of Jesus cut them off from the awakener of their desirability. After the execution of Jesus, God was no longer a living reality for them. Their dream had evaporated and nothing could make up for it. This descent into hell precluded any superficial resolution such as the emergence of another dream—an Easter dream!—coming after the disappointment occasioned by the first dream. It was pure desolation.

Besides the analogy of bereavement, Moore has recourse to the analogy of "bottoming-out" to suggest the kind of purification undergone by the disciples.[13] We have already seen that Jesus had awakened in them the desire for infinite life. That desire was bound to take the form of an addictive relationship to him, in the sense that their unlimited desire became hooked onto the person that seemed to promise satisfaction. Now the disciples went into a bottoming-out during the stage in which their addicted ego fell to pieces and the finitude of Jesus was revealed. The most noble form of idolatry had to be exploded before they could enter a third phase.

We have already indicated that according to the analogy drawn from the spiritual life, the second phase is envisaged as a condition for the third.

---

[13]"Jesus the Liberator of Desire: Reclaiming Ancient Images," *Cross Currents* 40 (1990–91) 495.

Mystics undergo death in the sense that they suffer from the fact that God is no experience, no image, no thought, no feeling, no reality in this world. Such a spiritual fasting is an extreme form of purification, opening up the soul to something radically other than what is ordinarily lived. "There is in this experience a radical spaciousness of the soul, a totally new capacity to perceive."[14] During Holy Saturday, the disciples began to enter into ego-death as they underwent a liberation of consciousness from its worldly limits.

Moore introduces the third phase in dialectic with the second one. After the horror of Good Friday, the disciples were on their way toward renouncing the Jesus who used to awaken them from outside. According to Moore, they encountered the risen Christ as the one who from now on would awaken them from within—that is, as God. In that new offer of love, Jesus was granting them what only God could give: a forgiveness that filled their inner void with a new being. Instead of seeing themselves as loved by God apart from their sinning, they perceived themselves as sinners who were forgiven and loved. The God who had raised Jesus from the dead was revealed as the One who accepts humans even at their worst.

By moving into death, Jesus entered a state in which no communication was possible between him and the disciples. He had descended into hell, namely, into sheol, the place where the dead are cut off from the realm of the living. As he appeared to his disciples, however, Jesus made them understand that the destruction of his body canceled the limit on his power to communicate fully with the world. Effective forgiveness entails this establishment of intimate communication among reconciled human beings, all of whom recognize themselves as both victims and victimizers.

Progressive ego-death is the expanding of desire. Only in physical death is there a complete de-limiting of desire, a falling away of all ties, a total disconnection with all. After his human desire has been de-limited by dying, the risen Jesus grants a delimiting of desire to anyone who would believe in him. The capacity to make such a transcendent offer corresponds with the exercise of a divine function. In contrast to modern apologetics, which used to go from the resurrection to the divinity of Jesus, Moore thinks the disciples went from the divinity to the resurrection of Jesus. As they experienced the divine role Jesus had begun to fulfill in their favor, they realized that he had been raised from the dead and exalted as Christ and Lord.

---

[14]"Death as the Delimiting of Desire: A Key Concept for Soteriology," *Concilium* 156 (6/1982), ed. Steven Kepnes and David Tracy, 53. Moore told me that what he actually means is "de-limiting."

The great breakthrough consists in encountering a transformed Jesus, who establishes a new relationship with human beings. In interaction with that positive experience stands a problematic experience: the women's discovery of the empty tomb. The profound shock of seeing that Jesus' body was no longer there affected their psyche and added to their confusion. Moore underlines the dramatic character of the symbolism: the removal of the corpse sends a direct message to our animality, which cannot but be acutely conscious of its fragility. Something totally unexpected happened to the body of Jesus, hitherto so weak in the vast universe, destined to "disintegration and reabsorption in the huge natural process of things."[15]

Faced with the harsh reality of biological death, mysticism can remain hesitant. For those who had seen the appearances of Jesus, the sign of the empty tomb was given as a concession of the mystery to their natural incredulity. It said: "Jesus is no longer among the dead." It did not say: "Jesus has been raised and glorified by the Father." It simply removed a visible, psychically powerful obstacle to their faith in the invisible reality of the resurrection. Neither the appearances nor the empty tomb constitutes proof. They are signs that enable the believers to affirm that religious experience is no illusion. They help us to see physical death as expressive of the death of ego. They allow Easter faith to validate human desire.

The Theological Validity of the Easter Experience

Moore has addressed the question, How can we know what was the early disciples' experience of Jesus? The answer to this question requires that we examine the experiential and cognitional accessibility of the resurrection. Such discussion will permit us to make a more general statement on the epistemological status of Moore's psychological theology. On those difficult issues, Moore offers us illuminating remarks, but he has not presented a systematic reflection on his own theological enterprise. Therefore I shall have to make certain points more explicit than they are in his writings, where they are just quietly assumed.

Because he is well acquainted with biblical criticism, Moore's approach to the New Testament equally excludes Protestant fundamentalism and Catholic apologetics. He knows that the stories of the appearances of the risen Jesus are not straightforward, uninterpreted reports of a single event that would have occurred to the first disciples. Notwithstanding this

---

[15]"An Empty Tomb Revisited," *Downside Review* 99 (1981) 239.

admission, Moore does not consider the various events surrounding the resurrection to be totally unknown to us. To make them intelligible, however, he does not engage in "the new quest for the historical Jesus." Only occasionally does he refer to a point made by a contemporary exegete. Although he displays great interest in, and respect for, historical criticism, his contribution does not rest on the findings of exegesis. The intellectual challenge he wants to meet is different and complementary.

Moore points out that we are shifting, in the study of the resurrection events, from an empirical to a subjective center of interest. Whereas the empirical center is variously defined by fundamentalism, apologetics, or by the historico-critical method, the subjective center is constituted by what takes place in the interiority of those who say, "The Lord is risen!" As far as this Easter faith is concerned, there is a continuity for Moore between the first- and the twentieth-century believers. His theological endeavor is based on the Church's conviction that, even though there is a difference, yet there is no rift between the faith of the first witnesses to the risen Christ and the faith of Christians down the ages. Furthermore, neither is there any chasm between what happened to Jesus after his death and what happens now to the believers. Like Jesus and thanks to the mediation of the risen Jesus, they participate, in an attenuated yet intense manner, in the mystery of God's life.

Besides that substantial identity in terms of religious experience, Moore believes a substantial identity also obtains in terms of the interpretation of that experience. Both the Holy Spirit and the pre-Easter Jesus guided the early Christian community. In particular, Jesus "must have seen to it that he was understood by his disciples sufficiently for their preaching to proclaim him. He must have seen to it that they got him right."[16] Moore's bold self-confidence in his attempt at making sense of the disciples' paschal experience rests on the conviction that there is a continuity of right interpretation, through enriching cultural diversity, from Jesus to his first disciples and to his subsequent disciples over two millennia. No doubt this represents a big claim. Nonetheless, it is no blind belief on the part of Moore, who is acutely aware of the distortions that have affected the handing-on of the Christian tradition regarding the resurrection. Rather, it is a faith assumption, many times confirmed by his own familiarity with the major church councils and theologians.

In his efforts at fathoming the subjective side of the Easter faith, Moore does not confuse what happened to Jesus after his death with what

---

[16] *Jesus the Liberator*, 77–8.

happened to the disciples when they realized that Jesus was present to them in a new and fascinating way. Yet he does not say much about the resurrection of Jesus, simply because he sees it as a unique event, and not as an instance in a familiar category. "It imposes the same condition of 'knowing unknowing' as does the Godhead itself."[17] Likewise, he does not say much about the appearances of Jesus to his disciples: "the encountering of Jesus risen is necessarily elusive. Its authenticity demands that it be so. There is a quality of *envelopment* about his presence to them, which cannot be pinned down."[18]

On the one hand, then, we must posit the independent reality of the resurrection of Jesus by God, and its capacity to make itself known in a way that eludes any precise analysis. As regards this revelatory capacity, perhaps Moore should have pointed out that a component of the disciples' recognition came from the risen Jesus himself, who was a real partner (though no longer in an earthly way) in the relationship. On the other hand, we must answer the question of the meaning of the resurrection. Moore has emphatically and honestly raised that question. This is the reason he emphasizes a subjective approach to the central belief of Christianity. For us humans, there is no access to the resurrection apart from engaging in a subjective quest for meaning.

Now a subjective approach is totally different from a subjectivistic point of view. From Bernard Lonergan, Moore has learned that, whenever conducted by a person healthy in mind and heart, a subjective approach tends to be objective. In human relationship, only deep appreciation allows someone to discover the profound qualities of another person. Whenever this is the case, we can say that the beauty of that person is present in the delighted awareness of the true friend. Subjectivity becomes objective as the real beauty of the other shows in the loving mind of the beholder.

Moore notes that the post-paschal warming of the heart, in the early disciples of Jesus, is amply documented in the New Testament and is ascribed to the work of the Holy Spirit. It is in order to shed some light on that transcendent experience that he has recourse to the interpersonal analogy. The glory of Jesus appears in the transformation it effects in the consciousness of the believers. *Noverim Te, noverim me.* To account for the conjunction of the Holy Spirit and the risen Jesus in the disciples' resurrection experience, he also borrows from Lonergan the pair "immediacy/mediation." The warming of the heart, the absolute forgiveness, the

[17]Ibid., 64.
[18]Ibid., 75.

great illumination are immediately given to the soul; at the same time, Jesus offers himself as the focus that mediates transcendence to the human imagination and intelligence.

What is crucial for theology, here, is the fact that both the immediacy and the mediation are subjective-objective. Of course, immediacy is not empirical: it cannot be perceived through the senses, for it does not come from the finite world. In this case of a transcendent immediacy, the objectivity is not conditioned by external data, but must derive from within, namely, from an intensification of the subjective life, which is a participation in the divine life. The non-illusory character of such intensification is guaranteed, in our world of human meaning, by something coming from outside, that is, from a consistent tradition that has crystallized in Scripture and has in turn been fashioned by it. This tradition employs various criteria in order to ascertain that a spiritual experience does register an objective reality.

Both being most real, then, the immediacy can be adequately experienced, while the mediation can be adequately interpreted. Far from being unavoidable, any subjectivistic interpretation is nothing but a deformation of a subjectivity that naturally heads for objectivity. Therefore, we must take exception to the widespread view that, because experience is molded by interpretation, we cannot but be uncertain about the nature of that experience. Even the rich variety of expressions that the resurrection experience has enjoyed should not be considered as buttressing a subjectivistic view of it.

In a "Review Symposium" on *Jesus the Liberator of Desire,* which includes a reply by Moore,[19] three thinkers offer penetrating and profound reflections on his book. But all three raise doubts as to the knowability of the early disciples' experience. It seems to me that those doubts stem from presuppositions that Moore cannot accept, and rightly so. As early as in 1980, he wrote: "the type of experience in question pertains to those deeper levels which always surprise us by their universality." He added:

> There is also a broader assumption behind this enterprise: a fundamental belief in a community of human experience across the great stretches of human time and human space. It is the sort of belief Eliot had. Eliot "knew" what Shakespeare was trying to do, knew it very accurately by his own attempts to create poetry.[20]

---

[19] "Review Symposium," *Horizons* 18 (1991) 93–129.
[20] *The Fire and the Rose,* 133 and 134.

By contrast, Elisabeth Koenig writes, "subjective categories are, from the philosopher's point of view, impossible to define because inner experience is never capable of being shared in its entirety."[21] On this issue, perhaps the following distinction could help diminish the distance between Moore and his critics. Personal experience as felt differs from personal experience as understood. The former is inaccessible, except to a few intimates, whereas the latter is shareable with many people. What is strictly individual in the experience of Jesus or of his first disciples is definitively lost and irretrievable. But that very same experience, as meaningful, has been communicated to generations of Christians. It can be reenacted without having to be felt in exactly the same manner. The reason why such communication can be successful is that there is, in human beings, a capacity for understanding situations, events, feelings, ideas. Therefore, although they do not exactly feel the same, good therapists understand their clients' experience, poets resonate to one another, critics discern what is excellent in works of art or literature, Christian mystics are on the same wavelength as non-Christian mystics, and so on.

Moreover, when Stephen Duffy and William Loewe talk of Moore's "historical reconstruction" of the disciples' experience, I have the impression that they consider his enterprise as precarious because it should rest on exegesis. Although in dialogue with biblical scholarship, Moore's theology does not depend on particular exegetical evidence, because he is explicating what Lonergan calls "foundations." By doing so, he provides us with a heuristic model, which is derived from an exploration of human interiority. Such a model is the upper blade in a scissors movement that also comprises a lower blade attentive to historical data.[22] The validity of the upper blade comes from what is universal in human interiority. It functions in interaction with the data provided by exegesis, literature, the arts, psychoanalysis, mysticism. Many of the highly perceptive observations on human life that we find in Moore's writings are due to his familiarity with those fields of human experience. Thus he sets an example of how the conjunction between the upper and the lower blade can work. However, since this conjunction is not systematically presented, he has initiated a pioneering movement that others can join and enlarge.

In conclusion, I rejoice, as do the three critics I have mentioned, in the fact that so many persons find inspiration in the works of Sebastian Moore. But I would venture to add that his writings are more than inspirational

---

[21]"Review Symposium," 112.
[22]See Bernard Lonergan, *Method in Theology* (New York: Herder, 1972) 284–5 and 293.

because the meanings they convey are true, once and for all. Of course, minor revisions will be made: details will be added or subtracted, items will be nuanced or qualified, in interaction with the wealth of data that will be met by the lower blade. Nevertheless, his metapsychological theology has universal validity, since the pattern of related concepts it offers can be trans-culturally translated in a continuity of understanding that, far from being abolished, is enriched by language diversity.

― 6 ―

Transcultural Knowers and Lovers

Joseph Flanagan, S.J.

Between publishing *Insight* in 1957 and *Method in Theology* in 1972, Bernard Lonergan made a series of important discoveries. While these discoveries did not invalidate his prior work, they certainly extended and recontextualized the contents of *Insight*. This was especially true of the last three chapters of *Insight*, on ethics and theology. In this paper I will attempt to rethink and reorganize chapter eighteen of *Insight* on ethics in the light of the developments that led to the publication of *Method in Theology*. My paper is divided into three parts. In the first section I will summarize the first seventeen chapters of *Insight*. Then in section II, I will discuss the transformation of Lonergan's ethics after *Insight*. Finally in section III, I will exemplify how Lonergan's transformed ethics operates.

I. Cognitional Theory, Epistemology, Metaphysics

In the first eleven chapters of *Insight* the reader is invited to appropriate the three levels of activities by which we constitute ourselves as knowers. A first level of experience sets conditions for us to wonder about the meaning of our experiences. This wondering directs us toward an anticipated understanding of experience and moves us to a second level of cognitional activities: the level of understanding and formulation of our understanding. However, we are not satisfied with simply understanding and formulating our understanding; we also want to know if our understanding is correct, and so the further question emerges on the second level and asks, "is this understanding really true?" This second question leads us to the third level of knowing, where we begin to reflect on our formulated understanding to test its accuracy. Only when we have satisfied our reflective wondering will we commit ourselves and make the judgment: "yes, it is so." Having appropriated these three levels of knowing and the various patterns within which we know in the first eleven chapters, the reader is invited in chapters twelve and thirteen to consider the object or goal that is sought whenever we seek to know. Here the reader discovers that any and every act of knowing has the same objective—whenever we seek to know we move through three related cognitive levels to know the real or being. Conversely, whenever we know correctly what we know is being in some restricted form. Or, being is that which moves knowers to question, understand, and judge and through such interrelated acts to become limited knowers of being or reality.

Being, then, is *why* knowing is what it is. Being grounds and provokes questioning; or, questioning is our responding to the presence of being. This identity or isomorphism of knowing with being is the cornerstone of Lonergan's philosophy.

In selecting the knowing of one's own knowing as the first step in self-knowledge, Lonergan invites each knower to discover within his or her own knowing his or her own spontaneous orientation to being and thereby appropriate the common objective or destiny of all knowers to seek being. Like Descartes, Lonergan begins with his own cognitional activities but would add to the Cartesian "I think" a prior lower level of experiencing and a higher level of judging. The actual existence of yourself or of other things is not known through thinking but through three distinct and functionally related levels of activities—experiencing, understanding, and judging. This leads to the surprising discovery that while you as a knower are a unity, you operate on three successive interrelated levels. Your own unity as a knower is a composed or structured unity and what unites the three distinguishable but related levels of acting is your own desire to know, manifested in a spontaneous wondering about your experience of yourself or of objects surrounding you. This wondering of yours sets the conditions for the emergence of a second level of activities which when completed triggers a further spontaneous critical wondering about the correctness of your understanding of your experiencing. This reflective activity issues in a judgment on the correctness of your understanding of your experiencing. Beyond any single act or set of acts your desire to know keeps recurring, seeking its objective—the totality of correct judgments. Only by allowing the spontaneous flow of questions to arise and only by intelligently selecting the relevant questions to ask and answer can any knower be faithful to his or her own self as a spontaneous or natural knower who desires to know correctly all that there is to be known.

Thus the answer to Kant's question about the objectivity of your knowing is given the ironic answer that a knower is truly objective in his or her judgments when they are authentically subjective. And "authentic" here means being faithful to the spontaneous goal of your own knowing.

Having answered the cognitional question—what am I doing when I am knowing?—in the first eleven chapters of *Insight,* and having answered the epistemological question concerning the objectivity or the "why" of knowing in chapters twelve and thirteen, Lonergan proceeds in the next four chapters to answer the metaphysical question—what do I know when I do knowing? For Lonergan, as for Aristotle and Aquinas, knowing reveals the being of the object in and through the being of the subject who is doing the knowing. Knowing does not change the object except when the object is the subject; then, knowing not only reveals the object but constitutes that object. To restate this claim: for all three there is between the knower and the known an identity, not a confrontation. Knowers share in the being of the object or objects known, and the more perfectly they know, the more perfect is their identity with that known. Thus all three philosophers would say that a perfect knower would be perfectly identical with the known. A perfect knower is an infinite knower and since human knowers are not actually infinite knowers, their knowing is an imperfect participation in the beings that they know. Since, however, our knowing is potentially unlimited we are always responding to being's invitation to come to a more perfect participation in being by pursuing the different patterns of knowing which are variations of the basic cognitional pattern of experiencing, understanding, and judging.

A key difference between Aristotle's and Aquinas's method of philosophizing and Lonergan's is that both Aristotle and Aquinas argue from a set of first principles which form the foundation of their metaphysics. Lonergan, on the other hand, begins not with principles that will serve as premises for metaphysical arguments, but with the concrete knowing subject and lets the knower discover, first, that his or her knowing is identical with and constitutive of his or her own being as a knower; second, that all knowing is responding to and seeking the same objective—being; third, that the knowing subject knows herself or himself through the same pattern of activities as one knows any other object. Therefore, not only do knowers develop a growing identity with themselves by repeated acts of self-knowing, but they also develop a growing identity with all beings insofar as they perform repeated acts of correct knowing. More importantly, in re-peated acts of correct knowing one comes to a more perfect identity with and participation of the infinite being that penetrates, underlies, unites, and transcends all limited beings.

For Lonergan, then, the basic principle of philosophy is the concrete knowing subject's identity with and orientation to being. In every correct act of knowing, either of oneself or of any other being, knowers constitute a more perfect act of identity with limited beings and with the infinite being that grounds and transcends every limited being. For Lonergan, then, the method for doing philosophy is to know yourself: (1) know your own knowing; (2) know the objective of all knowing; and (3) know that the objectivity of any subjective act of knowing depends on your actual re-sponse to that objective of all knowing. These three judgments, then, char-acterize the essential features of self-knowledge and together they form the foundation for doing metaphysics. They also differentiate Lonergan's method of doing metaphysics from that of other philosophers, including Aristotle and Aquinas.

Aristotle and Aquinas began philosophy with metaphysics and articu-lated their epistemology and cognitional theory in metaphysical terms. Lonergan reverses the order and begins with a theory of knowing, derives epistemology from his cognitional theory, and then grounds his meta-physical terms in the concrete knower's own cognitional activities as ori-ented to being.

Kant had argued that a philosopher's metaphysics depended on his or her epistemology. Lonergan went a step further and argued that both epis-temology and metaphysics depended on your cognitional theory and your cognitional theory depends on knowing that your own knowing is poten-tially unlimited, is oriented to and desires to be identical with an unlim-ited objective—being—and that this being penetrates, underlies, unites, and transcends all limited beings.

The bonus of this method of grounding metaphysics in self-knowing is that you have discovered a transcultural and transhistorical base for unit-ing every human being to one another since every human being is a born metaphysician insofar as every human being is born with a spontaneous desire to know everything about everything. From this transhistorical base one can anticipate the destiny of human history as the gradual realization by human beings of their infinite potential to know themselves and all other beings in their participation in and with being.

However, besides knowers responding to the invitation to participate in being there is also their refusal to know, and this can happen in four different ways, resulting in the formation of four different types of bias—dramatic, egotistical, group, and general bias. Metaphysics, then, can be conceived as the science that encourages persons to know their own knowing and their common objective in being and also to know how to reverse the positions of those who have become disoriented and distorted in their own spontaneous and immediately conscious desire to know through the different forms of bias.

The philosopher who knows his or her own knowing and its objective also knows the various ways this knowing can be distorted. More importantly, such a philosopher knows that one corrects mistaken philosophies, not by attempting to disprove their propositions or premises, but by a dialogue that invites a person to discover his or her own infinite desire to know and the way in which their own explicit philosophy is or is not in agreement with their own natural, cognitional spontaneities. A methodical metaphysician, then, knows how to develop those aspects of other philosophies that are in tune with the authentic orientation of all knowers as they move toward their common destiny in being, and how to reverse those aspects of those same philosophies that are not in agreement with the transcendental norms that one has appropriated within his or her own concrete, conscious activities.

II. Ethics in a Transformed Context

From this brief summary of the first seventeen chapters of *Insight* one would expect that chapter eighteen on ethics would follow somewhat similar methodical procedures. Readers would be invited to appropriate themselves as choosers by asking, first, what am I doing when I am choosing or deciding?; second, why do I do such choosing or deciding?; or what makes me a truly authentic chooser?; third, what do I choose when I choose authentically or objectively? However, these three steps, which I will sketch out in this section, are not what you find in *Insight*. There are reasons for this, which can be found in chapter seventeen, where Lonergan discusses the relation of truth to expression and points out that, while there is an important distinction between our thoughts and the way we express them, nevertheless there is a close interdependence between the way we reason and the language within which we reason and judge. In writing *Insight* Lonergan was trying to restate the scholastic metaphysical, moral, and theological traditions in terms of his new method of self-appropriation, but while his thought had moved beyond that context, his language to some extent was still within that context. This is especially true of his ethics in chapter eighteen and his theological perspective in the last two chapters. Only after *Insight* and his studies of phenomenology and existentialism did he begin his shift to what he called "intentionality analysis."

A key result of his shift was that the three successive levels of knowing were related to one another in terms of higher viewpoints or sublations. In this new context, acts on the level of understanding transform activities on the level of experiencing, placing them in the higher and richer context without in any way impairing these lower activities. The results of this shift are quite remarkable, especially in terms of the scholastic tradition in which Lonergan was working.

If the level of the self as a chooser sublates the three prior levels of self as a knower, then, this means that the science of ethics sublates the science of metaphysics. For Aristotle *Ethics* was done in the context of and under the control of his metaphysics, which meant that speculative intellect was given precedence over practical intellect. But in the new context of intentionality analysis, this relationship is reversed and practical intellect provides the fuller, richer, and more comprehensive set of meanings for speculative intellect. This also implies that the older definition of a person as a rational animal yields to the more concrete definition of the person as a choosing animal and even more significantly, as we shall see, a cultural choosing animal. It is in this transformed context of intentionality analysis that I shall set forth the three questions of Lonergan's ethics.

A. First Ethical Question, Symbolic Reasoning, and Culture

First, then, what am I doing when I am choosing? In choosing I am deliberating about a course of action or interaction that I may or may not decide to do. Deciding, then, and the deliberative process leading up to decision resembles judging and the reflective process that issues in a judgment, and so we can begin our analysis by comparing judging and deciding.

There are three key characteristics to the reflective process that grounds judgments: (1) it is related to the question, "Is it so?"; (2) it is personal; (3) it implies a context or horizon within which you reflect and judge. Deliberating has three similar characteristics. Deliberation begins with and is sustained by the question, "ought I to do this?" or, "is this a worthwhile course of action?" Second, deliberation involves a personal commitment to the proposed decision since you will begin to exist in a new way through the decisions that you make. Third, decisions, like judgments, are made in the context or horizon established by prior decisions. In other words, knowing and choosing are a function of your age and so both will depend on your accumulated wisdom and skills in performing these activities.

However, besides these three similarities between the reflective process that leads to judgments and the deliberative one that leads to decisions, there are significant differences. At each level of your knowing and choosing, your degree of control, freedom, and responsibility is qualitatively different. You sense, understand, judge, and choose; nevertheless, you have more control and freedom over understanding than sensing, more control and freedom in judging than in understanding, and more freedom and responsibility in deciding than in judging. And so, the "I" that you are aware of as you act on these four levels becomes more personal and intimate as you ascend from activities of experiencing through understanding, to judging and choosing.

A brief explanation of these degrees of interiority and freedom can be summarized as follows. If your eyes are open you see whether you like it or not. On the second level, while insights are not under your command, you can set the conditions for their occurrence and when they emerge you experience a new sense of your self. Judging, on the other hand, may always be exercised since you can stop reflecting at any time and judge just where you stand relative to the final certitude that you are seeking. Judging, therefore, is even more personal and free than understanding. Finally, deciding is still more personal than judging because in judging you are trying to discover whether or not the facts as you have understood them have been correctly understood, whereas in deciding you are deliberating about a course of action that is not a fact but only a possibility, and it will not become a fact unless you choose to bring it into existence. The same differences in interiority, freedom, and responsibility can also be experienced at successive stages of our personal development and most dramatically, as we shall see, in the successive stages in cultural history.

Another way of stating these differences in self-awareness and self-intimacy is in terms of conscience. Conscience for Lonergan is the conscious relation between different levels of our activities. We are all familiar with moral conscience but we also have a cognitive conscience concerning correct judging. Consciousness becomes conscience when you advert to your own freedom and responsibility in following your own spontaneous orientation to truth. As you wonder whether your understanding of your experience is correctly understood, you feel your own desire to state the truth as you have experienced, understood, and judged it, and if you do not so state it, then you are going against your own spontaneous and conscious orientation to truth. But on the fourth level you are aware of a different call—the conscious summons to value correctly. And to value correctly you must also make your choosing self-consistent with your knowing self. Just as in judging you consciously relate your three levels of knowing to one another and to your prior context of judgments, so on the fourth level you must harmonize all four levels of your intending self to one another and to the context of prior decisions in a consistent way if you are to satisfy your own spontaneous orientation to truly valuable objectives. In other words, "oughtness" is not only something imposed on us by social customs or traditional authority and precepts, but much more significantly it is a conscious experience of the summons we feel to harmonize our doing with our knowing. "Oughtness" is what we impose on ourselves. Knowing and choosing have their own built-in sanction. As one of my students put it, nobody gets away with anything.

Besides these differences in judging and choosing I have outlined, there is another major difference that needs to be analyzed and explained, namely, motivation. Motives provide the reasons for you to actually do what you think is the right thing to do. Motives or values give you the "why" for what you decide to do. Just what are these motives that cause you to decide whatever and whenever you do so decide?

Traditionally the scholastics taught that the intellect specifies the object or course of action to which our wills respond. However, when Lonergan shifted after *Insight* to "intentionality analysis" of the knowing and choosing subject, he realized that the fourth level of the subject as evaluating, deciding, willing and doing involved a new intentional term or object of the will, namely, value. Just as the intending subject operating on the first three levels seeks the transcendental term of infinite truth, so the same subject operating on all four levels longs for the transcendental goal of unrestricted value.

There is a further development in the traditional relation of intellect and will or between speculative knowing and practical knowing or between metaphysics and ethics. The fourth level sublates the prior three levels and so practical intellect similarly sublates speculative intellect and ethics subsumes metaphysics. In stating that the fourth level sublates the prior levels, Lonergan means "It goes beyond them, sets up a new principle and type of operation, directs them to a new goal but, so far from dwarfing them, preserves them and brings them to a far fuller fruition" (*Method in Theology*, 316). This sublation of the knowing subject by the choosing subject, then, brings about a new interrelation of the cognitional levels that needs to be explored.

To appropriate yourself as a chooser will involve a fairly extensive re-organizing of more familiar ways of thinking about the way we reason. Most readers of *Method in Theology* are familiar with Lonergan's analysis of common sense or practical reasoning as a specialization of knowing oriented to deal with concrete, particular situations as they arise in our day-to-day activities. But there is nowhere in *Insight* a similar detailed analysis of symbolic reasoning or the way we reason when we are deliberating about the values of a project we are considering to undertake. To appropriate what we are doing when we are deliberating and deciding, it is necessary to spell out this process of symbolic reasoning that shapes the motives that provide the sufficient reason for choosing what we choose to do or not to do.

To explain symbolic reasoning will require that we examine five topics. First, there is the difference between judgment of fact and judgment of value. Second, there is the order of love that Lonergan assimilated from Max Scheler and Dietrich von Hildebrand. Third, there is the central role that believing plays in deliberating. Fourth, there is the role of imagination and the way that symbolic images evoke conscious feelings and unconscious vitalities. Finally, there is the notion of culture and the way it brings together the prior four steps.

Judgment of Fact versus Value

It is one thing to design a battle plan or figure out how to cross the Rubicon, but quite another to decide such a battle or river crossing is a truly worthwhile thing to do. The difference is first of all the difference between a judgment of fact and a judgment of value.

Lonergan states in *Method in Theology* that judgments of value differ in content but not in structure from judgments of fact. In other words, the same procedures that Lonergan detailed in *Insight* regarding the process of judging can be applied to judgments of value.

In addition to the three properties of judging I have mentioned—(1) the question, is it so?; (2) personal commitment; (3) the context or horizon—there is a self-correcting process. Part of the reflective process initiated by the question "is it so?" involves testing or criticizing your insights, checking to see if things really are the way you have understood them. In judgments of value the same process is repeated, with the difference that you wonder whether you have correctly evaluated the worthwhileness of the project you are planning. Lonergan stressed that in making concrete judgments of fact, grasping of the invulnerability or correctness of an insight was the key event in the reflective process. The question "is it so?" becomes "is my insight invulnerable?" Or, do I have sufficient evidence to answer the question "is it so?" and assert "yes, it is so"? This of course leads to the question, when is sufficient evidence actually sufficient?

Lonergan's answer is that the process of critical reflecting heads toward a limit of familiarity and control when we no longer hesitate and feel quite comfortable in asserting "yes, it is so," or "no, it is not," or "it may be so." In other words, it takes time to judge correctly, and our ability to do so is a function of our temperaments and the stage of intellectual development we have achieved. This means that the context or horizon within which we reflect has to be developed. Just as it takes time to acquire physical skills, so it takes time to form reflective skills.

Using Piaget's research, Lonergan has specified stages of cognitive development. However, we are discussing affective understanding and judging, and in this context one cannot appeal to Piaget except in a very broad way since his research on development of feelings is quite sketchy.

Order of Love

To appropriate our feelings and the ways they respond to values and thereby ground our decisions, Lonergan turned to the writings of Scheler and von Hildebrand. It was in this context that Lonergan worked out his own context of the "order of love" and a way to recontextualize his writings in *Grace and Freedom.*

Since love is so central in human affairs it seems strange that the term appears so infrequently in *Insight.* The explanation is, as I stated earlier, that Lonergan wrote *Insight* in the language of faculty psychology, and in this context love is considered and analyzed as a virtue of the will. But in the context of intentionality analysis love is a dynamic state that embraces every level of our intentional being, including our lowest conscious and unconscious psychoneural patterns.

To understand the significance of this shift consider the context I set up in the first section, in which successive levels of cognitional activities give us successive levels of personal identity with ourselves and with the objects of our knowing. Each level sublates, transforms, and enhances the prior levels. Loving operates at the highest level of our being, giving us our most intimate and profound identity and the most intimate and profound identity with the objects of our loving.

Just as knowing reveals the intrinsic reality of subjects and objects, so loving reveals a new dimension of their realities that was not known prior to the state of being in love. Knowing reveals the intrinsic intelligibility of things, but loving goes a step further and reveals the intrinsic excellence or worthwhileness of persons and things. Knowing is a structured activity of a knower, but love is not only an activity but a way of being, a dynamic state that grounds, engenders, and orients activities. Love gives you a new context or horizon, and so, when we speak of making judgments of value within a context, we mean that for a person in love it is love that provides the horizon within which he or she judges the value of various courses of action. Such judgments of value provide reasonable motives for deciding to act or not to act in a certain way. Love thereby becomes the motive that directs and guides the activities that lovers choose. Being in love, then, helps to clarify the contextual aspect of our judgments of value and how these values form the motives for choosing our courses of action. But there are different types of love and a brief reflection on these different types will bring out a further fundamental character of values, namely, that they are hierarchical.

There are four different types of loves. First, there is the love of intimacy, the love of husband and wife that blossoms into the domestic love of parents and children for one another. Second, domestic love expands into social, national, and even historical loving. Third, there is the love of oneself that finds its ground in your own perfection as a domestic, civic, and historical lover. Finally, there is the love of God, who is the source and motive of all forms of loving. Implied in these four forms of love is a comparative judgment of the perfection implied in the different forms of loving. Just as true loving of family sets conditions for the broader love of country and fellow human beings, so such transcultural loving reveals your capacity for historical loving and of becoming a member of a wider historical community. Such potentiality reveals you to yourself not only as a social being but more significantly as a historical being whose origin and destiny belong to the beginning and end of all human history. To appropriate oneself as a potential lover of the total historical community is to set the conditions for seeking the infinite Lover in whom history begins and ends and to discover that the destiny of human history is to belong to a community whose love for one another is based on a love of self in love with God, the supreme value and infinite love that begins and ends all loving. To establish an authentic scale of values then depends on appropriating the love of God as the ground and basic orientation of all other loves.

This hierarchy of loves follows the traditional scholastic scale of virtues stemming from Aquinas and Aristotle with one exception. Both Aristotle and Aquinas insisted on the social nature of human beings but neither articulated our social being as historical, and it is the self as historical that needs to be clarified.

Belief

Aristotle took over and adopted Plato's famous principle that the state is the soul writ large and the soul is the state writ small. In the contemporary context we would say: a culture sets the conditions for developing the character of its people or: a culture is the people writ large. Between culture and the person stands the family, and the early acculturation of children is through the family. It is this transmission of cultural habits of values from parents to children that brings to light the centrality of belief or trust in the assimilation of a scale of value. As Freud and Erikson have noted, it is between the ages of four to seven that a child is taught the beginnings of a moral code and the manners of social behavior. The "generalized other" of the culture is mediated through the "super-ego" of the parents and both become the inner voice of personal and social conscience for the child. The child does not develop his or her own standards of behavior but obeys the commands of the parents in doing this and not doing that. The child desires to do what is correct because he or she fears and trusts the parents. It is the authority of the parents directing and controlling the behavior of the children that provides the reasons or motives for children to choose their activities and ways of cooperating which provide them with their roles and respective tasks. What needs to be stressed here is the role that belief plays.

Children do not develop their own norms of conduct nor do they formulate their own ways of acting and interacting. They act and interact the way that their parents command them, but such obedience is quite reasonable, even though it is not the sort of reasoning that emerges when you think out for yourself the solution to a problem. To believe in the reasoning of other people is a much more common form of reasoning than the more familiar use of the word "reason." The reason for believing in another is because you trust that person. You know he or she is trustworthy. Children know their parents are worthy of belief because they evaluate their parents through their own desires and fears. These desires and fears evolve and pass through stages detailed by Erikson, but the point is that these desires and fears are the contents for their value judgments which in turn provide the motives for children to choose to believe. Children trust the parents' code of prohibitions and permissions and this code becomes the normative ground for their behavior. This brief summary of the central role of belief in assimilating your social, cultural, and religious traditions leads us to the further question of just how we reason with our "hearts," which means for Lonergan how we deliberate and evaluate in such a way as to motivate ourselves to trust in the authority of others and actually carry out the actions and interactions that we choose to believe are truly valuable ways of behaving.

Symbolic Reasoning [The Role of Imagination]

Consider the example of a parent's, teacher's, or preacher's attempts to persuade a person or audience to carry out a sequence of actions. The key to persuading an audience is to speak symbolically with images that will reach down into the person's psychic underground and stir up subconscious vitalities and may also permeate higher levels to generate sufficient emotion to make an unwilling or indifferently disposed person become disposed to act. The result is that such symbols evoke feelings that not only are intentional but effectively intentional or motivational.

How do symbols or symbolic meanings operate? Or what is the logic of symbols by which we persuade ourselves or allow others to motivate us to act in a certain way? Why is one picture worth a thousand words? Because it is symbolic, and not univocal. The picture gathers a host of meanings embedded in a cluster of past experiences that are emotional and so resonate with rich and deeply moving meanings. Thus the home you lived in, the school, stores, and neighborhood where you grew up are all symbolic experiences reverberating with felt and remembered meanings that form part of that complex meaning world in which you live. Such symbolic meanings are spontaneous and primordial forms of meanings and they operated in human history long before logic was invented. In fact, a convenient way to summarize how symbols operate is to contrast symbolic meanings with logical meanings.

Logic seeks univocal not multiple meanings and it does so in order to clarify assumptions and argue carefully to conclusions that are reasonable because they have been proved by successive steps in a clear argument. But there is also an "argument" in a story, song, painting, temple, dance, and statue. That argument is symbolic and it does not reason inferentially but the way our hearts reason. Shakespeare, Beethoven, and Rembrandt are convincing not because they prove their premises and conclusions, but because they overwhelm with clusters of related meanings that do not abstract and exclude but evoke and condense endless lines of associative meanings. Such patterns of associations are frequently contradictory such as we find in the symbols of the four basic elements: earth symbolizes the source of life and womb of death; water refreshes and gives birth but the same dark waters may swallow up life; air is the breath of life but it is also the dreaded cyclone that destroys; and fire brings warmth and growth but it also burns and consumes.

Symbols do not therefore follow the logic of propositions but express the contradictions, tensions, conflicts, and rages of the human heart. Symbols express not the logic of the mind but the logic of motives that ground our actions and interactions, thereby revealing the logic of life itself and the basic tensions of our deepest desires and darkest fears.

While theoretical reason abstracts from images to deal in non-imaginable but highly intelligible meanings, symbolic reason employs images to evoke and direct feelings. Images speak simultaneously to our lower and higher knowing and evaluating self. Symbols speak to both body and soul and promise a destiny that will transform and glorify our minds and hearts.

Symbols, then, provide a people with the reasons of the heart that are the motivating meanings by which they live. And so we may distinguish between the institutional patterns that together constitute the communal practices of a people, and their cultural patterns which undergird these patterns and provide the motives that orient and direct their personal and social operating and cooperating. Institutions are what people do; culture is why they do it. Because symbolic reasoning and deliberating is more spontaneous and prior to the more familiar modes of reasoning, it is a more universal form of knowing and meaning. As I have noted, to define a person as a rational animal is to define a person abstractly. Concretely, we are cultural or symbolic animals. Just as the nineteenth century brought about a reversal in the priority of practical intellect over speculative intellect, so in the twentieth century we have come to realize that reasons of the heart have priority over reasons of the mind.

Culture

We do not experience the world spontaneously as knowers nor as choosers but in terms of our desires and fears. Such desires and fears are transcultural but how they are cultivated depends on the practices and symbols of the cultural world within which one is born and reared. Culture, then, is common to people at all times while the manners and mores, customs and beliefs of a people, are the cultural variables that change throughout human history. What does not change is the fact that people must be born, grow up, eat, work, sleep, marry, dream, get sick, and die. These are the basic events of human existence and they do not vary throughout history. What does develop and decline are the meanings and values that people give to these recurring events. Such meanings are expressed primarily in the stories and rituals of the people. Persons and communities live in the past, present and future; they remember and anticipate, and these memories and expectancies are expressed in cultural stories that explain the meanings and values that they have come to associate with their historical origins, their pilgrimages, and their final destiny. While such stories may be partially known, more importantly, they are lived and enacted and provide the basic context of motives for the people whose public institutional and private lives are oriented by them.

As twentieth-century phenomenologists have discovered, we live in language, and the languages we live in are formed and reformed by the continual flows of personal and communal knowings, choosings, lovings, and doings. But this language has a cultural history and while that history is being lived by individuals, it is not known in the usual meaning of the word known. It is known because it is believed, and it is believed because it is judged to be credible, and it is judged credible because it is valued and motivated by the cultural symbols that incarnate and articulate its history.

In other words, there is a fundamental distinction between the history of a people as it comes to be written down and that same history as it is being lived by those people. In primitive societies the only cultural history people know is through the recitals of their myths. Written history as we know it begins with the Greeks but even among educated people today only a small part of their lived cultural history is known through reading and reflecting. Most history is lived, and lived in the ordinary and symbolic languages of stories, songs, rituals, and other mediating images that evoke and cycle the emotional meanings and values that motivate daily living.

If we now repeat our first question—what am I doing when I am deliberating and deciding?—the answer can be briefly stated in the context we have just articulated. When we deliberate and decide, we are doing so in the context of cultural norms and standards that we believe are authentic and valuable. But such an answer reveals the significance of the second ethical questions: why do I decide or how do I know if I have decided objectively? i.e., how do I know if the cultural standards that ground my deciding are truly objective standards? In other words, what we are looking for is a transcultural norm or standard that is independent of any specific cultural norms and yet applicable to any and all cultures.

B. Second Ethical Question

The question we are considering corresponds to the question Lonergan asked in *Insight* about the objectivity of cognitional judgments, and the answer to that question was Lonergan's theory of epistemology. The problem we are dealing with in this section arises because the normative grounding for making judgments of fact or judgments of value depends on the desire to know and love being given free rein. As we have just seen, judgments of fact or value occur within a context or horizon, which means that such judgments are limited. But our desire to know and love is potentially unlimited, and so, how can I be sure that I have set the limits of my judgments correctly?

I have stated that reflecting heads toward a limit of mastery and familiarity when we grasp that the evidence accumulated is sufficient to assert or deny or qualify the judgment we are considering. In *Insight* Lonergan distinguished different patterns of knowing and therefore different patterns of judging. For example, if, as in science, you intend to judge whether your understanding of the order of the universe is correct or incorrect, then you cannot make such a judgment until you have completely understood all that there is to be understood about the universe—which, while possible, has certainly not been achieved. However, you can make a probable judgment and be certain about the fact that it is probable because you have sufficient evidence for the probability and you have the "mastery and familiarity" with the context within which you are reflecting to assert: this is probably true. In other words, whether you are making a practical judgment—"the cat is on the mat"—or a theoretical judgment—"Newton's theory of gravity is probably valid in limited cases"—you can always set your limits and judge correctly within those limits. What guarantees the validity of these limits is the proper development of the unrestricted desire to know as it unfolds in successive stages.

But how do you know if this desire, which is potentially unlimited, is developing as it should? Because our desire for truth is unlimited and because our achievement of truth is limited there is a continuous struggle that goes on within any human knower to go beyond the present state of self as knower and replace the present self with a more highly developed knower that does not yet exist but could exist in virtue of each knower's potentially unrestricted desire to know. To be an authentic or genuine knower, then, means one must not distort or disorient one's desire to know, but consciously accept the fact that one must always seek to transcend his or her present self.

There are, then, two norms of truth. First, the proximate norm or what Lonergan calls in *Insight* the "virtually unconditioned" or limited absolute. Second, there is the remote standard of truth, which depends on the proper development of one's unrestricted desire. Thus in explaining the proximate norm of truth Lonergan insists on the significance of an invulnerable insight, which is invulnerable because it answers your question, is it so? And it is invulnerable because you waited until the question, is it so?, had sufficient time to uncover sufficient evidence for your assertion, yes, it is so, within the limits you have set. And so setting the limits of any "limited absolute" is the key to the proximate norm, i.e., letting questions arise and wondering long enough for them to arise. But how do you know if your desire to know as operating in a limited context has properly developed? By knowing the different ways that you can interfere with that desire and thereby block it from raising questions that you prefer not to consider.

This is why Lonergan proposes three methods for dealing with the context or horizon within which you are judging. First, there is the method of logic that tests for clarity and consistency within any given context. Second, the genetic method that deals with the proper development of contexts by anticipating a continuous series of higher integrations, i.e., by controlling a continually moving viewpoint or context. And, third, the dialectical method that deals with the ways that you block your proper development as a knower and the ways by which you can not only correct a disoriented context but are able to reverse it, converting yourself back to a genuinely developing knower.

Summarizing the genetic and dialectical methods, then, we can state that as a genetically skilled knower you know how knowing develops through successive stages of intellectual growth. As a dialectical knower you know that there are four different ways that you distort the desire to know so that it does not develop properly. And so a genetic-dialectical knower is an authentic self-transcending knower who can critically judge the progress and decline of his or her own knowing as it advances toward its ultimate objective of unrestricted truth; and also can do the same for other knowers as the human historical community moves toward its final objective of unrestricted knowing. But this explanation deals with Lonergan's cognitive epistemology whereas the question I am raising— how do I know if my cultural valuing is truly objective valuing?—deals with moral not cognitive epistemology. Does Lonergan make the same distinction between the proximate and the remote norms of valuing as he does of knowing?

Lonergan does provide the context for distinguishing a proximate and a remote standard of valuing, not in *Insight* but in *Method in Theology*. Just as every operating knower is called to transcend his or her present stage of cognitional development, so every valuer or lover is continually invited to transcend his or her operating scale of valuing and become more lovable to self and others and to achieve a more perfect loving of God.

To do this one must transform these three methods of knowing into three methods of valuing or loving. I have already indicated how the logic of symbols differs from the logic of propositions, and I have indicated the direction of development in affectivity as one becomes more responsive and responsible, moving from special interests in one's own cultural community to broader concerns for a transcultural community, but I have not explained how dialectical method deals with and resolves moral conflicts.

In chapter seven of *Insight*, Lonergan discusses the dialectic of community as a tension between the spontaneous, intersubjective community and the larger deliberately designed community or institutional pattern that distributes cooperative tasks and roles among its member to achieve common goals. The motives for such common agreements are not discussed in chapter seven of *Insight* since Lonergan's intention is to analyze how common sense patterns of knowing develop and decline in the course of history through accumulation of practical insights and through the four-fold bias that blocks insights and brings decline. What is remarkable in Lonergan's analysis of how insights are blocked is the role of images. Much of what Lonergan later developed in his account of the logic of images and symbolic patterns of meanings is here clearly anticipated.

In *Method in Theology* Lonergan defined symbols as images of real or fanciful objects that evoke feelings or are evoked by feelings. Thus, symbols are a two-way street by which the higher levels of self speak to the lower conscious and unconscious levels of self, and vice-versa. Since the meanings of symbols are discovered in our feelings, symbolic forms of expressions provide the motives that persuade people to decide to operate or cooperate. In chapter six of *Insight* Lonergan transposes Freud's theory of repression, explaining that while neural demands, which become conscious desires and fears, cannot be directly controlled by the conscious self, nevertheless, they can be indirectly controlled or censored through images. How does one indirectly control spontaneously emerging feelings?

Insights emerge from sensible and imaginative data, and so, by controlling images you can indirectly control the way you interpret emotional images, thereby repressing questions and insights that would reveal you to yourself in ways you are not prepared to assimilate within the context of your present, emotional self. Freud's censoring becomes for Lonergan the way the different levels of your deliberating self interact. At any stage of your personal development there are continual psychosomatic changes to be assimilated into the emotional context of your deliberating self. If you do not successfully integrate these neurophysiological events but suppress them, redirecting them through a wide range of acceptable associations, there may develop a variety of abnormal patterns of behaviors. Lonergan refers to such neurotic behaviors as forms of dramatic bias.

Closely related to this dramatic bias is the individual bias by which a self-centered person exploits the social order for his or her own advantage at the expense of the common good. This is the familiar selfish person or egotist who develops her or his own desires for knowing and choosing sufficient to understand how a particular pattern of cooperation works and how it can be exploited, but at the same time blocks the further questioning as to whether such behavior is reasonable and valuable.

The third source of moral decline in a community is within the various groups that make up a community and the way they relate to one another. Just as a single person can block the desire to know and choose to suit his or her own advantage, so a class can distort the concerns of the cooperative community and thereby bring about their own group or class aggrandizement. Finally there is a general moral bias which leads all people to overlook the fact that the motives which direct practical choices toward the production of a standard of living form a specialized pattern of knowing and choosing since they tend to limit knowing and deliberating to the particular, concrete situations within which the community is developing and declining, and so tend to disregard and devalue long-term comprehensive issues. A community governed by practical knowing and choosing will not be interested in interpreting and evaluating correctly its own history but will continue to believe that its cultural standards are truly objective, not limited standards that stand in need of a genetic-dialectical interpretation and evaluation.

III. Transformed Ethics at Work: An Example

To exemplify how such a genetic-dialectical interpretation of the moral standards of a culture could be carried out, I will present a brief critique of American cultural standards, taking my cues from Lonergan's notion of a "cosmopolis" in chapter seven of *Insight* and his model of "stages of meaning" in chapter three of *Method in Theology*. This last section will indicate how the third ethical question—what am I choosing when I choose?—could be answered, suggesting the sort of *Ethics* we need to develop.

In the first part of section II we dealt with the question, what am I doing when I am choosing? In terms of American culture a brief answer to this question might be that when I choose to live as an American I am choosing to participate in my cultural community's pattern of collective habits in order to achieve a desired destiny and avoid the contrary doom. The motives for my practical choices are embedded in my personal class-oriented version of the American cultural story and the myriad mediating images that have formed the emotional habits that orient my day-to-day memories and expectancies.

In the second part of section II the question was—how do I know if the choices that I make according to the cultural norms I have inherited are truly valuable choices? Transposing this into the American context I might ask, how do I know if the American cultural story that orders the American communal memories and expectancies is in fact a truly valuable story and should serve as the basic motivating context for my choices? The answer assumes that you know the American story and that you possess a transcultural norm oriented to a transcultural objective by which you can evaluate to what extent the American culture is setting the conditions that will move you toward your transcultural destiny.

However, as we have seen in the second section, cultural stories are known not by personally generated knowledge but by believing in the worthwhileness of your cultural heritage and by actually living its meaning and values. During the past century there have been considerable efforts by scholars and historians to interpret, retrieve, and write down just what this story is that Americans are living. I can only give the briefest indication of these findings.

The best place to begin any investigation of the American story is with the classic study of American culture, *Democracy In America* by Tocqueville. In the opening of his second volume, Tocqueville makes the stunning observation: "So, of all countries in the world, America is the one in which the precepts of Descartes are least studied and best followed." In other words, nobody reads Descartes's philosophy in America, yet everyone lives and practices it. What is this Cartesian philosophy that Americans practice? It is an interpretation and evaluation of historical traditions and it suggests as a central normative principle "doubt everything." In America everyone tends to develop attitudes as if they come from Missouri, the "show me" state.

An important indication of cultural attitudes can be found in proverbs, maxims, advertising slogans, and bumper stickers. Thus Henry Ford remarked, "History is bunk." A similar cultural attitude is found in the familiar bumper sticker, "Question authority." Taken at face value these aphoristic statements of Cartesian philosophy are arrogant nonsense. As Einstein said, "ninety-nine percent of what a genius knows, he knows because he believes it." And he also said "don't pay any attention to what physicists tell you they do, rather watch them." Similarly, don't pay any attention to what Americans tell you Americans do, rather watch them. And what Americans do is what every other cultural community does; they believe in the history they are living, which is a way of life they have inherited and which they certainly did not invent. Without his historical heritage Henry Ford would have been living like a pre-Stone Age person without even knowing what a wheel was.

In other words, Henry Ford thought history was bunk and others think all authorities should be questioned because their own historical cultural community gave them those value judgments which they believed and, most ironically, never even thought of seriously questioning these popular American biases against authority and tradition. Just where did this American tradition against tradition come from?

To answer this question I shall turn to Lonergan's notion of a "cosmopolis." Lonergan developed the notion of a cosmopolis to meet the problem of the long cycle of decline which results from the intersection of general bias with group bias. General bias is the tendency for every society to disregard the long-term consequences of its decisions and pursue its own well-being, while group bias refers to the way people who belong to the same class tend to reinforce their own interests at the expense of other groups within their society. Karl Marx thought that group bias or class conflict resulted from the struggle between owners and workers, but because Marx did not grasp that group biases result from limiting the desire to know which brings about development and progress, he had little appreciation of general bias as the major cause of historical disorders.

Closer to Lonergan's model is Toynbee's analysis of historical progress as resulting from a group of people within a society who spearhead development and become the creative minority, but who in time change from a creative minority and become the dominant minority because they fail to realize that situations are always changing and that their former creative solutions are no longer working but have now become stagnant problems. The advantage of Toynbee's model is that the same group can be at one time the source of progress and later become the cause of disorder as their interest in knowing becomes a "vested or closed interest" blocking questions. However, Toynbee is still discussing the flow of history in terms of the rise and fall of creative and stagnant groups, which in Lonergan's context refers to the short cycles of progress and decline. But the notion of a cosmopolis requires a more universal viewpoint that identifies the four sources of decline as well as the sources of progress.

A cosmopolis is a group of people who can be characterized in three ways. First, they know the difference between the proximate and remote criterion of truth and value. Second, they understand the difference between specialized practical knowing designed to deal with concrete particular cases, and the disinterested, theoretical knowing of the natural and human sciences that are designed to be comprehensive and concrete. Third, they know that people whose knowing is dominated by practical interest can deal with short-term decline which can be corrected by reform or revolution, but they also know that every reform or revolutionary group has a tendency to elevate its own achievements by distorting and devaluing past historical results and thereby to carry forward certain aspects of the cumulative decline operating in history. Because the members of a cosmopolis have correctly identified the sources of historical progress and decline, they know how to advance progress and reverse decline.

An example of this can be seen in Lonergan's analysis of the long cycle of decline that began in the medieval period and kept accumulating down to our own time. Two major problems emerged in the medieval period—a practical one involving church-state relations, and a theoretical one involving the need for systematic theology to become hermeneutical and historical. Both problems failed to be solved. The historical results were as follows. The Church split into different groups, leading to conflicts and eventually to the wars of religion. In the theoretical context Machiavelli denied the possibility of development and progress and insisted that we must take the status quo as normative for choosing a social order. Hobbes went further and denied a transcendent good and demoted religious values below civic values. Bacon and Descartes failed to identify the nature of the "scientific revolution" in which they were involved. Instead of identifying what one of my colleagues has called "normative science," they began the "cover story" that set the stage for a number of major historical disorders including the "tradition against traditions" which permeates and conditions American cultural attitudes.

Bacon and Descartes failed to distinguish between the interested, practical knowing and deciding that develops and guides our day-to-day living, and the disinterested, scientific knowing that aims at a comprehensive understanding of nature and history. As a result, the notion of reason as practical and calculating came to be glorified as the cause of the Enlightenment while belief and tradition were "idols" of past, dark ages—a period of historical immaturity. The result was, on the one hand the formation of the new dogmas of secular liberalism and, on the other, the Marxist critique of that same secular liberalism as bourgeois capitalism.

This brief sketch of a historical sequence of disorders beginning in the medieval period and ending in the nineteenth century with a denial of the person as a transcendent knower and lover indicates the way a cosmopolis would function. Its purpose is to develop a new type of historical evaluative interpretation that would lead to a new collective responsibility of the human historical community.

With this notion of cosmopolis as a background, let us return to our critique of American culture. We can now understand how liberalism became the reigning philosophy of history in America during the nineteenth century and how we inherited this "tradition against tradition." For as Robert Heilbroner in *The Future As History* (New York: Harper, 1960) points out, "the idea of inevitability of progress sheds an important light on the philosophy of optimism whose roots we have been endeavoring to unearth. It makes evident the fact that a hopeful orientation to the future did not emerge solely from confidence in man's natural ability to shape his own destiny. On the contrary, it came with the growth of historical forces which promised to shape his destiny for him." Unfortunately it was also the very "blindness, the determinism of these forces which fortified men's faith in them." The theory of liberalism or automatic progress, however, was not just a flow of ideas changing practical living but also and more important it was a change in underlying cultural meanings and values. The major change in American historical community during the eighteenth and nineteenth centuries was the gradual emergence of a new lived story as well as the myriad civic and social rituals and customs that make up the common meanings and values of a cultural community. What was this new American story and how did it function in our day-to-day living?

Again the best way to answer this question is to return to Tocqueville. Tocqueville, like Aristotle, realized that there were two types of democracies—virtuous democracies and vicious ones. More important, he knew from Montesquieu that the laws of a people were expressions of the "spirit" of those people. In other words, he knew that institutional practices were motivated by the "spirit" of the people who lived those practices. And most significant, he knew that the spirit of a people formed their "habits of the heart." So the controlling question for Tocqueville in his first volume of *Democracy In America* was "just what is the spirit that informs the American cultural community?," a community that had already chosen its constitution and had been living its meanings and values for over forty years.

Implied in a constitution such as the Americans had drawn up was a scale of values, and the question I have been asking in this section is to what extent does our constitution as culturally lived encourage or discourage citizens to become authentic knowers and lovers? Authentic loving means you are open to an unrestricted loving of God. So to what extent, we might ask, did the biblical story inform the lived story of the American cultural community? Somewhat surprising for American Christians and Jews, the spirit of the Bible did not become the spirit of the American community, at least as far as Tocqueville interpreted that spirit in the nineteenth century. Quite the opposite, the people explicitly rejected the biblical spirit as that spirit was being lived by the original Protestant community.

The spirit of the American people "stands out in broad daylight" as Tocqueville liked to put it, and by that he meant it is revealed in the character, dress, speech, manners, and mores of the people, or as Lonergan would say, that spirit was expressed in the "incarnate meaning" of the person. That spirit for Tocqueville was the "sovereignty of the people," which in the twentieth century has become the "sovereignty of self."

American culture, then, cultivates its people to think of themselves as sovereigns. This value judgment neatly sums up the shift from the aristocratic culture of western history to the democratic culture of today. As Tocqueville in his prophetic and penetrating introduction pointed out, democratic culture started some seven hundred years ago in the medieval period and it has been building ever since like a great tidal wave sweeping before it kings, nobles, and every established authority. However impressive this fact seemed to Tocqueville in the nineteenth century, it was not characteristic of the America cultural community in the seventeenth and eighteenth centuries, as Michael Kammen's award-winning study *People of Paradox* (New York: Knopf, 1972) has suggested.

Americans in the seventeenth and eighteenth centuries were more medieval, less modern, and more English than American. This might seem obvious since the medieval English "habits of the heart" was what the early settlers brought with them to the shores of Virginia and Massachusetts. Kammen's *People of Paradox* and the series of brilliant studies on American cultural history he has published more recently underscore the importance of making a distinction between history as lived and the history that is written.

In his study *Season of Youth* (New York: Knopf, 1978) Kammen details how Americans during the nineteenth century were continuously reinterpreting and reorganizing their colonial history, the Revolutionary War, and their subsequent writing and ratifying of the Constitution. The title of Kammen's fourth chapter, "Reshaping the Past To Persuade the Present," sums up what cultural communities in general do, and what we as individuals do. What we do, as Freud discovered, is screen out our past memories to fit the motivations of our present wishes and decisions. Thus any generation will inherit the excuses, rationalizations, and lies of its ancestry, as well as its truths and achievements. And we generally choose to believe both because for the most part we trust our national community as it is given to us by our parents and other cultural authorities. When historians come to write our history they do so with "habits of the heart" and a scale of values they have received from their own families and other cultural sources. Historians writing history make myriad judgments of facts and values and numerous decisions about their research, its meanings and value, and about what narrative sequence or story they will construct. In other words, historians operate under the dialectical tensions of their own infinite potential for transcultural valuing and their own actual and inherited cultural norms. American historians, then, are always in the process of reading the written history of their own peoples' lived history and attempting to correct and expand it. What makes Michael Kammen's work so interesting is the sources he uses.

Kammen studies the manners and mores of our ancestors as he finds them in popular political oratory, sermons, bulletins, newspapers, letters, posters, pictures, and the popular literary genres, especially the best selling stories that provided the images that evoked the feeling that formed the "habits of the American heart."

In *A Season of Youth* Kammen found that the controlling image by which the American cultural community of the nineteenth century reformulated its past was a "rite of passage." The Revolutionary War period became a passage from youthful immaturity and dependence on cultural authorities to a mature manhood and political independence. The Atlantic crossing that for Cotton Mather in the seventeenth century was perceived as "a tribal response to a divine call" became secularized in the eighteenth and nineteenth centuries as the call to political action and the coming of age. What Kammen's studies explain is why Tocqueville discerned in the nineteenth century that the basic orienting spirit of American culture had become the "sovereignty of the people."

Kammen and Tocqueville are concerned with why Americans do what they do. It is necessary to add a word about what Americans actually did in the eighteenth and nineteenth centuries. Here I would draw on the work of a colleague who has discerned that behind the constitutional debate of the federalists and anti-federalists was a decision about whether we would become a small democratic republic, according to the vision of Jefferson, or a large commercial empire, according to the countervision of Madison. Madison's genius was to develop the popular political rhetoric that won the day. However, what sort of commercial empire we would be was not chosen. The southern states developed a way of life based on an international maritime trade and an interior canal-and-river-boat economy, while the north envisioned an industrial economy based on railroads. In what was one of the first specialized cultural histories of America, *The Virgin Land* (Cambridge: Harvard University Press, 1950), Henry Nash Smith has argued that the Civil War and the congressional debates surrounding it were as much about railroads and river boats as they were about slavery, since slavery was tied into the cultural vision of the southern commercial empire while the northern counter-vision was motivated by a different dream of our national destiny.

Following the lead of Henry Nash Smith, Leo Marx has given us a much broader perspective on these cultural themes as he explores in his study, *The Machine In The Garden* (New York: Oxford University Press, 1964), the fundamental dialectic of two transcultural images, the machine and garden, civilization versus nature, or the biblical dialectic of the garden and desert. As Moses put it to the Israelites, "Today I set before you life and death." And, as Marx argues, Americans, like the Israelites, chose both; they refused to let go of the Jeffersonian vision of turning America into a garden and "promised land," but they also insisted on building a "kingdom of force" so they could exercise and indulge the "sovereignty of the self."

How the sovereignty of the people became in our time the sovereignty of the self has been detailed by Mary Ann Glendon in her recent books on American legal history (*The New Family and the New Property* [Toronto/Boston, Butterworths, 1981]; *Abortion and Divorce in Western Law* [Cambridge: Harvard University Press, 1987]; *The Transformation of Family Law* [Chicago: University of Chicago Press, 1989]; *A Nation Under Lawyers* [New York: Farrar, Straus and Giroux, 1994]) and how legal decisions can be interpreted as expressions of American cultural meaning and values. What her studies and those of Robert Bellah have shown is that once again Tocqueville's premonitions may prove to be prophetic.

As Tocqueville grew older he became more concerned that Americans would choose equality rather than liberty and that the cultural results would be not the hard tyranny imposed on a community by tyrannical authority but a new kind of "soft tyranny" that a people would impose on themselves. This is the dark destiny of our American consumer culture, manipulated by mass media, suffering a loss of community, whose future seems to some apocalyptically dreadful.

Robert Heilbroner's book, *An Inquiry into the Human Prospect* (New York: Norton, 1980), opens with the question, "Is there hope for man" and he goes on to state: "the question asks whether we can imagine that future other than as a continuation of the darkness, cruelty, and disorder of the past; worse, whether we do not foresee in the human prospect a deterioration of things, even an impending catastrophe." Heilbroner's pessimistic perspective stems from his analysis of the way our institutional patterns are functioning, especially socio-economic forces. In answering this question of hope for our future, I would like to return again to the distinction between the culture we are living and that same culture as we reflect upon it and evaluate it. Here I will draw upon Lonergan's model of the "stages of meaning."

Lonergan suggests that the history of human culture can be studied in terms of the controls that a culture has over the meanings and values people are living. A similar distinction can be found in Piaget's model of personal, cognitive development. In the third stage of cognitive development, between the ages of eleven and fourteen, the child passes from the prior concrete operational stage to the formal operational stage. This new stage enables the young person to shift attention from sentences or propositions to the operations by which sentences or propositions are generated and communicated. This is a remarkable new stage of development, since in the prior stage the child was living in linguistic meanings but unaware of how these meanings were made and mediated. With the discovery of how to make sentences we acquire new controls and responsibilities. Similarly, if you assimilate Lonergan's genetic and dialectical method then you not only live your cultural history but you begin to wonder: what is the meaning and value of those historical meanings and values that you are living?

Just as Piaget suggests why children can become more responsible as they pass from the concrete operational stage to the formal operational stage, so Lonergan is suggesting that we are in a new stage of cultural history, since it is now possible for present cultural communities to begin to become collectively responsible for the human historical community. Lonergan would stress that this is a new possibility and only a possibility. But it may become not only possible but highly desirable, and then the problem will become: can we develop motivations that will be sufficient to carry out this collective responsibility? The best motive, as we have seen, is love, and not just domestic, civic, or historical love, but a world-transcending love that will effectively move the hearts of people to develop this kind of a new cultural community, a community that will be characterized not by a tradition that simply opposes an older tradition, but one that will set the conditions for its people to scale their values so that they will remain open to their own infinite potential as lovers while continuing to choose what they know to be a better way of seeking their final destiny in a community of unlimited lovers.

Reflections on the Terror of History

Glenn Hughes

History, Stephen said, is a nightmare from which I am trying to awake.
—James Joyce, *Ulysses*

History, if we wish to be precise about the term, is not everything that has ever happened, but the remembered and recorded past, the past judged worthy of reflection and narration. A "history" is a story comprised, not of all events, but of significant events. The weight of significance is something to be determined by the person trying to make sense of the flow of events; and the result is a tale, a story worth narrating, a pattern of the significant and essential.

This makes history a somewhat curious phenomenon, in that two components are required for its constitution: the occurrence of the significant events themselves, and the subsequent recognizing and telling of them. For this reason, when we speak of a "history" we might be referring to (1) a course of events, (2) the recorded narrative of those events, or (3) the combination of the two. Not only must there be a tale worth telling, but the tale must be drawn out or deciphered from the flux of events, and must be told, heard, and remembered, for history to exist.[1]

What makes events memorable? In general, we could say that memorable events are those that have the most explanatory, or revelatory, power.

---

[1] On this "double constitution" of history and its epistemological implications, see Eric Voegelin, "What Is History?" in Eric Voegelin, *What Is History? and Other Late Unpublished Writings* (Baton Rouge: Louisiana State University Press, 1990) 10–13.

A biographer eliminates the dross, the insignificant, from a life story, in order to expose the essential identity, the essential acts and influences, of a person. When Jean-Paul Sartre in his autobiography recollects that youthful occasion on which, after performing some mischief, he suddenly and painfully felt himself "seen by God," and reacted by flying into a rage "against so crude an indiscretion" as divine omniscience and by severing from that point on all relations with God, we do not wonder why he includes the episode in his memoirs.[2] He doesn't tell us, nor does he probably remember, what he ate for breakfast that morning; it is irrelevant to the formation of his character, and thus to his desire to understand himself. The same principle, the desire to understand the essential, guides the writing of the story of a political or cultural movement, or the history of a nation or civilization. And world history, too, is a narrative chosen in the hope or confidence that it is these recollected events that will most help us to comprehend ourselves and our human situation.

Historians disagree, of course, about which data have the highest explanatory value with respect to telling the comprehensive human story. A historian of Marxist persuasion, for example, might insist that economic factors and material conditions provide the most fundamental data for making sense of human history, on the assumption that these elements are constitutive of the human "essence."[3] By contrast, a Jewish or Christian portrayal of world history will be organized ultimately around shifting patterns of human response to divine presence (as understood within these respective traditions), as the key factors in making sense of the human story.[4] Disagreements arise because events recommend themselves as most pertinent to human history in direct relation to certain assumptions about the nature of reality. Such assumptions provide what we may call the "ground

---

[2]Jean-Paul Sartre, *The Words,* trans. Bernard Frechtman (New York: George Braziller, 1964) 102.

[3]"[A]t each stage [of history] there is found a material result: a sum of productive forces, an historically created relation of individuals to nature and to one another, which is handed down to each generation from its predecessor. . . . This sum of productive forces, capital funds and social forms of intercourse, which every individual and generation finds in existence as something given, is the real basis of what the philosophers have conceived as 'substance' and 'essence of man' . . . ." Karl Marx and Frederick Engels, *The German Ideology,* trans. Lawrence and Wishart (New York: International Publishers, 1972) 59.

[4]Cf. Josef Pieper, *The End of Time: Meditation on the Philosophy of History,* trans. Michael Bullock (London: Faber and Faber Ltd., 1954) 26, 22: "In the case of the philosophy of history . . . in so far as it declines to refer back to theology it does not descry its subject matter at all; it is altogether unable to obtain a serious view of the totality of history. . . . What really and in the deepest analysis happens in history is salvation and disaster."

of meaning" for a historian: a bedrock of meaning consisting of those realities that the historian is convinced are the most valid, stable, and enduring. The view of the Marxist historian, for example, is that human
meaning is, ultimately, to be determined in terms of material conditions
(these conditions are the ground of meaning); while for the Christian historian, human meaning is ultimately to be determined in relation to God
(God is the ground of meaning).

But professional historians and biographers are not the only ones who
construct histories. All of us do, to the extent that we fashion into coherent narrative wholes the stories of our lives, for telling to ourselves or to
others. And these stories are not without broader contexts of meaning that
we also interpret after some fashion, a context that includes family histories, national histories, and civilizational histories. We are all aware, in
other words, that the dramas of our individual lives unfold within broader
streams of meaning, and ultimately within an overarching history of humankind; and though few of us spend considerable time in the contemplation of what this ultimate history might mean, nevertheless, almost
everyone has at least a vague or inchoate interpretation of it. It is just this
comprehensive history that provides the ultimate backdrop of meaning for
making sense of one's life. And wherever this interpretation of the backdrop of history comes from, it too reflects, as does that of the professional
historian, assumptions about the nature of reality. In other words, every
mature self-understanding reflects some interpretation of human history,
and this interpretation of human history incorporates assumptions about
what constitutes the "ground of meaning." The ground of meaning, again,
may be defined as that which is most stable and enduring in reality.

Having established that one's sense of history and thereby one's sense
of identity is shaped by one's understanding of the ground of meaning, we
may begin our analysis of the phenomenon we call "the terror of history,"
with which this essay is concerned.

I

The search for the ground has always been, at bottom, a search for
some necessary mode of being. The ground sought for is reality or truth
that is stable and enduring; and only reality that *must* be the way it is,
which is immutable, fated, unalterable, is an absolute guarantee of stability of meaning. One such reality, for example, is the God of ancient
Hebrew faith: "The grass withers, the flower fades, but the word of our

God remains for ever" (Isa 40:8). The God Yahweh promises an eternal law and justice that are not subject to change, as are mere created things: "The heavens will vanish like smoke, the earth wear out like a garment . . . but my salvation shall last for ever, and my justice have no end" (Isa 51:6). The enduringness of the divine ground as newly revealed through the epiphany of Christ is again confirmed by the anonymous author of the Letter to the Hebrews, as he warns his readers not to put their trust in worldly things, which are subject to destruction:

> That time his voice made the earth shake, but now he has given us this promise: I shall make the earth shake once more and not only the earth but heaven as well. The words once more show that since the things being shaken are created things, they are going to be changed, so that the un-shakable things will be left. We have been given possession of an unshakable kingdom (Heb 12:26-28).[5]

The transcendent ground of meaning need not, however, be symbolized as a personal divinity. In the Chinese conception of the *Tao,* for instance, we find once again the confirmation of a reality that is a necessary and un-shakable law, and the measure for grasping the true meaning of all things and all actions. Since necessary reality is that which cannot be otherwise, the *Tao* is not subject to change, like finite things:

> There was something formless and perfect before the universe was born. It is serene. Empty. Solitary. Unchanging. Infinite. Eternally present. It is the mother of the universe. For lack of a better name, I call it the Tao. . . . Man follows the earth. Earth follows the universe. The universe follows the Tao. The Tao follows only itself.[6]

East and West, early and late in human history, the ground is con-ceived of as permanent and non-contingent—a necessary reality with which humans seek to establish a firm and truthful relation as the final ar-biter of personal and historical meaning.

Why is the search for a necessary ground of being ubiquitous in human culture? The search is impelled, certainly, by the natural human de-sire to understand the reality in which we find ourselves. But the search and its discoveries are scarcely disinterested intellectual exercises; on the

---

[5]Translations are from *The Jerusalem Bible* (Garden City, N.Y.: Doubleday and Company, 1966).

[6]Stephen Mitchell, *Tao Te Ching: A New English Version, with Foreword and Notes* (New York: Harper & Row, 1988) Chap. 25.

contrary, they are endowed with massive emotional value. Why this is so may be ascertained from a simple enough psychological fact: human consciousness, as it comes to an awareness of the human situation in reality, becomes aware that its own existence is derived, dependent on something other—in a word, contingent. As Descartes put it, we are conscious of occupying some sort of "middle ground" between "supreme being and non-being": we do not have the power either to create ourselves or to sustain ourselves in existence, and we participate in the temporal order whose law is that of coming-to-be and passing-away.[7] Human existence is precarious and fragile, a temporal emergence out of non-existence, hovering over the abyss of non-existence to which it may return at any time. The normal response to this awareness is anxiety: an anxious concern to diminish the threat of precariousness, to seek, if possible, a connection to what is more lasting in reality, to secure a more firm foothold in being.[8] Thus, it is primarily in response to the anxiety over precarious existence that the passionate search is undertaken for that which exists of necessity.

As previous references to the Hebrew and Christian God, and to the Chinese Tao, have indicated, the search has for most of humanity not been undertaken in vain: lasting and necessary orders of reality have been discovered, symbolized, worshipped, made the focus of meditation, contemplation, and prayer. But the Western God and the Chinese Tao are complex, sophisticated symbols of transcendent reality appearing quite late on the human scene. Earlier, so called "cosmological" cultures equally sought what exists of necessity, and found it in the forces and rhythms of the cosmic order, whose energy, lastingness, and regularity evidenced sacred power and intent.[9] In these cultures, the ground is not symbolized as a single transcendent principle, personal or impersonal, because the cosmological

---

[7]René Descartes, *Meditations on First Philosophy* (in a companion volume with *Discourse on Method*), trans. Donald A. Cress (Indianapolis: Hackett Publishing Company, 1983) Meditation Four, 79.

[8]For the classic philosophical texts on anxiety *(Angst)*, see Søren Kierkegaard, *The Concept of Anxiety*, ed. and trans. Reidar Thomte, in collaboration with Albert B. Anderson (Princeton: Princeton University Press, 1980), and Martin Heidegger, *Being and Time,* trans. John Macquarrie and Edward Robinson (New York: Harper & Row, 1962) especially 225–35. For an analysis of the relationship between anxiety and the search for the ground, to which the present essay is much indebted and which deserves a place among the basic philosophical texts on anxiety, see Eric Voegelin, "Anxiety and Reason," in *What Is History? and Other Late Unpublished Writings.*

[9]Cosmological cultures are here defined as those that predate the explicit recognition and symbolization of a transcendent ground of being. Thus, the whole of reality is the "cosmos," a cosmos bounded by spatio-temporal imagination. For an introduction to the cosmological

imagination has not yet explicitly differentiated transcendent and spatio-temporal being; rather, the ground is symbolized multivariously through the exotic refractions of the mythopoeic imagination, which portrays the necessary, originating sources of meaning as imaginable gods, their conflicts and relationships with each other, and their creative actions with and upon the familiar features of the natural world. The connection with enduring reality, then, for members of cosmological societies, is the connection with "intracosmic" gods and with the forces of nature with whom the gods are so closely identified; and the ritual activities that secure and maintain that connection are the central scenes in the drama of cosmological existence.

Mircea Eliade has explained in persuasive detail how the essential goal of religious activities in archaic societies, which is to forge a connection with the power and enduringness of sacred reality, involves the repeated overcoming or annihilation of time through ritual participation in archetypal actions, situations, and events. The archetypal persons or actions are those enduring powers that established the world and its features "in the beginning," and which even now grant meaning to whatever imitates them or participates in them. They are true reality, efficacious, necessary, perfect—and immune from the deteriorating effects of time. Human existence, however, is lived in time, or in "history," which Eliade defines in this context as "a succession of events that are irreversible, unforeseeable, possessed of autonomous value."[10]

From a modern perspective, one of the most striking characteristics of the archaic or cosmological outlook is its refusal to place a value on history so defined, and, indeed, a desire to annul it, to leave it behind, at every opportunity. It is, first of all, desirable to annul the effects of time, because the temporal is that which has no lasting or self-sufficient being, and is therefore always threatened with the meaninglessness of non-existence. The need to transcend time is especially acute where suffering is concerned, since suffering that is merely of time, unconnected with the meanings associated with sacred purpose or intention, is arbitrary and, consequently, meaningless. As Eliade emphasizes, it is possible to tolerate such sufferings as those inflicted by disease, natural disaster, or the cruelties of warfare, only so long

perception of reality, see Eric Voegelin, *Order and History, Volume 1: From Israel to Revelation* (Baton Rouge: Louisiana State University Press, 1976) 145.

[10]Mircea Eliade, *The Myth of the Eternal Return; or, Cosmos and History*, trans. Willard R. Trak (Princeton: Princeton University Press, Bollingen Series XLVI, 1974) 95. The present essay owes its conception in part to Eliade's detailed analysis of what he calls "the terror of history" in this book (see Chap. 4).

as these have a meaning that raises them above the level of blind chance, so long as they are not absurd. Purely historical suffering, however—suffering unrelated to any transtemporal meaning—is unbearable.[11]

Second, it is possible to annul the effects of time, because in cosmological experience the ground of reality, what exists originally and of necessity, is identified with the powers and rhythms of the natural cosmos. That is, the ground is conceived in terms of spatio-temporal entities and events, and therefore the time and events of everyday life can be followed by the imagination to where they seamlessly merge with, and dissolve into, primordial, sacred reality. Thus, a return to pristine origins, for society as for nature, can be experienced as a fact. Through the efficacy of rituals of renewal and return, time, with its attrition and threat of meaninglessness, and its accumulation of imperfect action, suffering, and guilt, is periodically annihilated, and time is experienced as starting over.[12]

It is a commonplace in historical studies to assert that, as a consequence of this cyclical experience involving the periodic destruction and renewal of time, cosmological cultures had no real experience of "history" as a unique, irrecoverable, linear progression of human events. History, we are told, was a discovery of the ancient Hebrews, through their experiences of a transcendent God, in relation to which human events for the first time took on the character of a unique series of unfolding situations, the story of a one-time creation and its career in time. While this view reflects a solid core of insight concerning the decisiveness of the Hebrew experience of transcendence and its accompanying radical insistence on the significance of historical particularity, it is also somewhat misleading because it oversimplifies the cosmological experience. While that experience is dominated by cyclical time, linear time is not utterly excluded from awareness or concern. Voegelin has sufficiently established this through his analysis of the phenomenon, present among the cosmological societies of the ancient Near East, of what he calls "historiogenesis."

Historiogenesis, like cosmogony, theogony, and anthropogony, is a mythopoeic speculation on ultimate beginnings; in this case, on the ultimate beginnings of the presently experienced social order. Its function is the same as all myth: it explains how this present society came to be in an ultimate sense. It does this by telling the story of this society, beginning at an absolute point of cosmic origins, proceeding through mythical and legendary

---

[11]Eliade, *The Myth of the Eternal Return,* 95–102.

[12]See Mircea Eliade, *The Sacred and the Profane,* trans. Willard R. Trask (New York: Harcourt, Brace & World, 1959) 69–80.

events that merge into the known events of recent history, and concluding with the establishment of the society in which the author is writing, now firmly revealed in its inevitability.[13] There is no getting around the fact that unrepeatable time is the object of interest here; historiogenesis, with its rigid documentation of the inevitability of the step-by-step process leading from cosmic beginnings to the current social order, is a "ruthless construction of unilinear history."[14] The cosmological experience of time, then, is somewhat more complex than is usually assumed by scholars. Somehow, the cyclical experience of time, and of time's periodic abolition and renewal, dominates a perspective that also, however, accommodates the recognition of linear, one-way time, the time "where opportunities are lost forever and defeat is final."[15]

But is such an accommodation truly possible? It would seem to be a psychological impossibility. It has the appearance of an impossibility because we have so completely lost the cosmological perspective, which is characterized in part by the absence of certain conceptual differentiations. Most crucially, there is as yet no differentiation of a transcendent ground of reality, or, correspondingly, of an immanent, worldly reality distinct from the sacred.[16] The cosmos is still saturated with the timelessness of divine presence. With respect to the experience of time, we might say that the experience of irreversible time is not yet sufficiently differentiated as a distinct concern from the experience of the cyclical dissolution of time in the ever-present sacred as to present a challenge to that experience—or,

---

[13]Voegelin makes clear that historiogenesis is not universally found in cosmological societies: "As a matter of fact, wherever it can be dated, historiogenesis proves to develop later than the speculations on the other realms of being [i.e., the gods, the world, and human being]; and in some cosmological societies it does not develop at all." "Anxiety and Reason," 55. Nevertheless, its presence in those cosmological cultures in which it is found confirms that the concern with irreversible time, and thus with "history," is not entirely absent from mythopoeic societies. Even more fruitfully, Voegelin finds historiogenetic speculation to be "virtually omnipresent" in all later developed societies, East and West, from ancient Israel, China, and India up to and including the modern West (56). It thus appears to be a symbolic form of considerable importance for the understanding of historical self-interpretation. For Voegelin's analysis, see Eric Voegelin, *The Ecumenic Age* (Baton Rouge: Louisiana State University Press, 1974) Chap. 1: Historiogenesis (59–113). "Anxiety and Reason" is an earlier version of this chapter.

[14]Voegelin, "Anxiety and Reason," 55.

[15]Ibid.

[16] The discovery of transcendent reality in Western cultures has been most helpfully analyzed by Voegelin, in a large body of writings. For a summary introduction to his analysis, see my *Mystery and Myth in the Philosophy of Eric Voegelin* (Columbia, Mo.: University of Missouri Press, 1993) Chap. 2: The Question of the Ground.

that the experience of irreversible time is enough of a concern to prompt the creation of such forms of speculation as historiogenesis, without yet posing a logical or conceptual threat to the validity of the experience of the cyclical abolition and renewal of time. This would appear to be the only explanation compatible with the harmonious co-existence in some cosmological cultures of historiogenetic speculation with the rich body of rituals and symbols the primary purpose of which is the annulment of time.

Moreover, a single and fully understandable motive can be discerned behind both the ritual return to timeless, archetypal being *and* the indulgence in historiogenetic speculation. That motive is the desire to overcome the precariousness of existence and its attendant anxiety. We have noted how the archaic religious rituals, by connecting the participants with real and necessary being, overcame the threat of meaninglessness associated with merely temporal, contingent existence. In a related way, the firm linking of the present state of society through historiogenetic accounts to the original divine ordering of reality, in a manner indicating that no other course of events was possible, removes the index of contingency from social existence, and confers upon it the sanction of necessity and the aura of predestination. Both symbolic forms, then, assuage the anxiety that arises from an awareness that the meaning of particular, contingent existence is dependent on a self-sufficient and necessary ground of meaning. Both defuse the threat of "mere" historicality—the threat, that is, of existence in time divorced from real, exemplary, timeless being.

The cosmological achievements in ordering human existence into a proper relation to necessary being were therefore successful—up to a point. That point was the revelation of the transcendence of the ground. In ancient Israel, in Hellas, and in the cultures of ancient China and India, roughly during the time of what Karl Jaspers has dubbed the "axial period" of human history (800–200 B.C.E.), there occurred the breakthrough discoveries that established the ground of reality as lying beyond the orders of space and time and thus beyond the horizon of full human comprehension.[17] In Israel, Yahweh reveals himself to Moses as the "I AM WHAT I AM," separate from all created things, and to later prophetic understanding as the God of all the nations; in Greece, the poets and philosophers discern with increasing clarity the transcendent universality of the first principle of reality, culminating in Plato's conception of a "being beyond being" (*Republic* 509b) and Aristotle's "unmoved mover"; while in India the Upanishadic

---

[17]On the "axial period," see Karl Jaspers, *The Origin and Goal of History*, trans. Michael Bullock (London: Routledge and Kegan Paul Ltd., 1953) 1–77.

texts on Brahman and the teachings of the Buddha, and in China the
Confucian and Taoist insights, affirm that the ground of reality is not to
be identified with any "intracosmic" thing or things but rather with a mysterious non-thing "behind," "underlying," or "beyond" all natural things.

The consequences of these discoveries, as they advanced through their
respective cultures, can hardly be overestimated. The solace-providing
myths and rituals that secured attunement with ultimate reality for cosmological societies shattered or dissolved in the face of symbols of transcendent reality. In each of these cultures, a massive reordering of human
existence was initiated that involved assimilating the fact and the implications of the revelations and the restructuring of social, political, and religious life in accordance with their truth.

A first, brutal consequence of the differentiation of transcendence was
the raising to explicit consciousness of the essential unknowability of the
ground and of its relative inaccessibility. Human existence is no longer in
direct contact with its own ground; the ground has receded to a "beyond"
of space, time, and imagination, leaving a heightened awareness of the precarious contingency of existence in time, and a corresponding heightening
of anxiety over securing the meaning of that existence. The new dispensation is characterized, above all, by "existential uncertainty" about the status of one's relationship to the ground of all meaning.[18]

A second consequence pertains to the relationship between temporal
and timeless being. As the case of Israel shows most clearly, when the
ground ceases to be identified with the natural world—when the "cosmos"
conceptually splits asunder, as a result of the differentiating insights, into
(1) the world of spatio-temporal or immanent nature, and (2) a transcendent beyond of nature (a Creator-God, in Hebrew and Christian
thought)—then the finite (or created) world is indeed released into "history" in the pregnant sense. That is, objects and events of the physical
world can no longer themselves embody the timeless, can no longer themselves be archetypal; rather, they are understood as *related* to the timeless
ground, in a kind of tension of relatedness.[19] But this places them solidly
under the index of temporal, one-time only events. Thus, the course of
worldly events becomes a unique, unrepeatable sequence, and the course
of human events a history of unique, unrepeatable situations.

A third consequence is that access to permanent, necessary, transtemporal meaning is now to be found only through the internal processes of

[18]Voegelin, "Anxiety and Reason," 69–70.
[19]Voegelin, "What Is History?", 21–3, 35–6.

the soul, because the only access to transcendence is through that interior element in human being that is capable of discerning and responding to transcendence. In the Hebrew and Christian traditions, this element is the "spirit"; the Greek philosophers identify it as *psyche* and, more precisely, *nous;* the teaching in the Upanishads stresses the recognition of *Atman* (the true self) in its oneness with *Brahman* (the transcendent principle). Thus, the search for the ground is forced to turn inward, and to develop those subtle powers of self-reflective discernment that will lead one to truth only by exposing one also to the many dangers of spiritual self-deception. Not the least significant obstacle to such a search is the need to develop the emotional capacity to embrace its permanent uncertainties.

In the new dispensation, then, access to the timeless is still possible, but only under the conditions of what Christians call "faith": the effort to order one's existence through a hopeful and loving relation to an essentially mysterious ground of reality that, in relation to the natural world, is a "nothing," nothing. Under these conditions, the experiences of ritual renewal and regeneration are still accessible, though, of course, only in the realm of interiority, and so only on the level of the individual person, not on that of nature or society *en masse.* The clearest example of this is the Christian experience of personal regeneration through the ritual participation in the birth, passion, death, and resurrection of Christ, which allows the believer to transcend "mere" history and its threat of pointless action and meaningless suffering, and which valorizes historical reality by infusing it with divine participation.[20] The Hindu teachings on *moksha* ("liberation") and the Buddhist paths to "enlightenment" likewise promise an escape from time, through appropriate self-discipline, attentiveness, right-mindedness, and spiritual struggle. The anxiety over contingent existence, heightened now through explicit recognition of the nothingness implicit in particularity, need not remain unassuaged; the anxious soul can adjust itself, through "faith," to proper performance of its role as a temporal existence in whom a conscious relation to transcendent meaning is capable of being realized. It is still possible for history to be annulled, in the invisible silence of the soul.[21]

"Faith," so understood, has a limited appeal. Most people, it turns out, are incapable of embracing its high demands, particularly its permanent uncertainty, so memorably characterized by Kierkegaard:

---

[20]Eliade, *The Myth of the Eternal Return,* 129–30.

[21]There are, of course, extremely important differences between Western and Eastern views on access to transcendent timelessness, and salvation from time, the most important of which derive from the Western experience of the ground as mysteriously "other" yet still

Faith is precisely the contradiction between the infinite passion of the individual's inwardness and the objective uncertainty. . . . If I wish to preserve myself in faith I must constantly be intent upon holding fast the objective uncertainty, so that in the objective uncertainty I am out "upon the seventy thousand fathoms of water," and yet believe.[22]

A further demand has to do with the transformation of world-time into history, an unrepeatable sequence of unique situations. If all world events are singular, unfolding once only in relation to a transcendent ground, then each individual life is also a sequence of unique moments in which the willingness and ability to attune oneself to transcendent meaning take on decisive importance. Religious life no longer has the "general" character, as Eliade puts it, of periodic dissolution into archetypal meaning for the purpose of assuring the overall functioning of the divine economy; now religious demands are personal, isolated, irreversible. The pressure of such responsibility is too great for most people to endure.[23] The alternative, though, to adjusting to at least some of the demands of faith, in a culture where cosmological myths and rituals have been rendered inefficacious and the intracosmic gods unbelievable due to the advancing influence of symbols of transcendence, is the relinquishing of access to the timeless, and experiencing solely the time of "mere" history—that is, the time of one-way history unredeemed by absorption, dissolution, into the eternal present and its self-sufficient meaning. This, too, is existentially daunting; perhaps, in a strictly psychological sense, impossible.

What in fact has emerged for most people in cultures East and West are ways of living that succeed in fending off the anxiety of historical con-

---

personal, while the classic Taoist, Buddhist, and Upanishadic teachings portray the ground as impersonal mystery. This leads to a difference in the value placed on the finite world: in the West, as the creation of a personal God, the imperfect world with its inevitable suffering is still sacred and good; while in Eastern thought there is a tendency to devalue the world and the suffering existence naturally entails. And, importantly, it leads to different experiences of history. In the West, the concept of a Creator-God who creates the world *ex nihilo* separates the ground so radically from finite being, while simultaneously establishing it as the work of free and loving divine intention, that world history enjoys a high degree of autonomous value; in comparison, the Eastern concern with history is mild: the "nearness" of transcendence limits its value. In this context, Voegelin speaks of Eastern traditions as evidencing "incomplete" differentiations and breakthroughs. See *The Ecumenic Age,* 285, 321.

[22]Søren Kierkegaard, *Concluding Unscientific Postscript,* trans. David F. Swenson (Princeton: Princeton University Press, 1941) 182. The "objective uncertainty" here referred to by Kierkegaard is the very Western problem of the existence of God, but it can just as easily be applied to the question of the existence of the *Tao,* or *Brahman,* or *Nirvana.*

[23]Eliade, *The Myth of the Eternal Return,* 108–10.

tingency while not fully embracing the adventure of faith. These include nurturing a partial faith, which acknowledges to some degree the transcendence of the ground and the implications of transcendence, while nevertheless continuing to some degree to invest temporal objects and events with sacred power or the value of necessity (including all forms of belief in "magic," in strict intracosmic *karma,* and in "fate"); transferring to representative religious institutions the absolute authority corresponding to the perfection of the ground, thereby rendering the ground comfortably "visible"; and tolerating history by anticipating the end of time, taking refuge from the uncertainties and sufferings of existence in the thought of the *eschaton,* which annuls history from the future, anticipatorily.[24]

In the West, the discovery of transcendence establishes God as the ground of meaning and the backdrop of history, the ultimate reality in relation to which events have historical significance. In Jewish, Christian, and Islamic cultures, history is a story told by God, or rather, co-told by God and humanity, which has been lovingly allowed to share in the privileges of divine freedom and creativity. Accordingly, the core of historical meaning is constituted by what takes place in human-divine interchange, in human response to divine initiative, in the dialogue between God and creature repeatedly provoked by God's manifestations of divine truth and will. History is the history of theophany.[25]

Also in the context of these traditions, with respect to the need to anchor the sense of precarious existence in permanent being, two consequences of enormous importance follow from the discovery of divine transcendence. First, the entire world becomes a contingent affair: it is not being that *had* to be, none of its events has an intrinsic necessity, and the meaningfulness of worldly action and suffering are thus not self-evident, but are guaranteed only through faith. Secondly, since every existence is unique and unrepeatable, a one-time appearance in a one-time story, each individual carries the burden of responsibility for successful action in history—for either investing life with the truths of transcendent meaning, or dissipating it in a flourish of irrelevancies. These features combined make up the frightening aspect of "history," which we may now characterize as the conscious exercise of unique and contingent existence. It is this aspect of history that leads people to ignore or deny it, in favor, for example, of attempted reintroductions of intracosmic notions of the sacred, or adherence to a rigid belief in "fate" or "destiny," or hope for an imminent end

[24]On eschatological hope as an anti-historical attitude, see ibid., 111–12.
[25]Ibid., 102–12; Voegelin, *The Ecumenic Age,* 226, 252.

to history, or the practice of techniques for being released from this world into a better—all of them forms of escape from history. And it is this aspect of history, finally, that is able to be recognized, affirmed, and assimilated into action and belief only so long as the religious teachings that convey the truths of transcendence, and that inform the institutions that seek to guide human living in accordance with those truths, remain effective and regarded as worthy of belief.

II

The most recent act in the drama of the Western historical imagination involves the wide-scale dwindling of belief in transcendent reality. Images and symbols of divine transcendence have become, for increasing numbers of people, ciphers that fail to mediate a genuinely intelligible or felt sense of truth. The reasons for this transformation are, needless to say, many and complex: they include the rise of the modern mathematical sciences and the impact on popular imagination of the growing use of their methods as an ultimate measure of truth and reality; the failure of the Jewish and Christian theologies of history to respond adequately to changing political and economic circumstances involving world commerce and exploration, the emergence of nation-states, and the rise of industrial technologies; the defensive hardening of religious doctrines concerning transcendence into various types of fundamentalist assertion, that respond to the challenge of secular worldviews only with increasingly inexplicable commands; and, with the philosophical "turn to the subject" and the growth of modern historical consciousness, a steadily intensifying awareness of the human role in the constitution of meaning. The upshot has been a decreasing ability or willingness to understand history as a story that begins and ends in God; and consequently, modernity has been characterized by a vigorous search for a genuinely believable ground of meaning and historical significance.

The last couple of centuries have produced a wide variety of fresh answers to the question about the ground. In the climate of Enlightenment thought, a rapidly expanding faith in the modern scientific method as the sole arbiter for determining what is true or real, together with the denial of transcendent reality, led the search for the ground to the structures of the physical world and the laws that govern their motions. Various forms of materialism and physical determinism (the ground of meaning is matter and the laws of physics) make their appearance. More sophisticated types of determinism emerge that take the human subject as agent more fully into account: the ground of meaning lies in the laws that govern the human use of material circumstances, that is, in economic forces (Marx); or the ground lies in sources of psychic energy that, operating below the level of consciousness, guide the direction of human thinking and human action with the inexorability of physical laws (Freud). What such answers have in common is their imputation of the ground to some world-immanent order of being. From the point of view of the religions of transcendence, they are forms of reductionism, in that they attempt to reduce transcendent meaning to purely worldly meaning; they are efforts at the radical immanentization of reality.[26]

The reductionisms necessitate new answers about where history is headed. World-immanent history must have a world-immanent goal. There develop secular doctrines of progress, of the relentless improvement of the human condition, perhaps to culminate in a perfected state of fully enlightened human relations, of global oneness and permanent peace, undergirded by the miracles of technology. Alternately, some, like Freud, see history as a battlefield between forces of life and civilization, on the one hand, and those of human destructive urges, on the other, a scenario that relocates the traditional apocalyptic struggle for spiritual salvation to the natural and social world. Or, history is organized like a drama into a sequence of discrete acts—ancient, medieval, modern, postmodern—that, if not leading to some permanent and perfect finale, still establish a set of evolutionary categories for classifying its world-immanent mutations. What is clear in all this speculation is the heightened concern with temporal history itself, along with a readiness to invest the immediate present with the highest degree of historical significance. The philosophies of history that burst upon the scene in the eighteenth and nineteenth centuries, such as those of Condorcet, Kant, Comte, Hegel, and Marx, invariably assert, in one fashion or another, that the meaning of history lies in the improvements of progress, and that the justification of earlier stages of history is to be found in later (especially contemporary) achievements.[27] Insofar as

---

[26]See Eric Voegelin, "In Search of the Ground," in *Conversations with Eric Voegelin,* ed. R. Eric O'Connor (Montreal: Perry Printing Ltd., Thomas More Institute Papers/76, 1980) 13–6.

[27]See Karl Lowith, *Meaning in History* (Chicago: University of Chicago Press, Phoenix Books edition, 1964). Kant, in his "Idea for a Universal History from a Cosmopolitan Point of View," writes: "It remains strange that the earlier generations appear to carry through their toilsome labor only for the sake of the later, to prepare for them a foundation on which the later generations could erect the higher edifice which was Nature's goal,

they assert, as well, that history had no alternative but to arrive at the present state of things, we again come across the comforting conceits of historiogenetic speculation—a form of speculation that, as Voegelin comments, "displays a curious tenacity of survival."[28]

The modern fascination with permanent progress and with the idea that there might be ironclad laws governing the course of history is not difficult to fathom. It comes above all from the desire to find necessity operating in history. The legacy of the Western religions of transcendence is an inescapable awareness of the contingency of temporal existence and of the responsibility humans share for history. Faith in transcendent divinity, however, keeps the threat of impermanent meaning and of responsibility for a disastrous mismanagement of history at bay: God, finally, has the power to redeem history. With God eclipsed, however, the responsibility for history falls completely on human shoulders. But more troubling than the increasing consciousness of this burden of responsibility, there is the perhaps inarticulate but creeping awareness that, if God or timeless being is no more than an illusion, there can be no ultimate or lasting meaning to the enterprise anyway. History becomes now a story told by human beings in the interim between darkness and darkness, on a stage that will be wiped clean with nothing remaining. The search for necessary laws governing history must be diagnosed as a search for a historical meaning that transcends human intention and action, that will relieve individuals of ultimate responsibility, provide a measure of forgiveness, and re-establish a sense of permanence to meaning. It is, of course, a doomed search. For it is yet another reductionism. Rather than achieving the timeless, it unsuccessfully attempts to impose necessity—which, after the religious differentiations, can only belong to the timeless transcendence of the ground—onto a world history whose intrinsic contingency remains all too assuredly felt.

The modern, secular philosophies of history, then, are an unsatisfactory solution to the anxiety of contingent existence, which can only be adequately assuaged by experiences of timeless being. Eliade has again put the matter succinctly: all viewpoints that reduce historical meaning to

---

and yet that only the latest of the generations should have the good fortune to inhabit the building on which a long line of their ancestors had (unintentionally) labored without being permitted to partake of the fortune they had prepared. However puzzling this may be, it is necessary if one assumes that a species of animals should have reason, and, as a class of rational beings each of whom dies while the species is immortal, should develop their capacities to perfection." Immanuel Kant, *On History,* ed. Lewis White Beck (Indianapolis: The Bobbs-Merrill Co., Inc., The Library of Liberal Arts edition, 1975) 14.

[28]Voegelin, *The Ecumenic Age,* 67.

merely worldly conditions are frustrating, and finally terrifying, because by removing timeless meaning from those conditions they "empty them of all exemplary meaning," so that what is "valid and significant in human history disappears": the result is a "terrible banalization of history."[29] Human actions are reduced, in effect, to temporary maneuverings in the void; and most distressingly, there is no protection against the horror of meaningless suffering. When the calamities of misfortune, disease, oppression, and cruelty, not to mention the collective victimization resulting from totalitarian warfare and policies of mass intimidation, incarceration, deportation, and genocide, are experienced as having none other than "merely" historical meaning, they can scarcely be considered more than accidents of history, mistakes along the way.

From the victim's perspective, this is hardly supportable. Here we can identify one of the sources of the explosion of revolutionary terrorism during the last century. If suffering is not felt to be redeemed through its participation in exemplary, divine meaning, then history must be forced, on pain of meaninglessness, to yield an outcome that justifies that suffering. History must be made to achieve a just solution, the debts of suffering must be paid in history; and only the victims, fighting for their due through violent revolutionary action, can ensure the proper result. And if social and political reality prove stubbornly resistant to being shaped by the revolutionary will, there is at least the recourse to the democracy of fear regardless of any politically realizable goal; through arbitrary acts of terrorism the victims of historical terror can reduce representative others to their own state, thus achieving historical parity. The terrorist psychology is quite intelligible as a natural response to being cornered by the terror of history.

Of course most people who suffer from the terror of history, even excessively, do not become terrorists. They find other ways to cope with the threat of meaninglessness. As Thoreau noted, many an existence is lived in "quiet desperation." Many others seek out evidence of a fateful necessity that orders the patterns of their lives. In *Four Quartets*, T. S. Eliot has given us a catalogue of some popular antidotes to the burden of historical contingency:

> To communicate with Mars, converse with spirits,
> To report the behaviour of the sea monster,
> Describe the horoscope, haruspicate or scry,
> Observe disease in signatures, evoke

[29]Mircea Eliade, *No Souvenirs: Journal, 1957–1969,* trans. Fred H. Johnson, Jr. (New York: Harper & Row, 1977) 55.

Biography from the wrinkles of the palm
And tragedy from fingers; release omens
By sortilege, or tea leaves, riddle the inevitable
With playing cards, fiddle with pentagrams
Or barbituric acids, or dissect
The recurrent image into preconscious terrors—
To explore the womb, or tomb, or dreams: all these are usual
Pastimes and drugs, and features of the press:
And always will be, some of them especially
When there is distress of nations and perplexity
Whether on the shores of Asia, or in the Edgware Road.

They are "pastimes and drugs," and not solutions to the question of personal and historical meaning, because they seek answers within the dimension of time, of imaginable past and future, whereas redemption from the terror of history can only be found where the human search for meaning encounters its transcendent ground, at

The point of intersection of the timeless
With time. . . .[30]

We might add to Eliot's list the pastimes of terrorists and neighborhood gangs; the drugs of television and shopping; and the perennial belief that a New Age, with all its consoling perfections, is upon us at last.[31]

Another coping mechanism has been found by "postmodernist" intellectuals, who have decided to make the most of the death of God and the absence of necessity by announcing the apotheosis of contingency. Trained to think things through and to eschew outmoded solutions, they are consistent enough to realize that, without transcendent meaning, there can be

---

[30]From "The Dry Salvages," in T. S. Eliot, *Four Quartets* (London: Faber and Faber, 1970) 43–4.

[31]In 1930 the Austrian novelist Robert Musil described those who in every age are ready to proclaim "the pernicious nonsense known as the New Age": "This sort of people had in all ages regarded themselves as constituting the New Age. . . . In these people there lived, in the queerest way, the conviction that it was their mission to bring order into the world. . . . It shook them, it blew like a gust through their heads. . . . Ulrich had once, for the fun of it, asked them for exact statements of what they meant. They had looked at him disapprovingly and called his demand a mechanistic view of life, and skepticism, asserting that the most complicated things of all could only be solved in the simplest way, so that the new age, once it had sloughed off the present, would look quite simple." Robert Musil, *The Man Without Qualities,* Volume II, trans. Eithne Wilkins and Ernst Kaiser (London: Pan Books Ltd., Picador Edition, 1981) 184, 190–1.

no "ground" of historical relevance at all. It has become, therefore, intellectually *au courant* to insist that a historian's criteria for selecting pertinent materials are irredeemably subjective and arbitrary—that unconscious motivations and biases, social and linguistic networks, the sheer historical situatedness of any historiographer, render his or her construction of historical narratives unique and contestable at best, self-serving and reactionary at worst. The logical conclusion is that all principles of selection for telling a history, all "backgrounds of meaning," are equally valid—or, with respect to the desideratum of a "true" account of significant events, equally invalid.

It is, without question, exciting to deny that there is any ultimately stable meaning within the scope of human experience. Exciting in the short run, anyway. A more profound understanding of the position leads to different qualities of feeling. The denial, if analyzed, reveals both an ontological and an epistemological component. Ontologically, it asserts that there is no stable meaning in reality (read: God). Epistemologically, it asserts that because all human understanding proceeds by way of language, and language is intrinsically imperfect and unstable, all meanings grasped by human understanding must also perforce be unstable. Does the epistemological stem from the ontological component, or vice versa? The answer is not really important. What is important is to recognize that they imply each other, and that if true—if there is no human connection whatsoever with permanent or timeless meaning—then no event can really be more meaningful than any other; and to reduce all events to equal status and to decree the radical arbitrariness of the storyteller's perspective is tantamount to reducing experience to meaninglessness. The idea of radical meaninglessness, or more accurately, the idea of the threat of radical meaninglessness, as a counter in the games of postmodernists, has little real purchasing power: despite the brilliance of thought displayed, people will continue to search for a meaningful ground to personal and human history. But, as we have already observed, the idea does correspond to certain very real moods of existential despair, brought on by those who genuinely suffer the terror of sheer contingency. Eloquent voices of that despair are to be found throughout Western literature of the nineteenth and, especially, the twentieth centuries, with none, perhaps, more fluent than those of the characters in the works of Samuel Beckett. With anguished precision they speak of historical time as an interminable piling up of valueless moments, each as pointless as the next:

> Have you not done tormenting me with your accursed time! It's abominable! When! When! One day, is that not enough for you, one day he went

dumb, one day I went blind, one day we'll go deaf, one day we were born, one day we shall die, the same day, the same second, is that not enough for you?[32]

Moment upon moment, pattering down, like the millet grains of . . . that old Greek, and all life long you wait for that to mount up to a life. Ah let's get it over![33]

As Beckett and other artists who speak for countless victims of the terror of history attest, the apotheosis of contingency has a shadow side: the neuropathologies born of authentic spiritual despair.

III

In the course of the preceding reflections the term "history" has undergone more than one change of meaning. At the start, it was defined as (1) a pattern of memorable events with explanatory power, whose significance is determined in relation to some ground of meaning, however the latter may be conceived. Later, in the context of the analysis of cosmological culture and its breakdown through the differentiation of transcendence, it was used to designate (2) the experience of time as a one-way succession of irreversible events, sharply distinguished from the timeless dimension of reality—the concept generally referred to in the foregoing as "mere" history. And finally, history has been referred to as (3) a pattern of decisive events unfolding in relation to a transcendent ground: the history of theophany and of the human search for timeless meaning.

In the popular mind, as well as in the writings of most historiographers, history is understood in the sense of (2) above; even if a permanent ground of meaning is assumed, there is no explicit reflection on the fact, and history is simply identified with some immanent course of events. But we have seen that it is this conception of history, or rather this *experience* of history, that provokes terror and the fashioning of escape-routes, existential and intellectual, from the burden of contingency. It will be noted, further, that history in the sense of (3) is a specific variant of the more general definition of history (1) with which we began. It is, in fact, a refinement corresponding to an appreciation of the "axial period" discoveries that the permanent ground of meaning can only have the character of tran-

---

[32]Samuel Beckett, *Waiting for Godot* (New York: Grove Press, 1954) 57B.
[33]Samuel Beckett, *Endgame* (New York: Grove Press, 1958) 70.

scendence. At the level of historiographical reflection, then, history in the sense of (3) is a more adequate conception than history in the sense of (1), in that it corresponds most precisely to actual human experience; although history in the sense of (1) represents a significant advance over the jejune conception of history in the sense of (2), which fails even to recognize that an enduring ground of meaning is assumed in every act of historiographical judgment. Finally, at the level of the personal experience of history, we might suggest that it is again history in the sense of (3) that alone offers a cure for the terror of history; that is, it is only possible to overcome the imbalancing effects of the anxiety of contingency in the modern world by gaining access to the timeless through experiences of transcendence. "Man probably cannot rejoice over the gifts of existence," writes Eliade, "if he does not take them as signs that have come from the beyond." For only then can one "build a structure and read a message in the formless flow of things and the monotonous flow of historical facts."[34]

Eliade describes how, in Australian aborigine culture, the anxiety over what we have identified as the implicit nothingness of contingent particularity becomes assuaged through initiatory rituals, in which the neophyte learns that he or she is a repetition or reincarnation of a mythical ancestor; in other words, that what is experienced as personal identity is in fact timeless and necessary.[35] Such are the types of solution available to cosmological consciousness, which is not yet explicitly aware of the mystery of transcendence, and of the radical gap between temporal existence, on the one hand, and the timeless ground of existence, on the other. We who are inheritors of the perspective deriving from the differentiation of transcendence do not find relief from our historical identities so easily. And yet, we too need conscious access to the emotions that connect us with a nontemporal sense of identity. There are many, certainly, whose faith enables them to in some measure "put on the mind of Christ" (or "find their original Buddha-mind"). But for many others, such experiences have become all but inaccessible, or at best glancingly encountered. What is their hope for relief from the terror of history?

Apart from the intrinsic difficulties of faith, the primary obstacle in contemporary life to experiencing existence as an encounter of temporal with timeless meaning, is the inefficacy of the words and symbols that have traditionally functioned to mediate a sense or understanding of transcendence. The language of transcendence has become devitalized and opaque.

[34]Eliade, *No Souvenirs,* 94, 85.
[35]Ibid., 182.

Words such as "God," "spirit," and "faith" have become, like cosmological myths, a dead letter for many, in whom they no longer awaken or engender affective recognition of personal participation in a timeless ground. It is more difficult to explain why this is so than to direct attention to the fact itself. Mythic and religious symbols, it can only be stressed, are not effective upon command.

Today there is an indisputable longing for symbols that will help us recover experiences that consolidate for us a felt recognition that we exist in the "in-between" of time and timelessness, of contingency and necessity, of unique and exemplary identity. As Voegelin writes: "The return from symbols [for the 'in-between'] which have lost their meaning to the experiences which constitute meaning is so generally recognizable as the problem of the present that specific references are unnecessary."[36] It only remains to emphasize that the first step in such a return will be a renewed capacity to suffer existential openness to the mystery of transcendence. That openness has been undermined not only by a receding of traditional symbols of experiences of transcendence into unintelligibility, but also by modern secular fantasies, both philosophical and scientific, of absolute control over reality and the course of history, and again more recently by postmodern declarations that sheer contingency is all there is. Only through openness to the mystery of transcendence has post-cosmological historical existence ever been found to be, not a nightmare, but a meaningful adventure—and sometimes even a blessing.

---

[36]Voegelin, *The Ecumenic Age,* 58.

— 8 —

Nature, History, and Redemption

Matthew L. Lamb

Dom Sebastian Moore, O.S.B., has dedicated most of his theological work to deepening his understanding of the experience of redemption revealed in the life, death, and resurrection of Jesus Christ. His exploration of the psychological dimensions of redemption concedes nothing to the all too facile subjectivism of much new age pop-psychologizing of the spiritual. Quite the contrary. For Moore the objective reality of the Triune God's infinite understanding and love is the origin and goal of creation, of the redemptive mission of the Son and of the sanctifying mission of the Spirit. Moore does not confuse symbol and metaphor with divine Infinite reality. God is infinitely more than paltry human images and ideas. For all of creation "to be" is "to be received," to be loved into existence. Human subjectivity, as Moore repeatedly reminds us, is radically a desire, a thirst, an inner longing which can find complete fulfillment only in the Triune God.

In Moore's meditative writings the narrative addresses God and the Lord Jesus directly, prayer flows effortlessly from the quest for theological wisdom. The classical trinitarian and christological dogmas are not "mere ideas" or "propositions." They state the revealed divine reality of Father, Son, and Holy Spirit, and the incarnation of the Son as truly God and truly man. The realism of the dogma is not watered down but preserved in the realism of Moore's critical explorations of the transformation of desire through the grace of redemption. Desire is liberated from the alienation and distortion of sin.

Sebastian Moore's theological explorations, and some of the problems he has encountered, illustrate a point made by Bernard Lonergan in his essay on "Revolution in Catholic Theology." Lonergan discusses the major changes which historical consciousness requires of Catholic theology. The concern for interiority and self-appropriation make large demands that revolutionize Catholic theology. Surprisingly Lonergan ends this essay stating that this revolution is also a restoration, for it will enable theologians to understand the great achievements of the past. Lonergan concludes the essay on the revolution in Catholic theology by writing:

> To theology as governed by method and as an ongoing process the present situation points. If that pointing is accurate and effective, then the contemporary revolution in theology also will have the character of a restoration.[1]

There is an aspect of this revolution in theology which challenges modern Enlightenment and contemporary postmodern horizons to change. Indeed, taking historical consciousness seriously will enable us to restore a proper systematic appreciation of the relation of time to eternity. Moore has been puzzled by the failure of many contemporary theologians and Christians to appreciate how Catholic doctrines challenge us to a deeper understanding of the human and historical condition. In this essay I wish to indicate how modern theories of nature and time have promoted misunderstandings which have led to a truncation of consciousness to the data of sense, with the result that moderns and postmoderns are unable to measure up to scientific advances in the understanding of nature and time. In some ways this parallels Moore's analysis of desire, showing how a proper appropriation of the dynamics of desire occurs within the context of a conversion which both reveals revolutionary dimensions of human experience and restores a proper grasp of Catholic doctrine and theology.

The Openness of Nature and Historical Time

As Helmut Peukert asserts, there is the openness of history, in anamnestic solidarity, to redemption. The past is not closed off, any more than the future is.[2] Sebastian Moore's narrative appropriation of redemption can be systematically understood only if nature and history are under-

---

[1] Bernard Lonergan, *A Second Collection* (Philadelphia: Westminster, 1974) 231–8.

[2] Cf. Helmut Peukert, *Science, Action, and Fundamental Theology*, trans. James Bohman (Cambridge: MIT Press, 1984) 176–82, 202–45. Also his "Enlightenment and Theology as Unfinished Projects" in Don Browning and Francis Fiorenza, eds., *Habermas, Modernity, and Public Theology* (New York: Crossroad, 1992) 43–65.

stood as both ordered wholes, so that one has an ontology or metaphysics open to the new.

We have yet to grasp the fullness of how the four-dimensional universe uncovered by Einstein and Heisenberg[3] has deconstructed the Newtonian separation of space and time which deeply influenced the secularist truncation of modern historical consciousness. An irony of historicism is that it is a remnant, not only of nominalism, but also of a Newtonian worldview that played well into the prejudices of the Enlightenment's rejection of the past.

A fundamental issue in any systematic understanding of the human condition requires us to overcome the modernist truncation of modern horizons trapped in the false alternatives of either a conceptualist universalism, so typical of Kantian ethics, or the historicism of postmodern rejections of that universalism. These are merely two sides of the same failure to grasp the concrete universal which Lonergan retrieved from the philosophical and theological orientations of classical Greek, Roman, and Christian medieval cultures.

With the false choices of an idealist universalism or an empiricist historicism, the past and tradition are effectively silenced in their ability to challenge and question our present. The dead are for all intents and purposes ex-communicated. The human unity of communication is broken. The conversation and debates that constitute the history of human civilizations, philosophies, religions, is interrupted by a rejection of the past as "unenlightened," as hopelessly a product of "the dark ages."

The earnest dialogue that constitutes genuine dialectics is broken by too easy dismissals of the political and intellectual achievements of the past. There are many ways of silencing the dead. The most usual is the "Besserwisserei" of moderns over ancients. Contradictory epitaphs witness to the distortions: the end of classical metaphysics is proclaimed while in the next breath it is accused of a forgetfulness of being; progress is proclaimed only to turn into a nihilism with a happy ending.

Indeed, serious philosophical and theological transformations of historical consciousness uncover systematic distortions of communication in the Enlightenment privatization and negation of religious faith and practice. The loss of theology as a serious collaborator in the enterprise of the natural and human sciences has systematically distorted the efforts of the

---

[3]Cf. Patrick Heelan, *Quantum Mechanics and Objectivity* (The Hague: Nijhof, 1968); Stephen Hawkings, *A Brief History of Time* (New York: Bantam, 1988); Stephen Toulmin and June Goodfield, *The Discovery of Time* (Chicago: University of Chicago Press, 1982³).

natural and human sciences in their practical tasks of transforming societies. Empiricism and instrumentalism are not just abstractions; with their
loss of the classical difference between technique and praxis, they are manifest in post-Enlightenment cultures that exalt the machine over the
human. In all areas of politics, culture, art, and religion there is a domi-
nance given to procedure over substance, to products over friendship, to
roles and skills over virtues.[4]

A major reason for the mechanization and fragmentation of modern
and post-modern cultures lies in the loss of wisdom. Modern science has
vastly extended human knowledge of the empirical and particular. But
there is no cognitive and philosophical mediation of the whole. The traditional task of wisdom, to order all things in light of the whole of reality,
has been declared void.

This is the usual "end of metaphysics" dirge in modernity. Indeed, a
danger in the modern period is precisely the tendency to see all ordering
of things as springing, not from a love of wisdom, but from a disordered
desire for power. Adorno's negative dialectics calls attention to the danger
of a power-centered totality that is a lie. But metaphysics need not be defined by its abuse any more than science or religion should only be defined
by the abuses they have suffered. Today especially there is need of a metaphysics that can rescue the love of wisdom from the conceptualism and
denigration of the power plays of sinful human history. As I argued elsewhere, attention to the victims of history requires a mediation of the totality of history that is both intellectually compassionate and open to the
transformation of the revealed Word of God.[5] For, as Bernard Lonergan
writes, divine wisdom ordained, and divine goodness willed, not to remove
the many evils afflicting human history through an exercise of power, but
according to the just and mysterious law of the Cross of Christ to transform, as only God can, all those evils into the highest good of the eternal
life of the kingdom of God.[6]

---

[4]Cf. Charles Taylor, *The Sources of the Self: The Making of Modern Identity* (Cambridge: Harvard University Press, 1989); Alasdair MacIntyre, *After Virtue* (Notre Dame: Notre Dame University Press, 1984); Neil Postman, *Technopoly: The Surrender of Culture to Technology* (New York: Vintage Books, 1993).

[5]Cf. *Solidarity with Victims: Towards a Theology of Social Transformation* (New York: Crossroads, 1982) 116–43.

[6]Bernard Lonergan, *De Verbo Incarnato* (Rome: Gregorian University Press, 1964) 552–93. This will be published by the University of Toronto Press, with an English trans-lation, as Volume 8 of his Collected Works.

How can a wise recovery of metaphysics be genuinely open to the new, which faith in the redemptive transformation of history requires?[7] How can the mediation of totality do justice to the vast diversity of history? One requirement will be a metaphysical wisdom capable of accounting for an understanding of time which is open to messianic interruption and transformation.[8] One aspect of such a recovery will be to discover how the modern understanding of time has been derailed by an imaginative separation of time from space. What this separation did was twofold.

First, it made any wise understanding of time as an ordered totality of concrete durations impossible by insisting upon only the momentary and incessant becoming of these fragments of time. In some ways the modern Enlightenment version seemed commonsense enough. We can imagine the three dimensions of Euclidean geometry (height, width, length), and we can see simultaneously all three dimensions. But we cannot imagine or visualize four dimensions, the dimensions of space *and* time, as in $ds^2 = dx^2 + dy^2 + dz^2 - c^2dt^2$. These are highly intelligible, but not imaginable. Commenting on Newton, Stephen Hawkings writes: "Time was completely separate from and independent of space. This is what most people would take to be the commonsense view."[9]

Second, instead of an ordered totality of concrete durations the Enlightenment commonsense view projected an imaginary and inexorable continuum of time moving from the past in the present into the future. Such a misunderstanding of time fits in well with a naturalism and historicism which can only conceive of order, not as an intelligible pattern, but as an exercise of dominative power and force. This owes much to Newton.[10]

The influence of Sir Isaac Newton on the development of modern mathematics and physics can scarcely be exaggerated. Less attention has been paid to his contributions to the seventeenth-century convergence of an empirical-mechanistically conceived science and theology.[11] Michael

---

[7]This is the problem posed to metaphysics by Johann Baptist Metz. Also, cf. Sebastian Moore, *The Fire and Rose Are One* (New York: Crossroad, 1980) 94–6, 151–8; also his *Jesus the Liberator of Desire* (New York: Crossroad, 1989) 109–16

[8]Cf. also M. Lamb, "Kommunikative Praxis und Theologie," in Edmund Arens, *Habermas und die Theologie* (Düsseldorf: Patmos Verlag, 1989) 241–70. English version published in Don Browning and F. Fiorenza, eds., *Habermas, Modernity, and Public Theology* (New York: Crossroad, 1992) 92–118.

[9]Stephen Hawkings, op. cit., 18.

[10]Cf. Bernard Lonergan, *Insight: A Study of Human Understanding* (Toronto: University of Toronto Press, 1992) 163–95.

[11]Cf. the studies of Michael Buckley, *Motion and Motion's God* (New Haven: Yale University Press, 1971) and his *At the Origins of Modern Atheism* (New Haven: Yale

Buckley has shown how Newton's universal mechanics, with its emphasis upon motion and force, issues in a doctrine of God as the "Universal Commander" of a universe that is totally under divine domination *(dominatio entis spiritualis).*[12] The divine *sensorium* permits all things to be present to God and allows God's dominion to rule or command all things. Space as the sensorium of God privileges a Euclidean three-dimensional extension over time and duration. Space is always, but only moments of time are everywhere. There can be no ordered totality of concrete durations, so Newton relies on the fiction of absolute space and time. As he writes in the General Scholium to the second edition of his *Principia:*

> God "is not eternity and infinity, but eternal and infinite; he is not duration or space, but he endures and is present. He endures forever, and is everywhere present; and, by existing always and everywhere, he constitutes duration and space. Since every particle of space is *always*, and every indivisible moment of duration is *everywhere,* certainly the Maker and Lord of all things cannot be *never* and *nowhere.*"[13]

While there is an "always" of all space, there is not a corresponding "everywhere" of all time. Instead, only indivisible moments of time are everywhere, by which Newton means that at any instant of time the entire spatial universe exists. Totality is a characteristic of space, but not of time. One instant will follow another, but the three dimensions of space (width, height, length) are simultaneously all present. Thus, even in Newton's discredited notions of absolute space and time, it is clear that space has a situational totality while absolute time flows successively.[14] That the imaginal matrix of Newtonian universal mechanics is spatial is evident in how "to order" for Newton is "to place."[15] Force and power moves things in space, and this

---

University Press, 1987). Also Amos Funkenstein, *Theology and the Scientific Imagination from the Middle Ages to the Seventeenth Century* (Princeton: Princeton University Press, 1986).

[12]Buckley, *Motion and Motion's God,* 193–204; *At the Origins of Modern Atheism,* 129–44.

[13]Isaac Newton, *Principia,* trans. Motte and Cajori (Berkeley: University of California Press, 1962) vol. II, 545.

[14]Cf. Lonergan, *Insight,* 181: "As absolute space, so absolute time is the result of looking for the absolute where the absolute does not exist."

[15]"Absolute, true, and mathematical time, of itself, and from its own nature, flows equably without relation to anything external, and by another name is called duration. . . . For times and spaces are as it were, the places as well of themselves as of all other things. All things are placed in time as to order of succession; and in space as to order of situation." Ibid., vol. I, 6 and 8.

is then projected infinitely onto God. Three-dimensional space is open to God's power, but does not manifest God's wisdom. Time is a fortiori not open but closed in an inexorable continuum of fragmentary moments.

Although there are major differences between Descartes's quest for a universal mathematics and Newton's universal mechanics, these differences do not mean that Descartes was any less inclined to give priority to spatial simultaneity and order. The "res cogitans" ceded power to the "res extensa"— time is merely thought, and so of lesser ontological value than space. Later, Leibniz, who rejected Newton's notion of absolute space, made explicit the fact that the past is past, gone, and so clearly separated a spatial order of nature, to which simultaneity applies, from the order of time, which is not:

> Given the existence of a multiplicity of concrete circumstances which are not mutually exclusive, we designate them as *contemporaneous* or *co-existing*. Hence, we regard the events of past years as not co-existing with those of this year, because they are qualified by incompatible circumstances. *Time is the order of non-contemporaneous things.* It is thus the universal order of change in which we ignore the specific kind of changes that have occurred.[16]

What defines time is a non-simultaneity which is itself derived from a priority implicitly given to spatial simultaneity. Synchronicity is normative, and diachronicity is only derived, as constituted by mutually exclusive events. Instead of understanding time as an ordered totality of concrete durations, Leibniz projects a "universal order of change" in which the present and past are "mutually exclusive." The present cannot affirm or continue the past, but must exclude it. The Enlightenment prejudice against the supposedly unenlightened past is evident.

Hegel transposed the priority of space and time, but only by defining time as a totality that is abstract and ideal, the negative unity of being as becoming other than it is. Time is a momentary becoming, and so "Sie ist das Sein, das, indem es *ist, nicht* ist, and indem es *nicht* ist, *ist*."[17] The negativity constitutive of time is transposed into the centrality of negation in the process of historical sublation ("Aufhebung") in which the present can preserve and elevate the past only if it negates the past as well. The genius of Hegel was to internalize all the contradictions of modernity into the ongoing dialectic of absolute spirit externalizing itself into history only to return to itself through struggles and conflicts of history by the sublating power of absolute knowledge in which spirit knows itself.

---

[16] P. P. Wiener, ed., *Leibniz: Selections* (New York: Scribner, 1951) 201–2.
[17] Hegel, *Enzyklopädie der philosophischen Wissenschaften*, ¶ 258.

The speculative Good Friday of the spirit foams forth, not in a wisdom open to an ordered totality of concrete durations, but in a science that replaces contingency with the necessity of an inexorable logic of progress. Reality and truth are recognized only in "the certainty of the throne of Absolute Spirit."[18] Totality and order in Hegel are always dialectical, and dialectics is marked by the struggle for domination and recognition.

The contingent and particular is erased in the quest for a dominative totality. Individuality and universality are contrasted, *Eigentlichkeit* and *Allgemeinheit,* as though one necessarily negates aspects of the other. Objective time of universal process can be "subject-ified" only by making the subject, with Hegel, absolutely objective *Geist,* or, with Heidegger, by denouncing this project as a denial of the subject's ultimate being-toward-death and finitude. In neither of these options is there recognized a concrete intelligibility of space and time as ordered totalities of concrete extensions and concrete durations in their particularities and novelties.[19]

Walter Benjamin's and Theodor Adorno's constellations, clusters of terms and images which render present some weak premonitions of redemption open a path that requires more than the expressivist rejection of totality and universality. Indeed, being faithful to the wisdom of those constellations means rescuing them from the historicism and relativism which consigns those redemptive fragments to the "wreckage upon wreckage" which the angel of history longs to make whole.[20] Such "framing epiphanies," as Charles Taylor calls them, are too exposed to the nihilism which is so deeply ingrained in modern cultures.[21]

Space and time are the ordered totality of concrete extensions and durations. This totality is the four-dimensional concrete universe in which both space and time, both nature and history, in all of their particular and unique things and events, exist. This means moving beyond the imaginal matrix that places the universe in a three-dimensional Euclidean framework with time as merely incidental. While we cannot imagine the four-

---

[18]Cf. the end of Hegel's *Phenomenology of Spirit.*

[19]This is how Lonergan understands space and time, cf. *Insight,* 172–95.

[20]Cf. Walter Benjamin, *Illuminations,* trans. Harry Zohn (New York: Schocken Books, 1978) 257–8: "This is how one pictures the angel of history. His face is turned toward the past. Where we perceive a chain of events, he sees one single catastrophe which keeps piling wreckage upon wreckage and hurls it in front of his feet. The angel would like to stay, awaken the dead, and make whole what has been smashed. But a storm is blowing from Paradise; it has got caught in his wings with such violence that the angel can no longer close them. This storm irresistibly propels him into the future to which his back is turned, while the pile of debris before him grows skyward. This storm is what we call progress."

[21]Charles Taylor, *Sources of the Self* (Cambridge: Harvard University Press, 1989) 468ff.

dimensional universe of Einstein's special relativity, it is highly intelligible. Nor is it a totality which ignores or belittles the particular and unique, for the totality is known only as a heuristic anticipation of ordered things and events open to whatever occurs.[22] For all time is included in this heuristic just as readily as all space.

This understanding of totality replaces continua of force and unilinear progress with freedom open to both success and failure, both progress and decline. So, for example, the technological application of special relativity in nuclear weapons has made abundantly clear that we humans will either renounce the international use of such force as a means of settling disputes or such force will destroy the possibility of human life on this planet. Nuclear weapons confront humankind with the need either to grow in wisdom and recognize the stupidity of violence or perish. What in fact will happen we do not know, we can only surmise various probabilities, and those are always open to revision. Who would have, for example, predicted the sudden collapse of the Soviet Union, and the lessening of tensions regarding nuclear war? History is not locked into "iron laws" of nature or progress. Rather, history is open to both progress and decline.

A contemporary understanding of nature in the natural sciences since Einstein, and especially since Heisenberg's Quantum Theory, requires an openness to the statistical and change in a way that Newtonian mechanics could not allow.[23] As Kant simply transposed Newton's absolute time into an *a priori* form of human sensibility,[24] so Hegel broke with Kant's reliance on sensible intuition only to develop intellectual intuitions into a dialectic that is "conceptualist, closed, necessitarian, and immanental."[25] The closed Hegelian system left history in the inexorable continuum of time, now unfolding according to the necessary laws of the Absolute Spirit, among which was the struggle to the death of master and slave, and the negativity of war.[26] Little wonder, then, that some would see in the end of the cold war

---

[22]This is further analyzed in Bernard Lonergan's notion of emergent probability, cf. *Insight,* 126–62.

[23]Cf. Patrick Byrne, "Teleology, Modern Science and Verification," in Fred Lawrence, ed., *The Legacy of Lonergan* (Boston: Boston College Lonergan Institute, 1994) 1-45.

[24]Cf. *Insight,* 177–81.

[25]Ibid., 446

[26]Cf. E. Wyschogrod, *Spirit in Ashes: Hegel, Heidegger, and Man-Made Death* (New Haven: Yale University Press, 1985) 148: "Using the struggle to the death as a paradigmatic pattern of Spirit's activity Hegel tries to show that war is necessary for the sublation of individual ego on behalf of the state, which he considers to represent a higher form of reason, and for states themselves, whose honor depends upon their willingness to risk their sovereignty. For Hegel war is not absolute evil but necessary for the life of polity."

an Hegelian intimation of the end of history.[27] The need to move beyond these modern, post-Enlightenment parameters is evident if political life is to overcome the violence that is fundamental to modern nation-states.[28]

In a four-dimensional universe where time is intrinsic to nature, and time is defined, not as only momentary, but as the ordered totality of concrete durations, then the openness of time and history becomes more evident. We can no longer separate the past from the present, nor them from the future. Indeed, from a theological perspective, we can appreciate how God's act of creation embraces the totality of the entire spatio-temporal universe. All of creation, including the totality of concrete durations with all of the events occurring in them, is present in the Divine Eternal Presence. Indeed, we now may be able better to understand the theoretical achievements of Augustine, Boethius, and Thomas Aquinas in their understanding of God's eternity as the total simultaneous presence of all that is. There is no "before" or "after" in God. In the Triune Presence the whole of the universe, and the whole of history, is present.[29] Similar to the four-dimensional universe, this understanding of eternity is highly intelligible, but not imaginable.

Failure to understand this systematic breakthrough led to the imaginable rhetorics which opposed a "static eternity" to dynamic history. This breakthrough was neither Platonist nor Plotinian, for both of these imagine a contradiction between eternity and time. In Augustine, Boethius and Aquinas eternity does not negate but creates time, there is no contradiction. Preaching eternal life, Jesus was not denigrating time or history. As Augustine puts it, contrary to the Platonists, the eternal Word became man, revealing how the eternal God, as "totum esse praesens," creates and redeems all time.

Nominalism paved the way for the Enlightenment to set eternal life in opposition to history, so that those seeking eternal life were despising the good life on earth. The beyond as "Jenseits" was opposed to the here and now as "Diesseits." From this loss of a grasp of the simultaneous totality of time in God's presence, there was a dissolution of time itself into a continuum of isolated moments. The present was set in opposition to the past. Memory and tradition were disparaged; the apocalyptic expectation that

---

[27] F. Fukuyama, *The End of History and the Last Man* (New York: Free Press, 1992).

[28] Cf. Bruce Porter, *War and the Rise of the State: The Military Foundations of Modern Politics* (New York: Free Press, 1994).

[29] For further reflections on this, cf. M. Lamb, "The Resurrection and Christian Identity as *Conversatio Dei,"* in *Concilium,* vol. 249 (October 1993) 112–23; also Frederick Crowe, "Rethinking Eternal Life" in *Science et Esprit,* vol. 45, no. 1, 25–39 and no. 2, 145–59.

awaited the advent of the kingdom of God was emptied into what Metz calls a softened evolutionary eschatology.[30]

These all result from a faulty understanding of time and history, a failure to mediate a totality which is genuinely open to the new without negating the old. The fixation of the Enlightenment upon the present moment, set up in opposition to the past, not only mirrored the hyper-individualism of autobiography in the Enlightenment (e.g., Rousseau's *Confessions*),[31] but also accounts for the emergence in Spinoza's *Theological Political Treatise* of the historical-critical methods.

Neither nature nor history is open for Spinoza. They both are fixed and necessary chains of events. Confronted with the religious pluralism of his day, Spinoza sought to privatize faith and show how the Scriptures were to be empirically studied, as nature is.

"I may sum up the matter by saying that the method of interpreting Scripture does not widely differ from the method of interpreting nature—in fact, it is almost the same."[32] Such an interpretative study of the Scripture restricts itself to the texts alone. No appeal can be made to faith, for that is private and personal, sharply separated from reason.[33] Faith plays no role in the interpretation of Scripture, for the universal rule is to only accept as meanings of the texts what anyone can perceive from studying the history of that text. Spinoza makes clear that biblical interpretation does not concern itself with the truth of the texts, but only with perceptible meanings.

Thus the birth of the historical-critical methods is to treat the Bible as any other text. As Newton's mechanics sought only three-dimensional perceptible motions, so Spinoza's canons of interpretation recognize only those perceptible textual meanings found in the Scriptures as a perceptible book.

> We are to work not on the truth of passages, but solely on their meaning. We must take especial care, when we are in search of the meaning of a text, not to be led away by our reason in so far as it is founded on principles of natural knowledge (to say nothing of prejudices): in order not to confound

---

[30]Cf. Johann B. Metz, *Glaube in Geschichte und Gesellschaft* (Mainz: Grünewald, 1992⁵) 149ff.; "Ohne Finale ins Nichts," *Frankfurter Allgemeine Zeitung* (13 Juli 1991).

[31]Cf. M. Lamb, "The Resurrection and Christian Identity,"112–23.

[32]Spinoza, *A Theological Political Treatise*, trans. R. Elwes (New York: Dover, 1951) 99.

[33]Ibid., 10: "Furthermore, as men's habits of mind differ, so that some more readily embrace one form of faith, some another, for what moves one to pray may move another only to scoff, I conclude . . . that everyone should be free to choose for himself the foundations of his creed, and that faith should be judged only by its fruits."

the meaning of a passage with its truth, we must examine it solely by means of the signification of the words, or by a reason acknowledging no foundation but the Scriptures themselves.[34]

The deconstructionist insistence upon severe restriction to intertextuality, "all we have is texts," is here anticipated by Spinoza. Little wonder, then, that Spinoza would restrict faith to an obedience and piety; the assent of faith is only obedience, an act of will, not an intellectual act. Theology is founded on obedience to revelation and has no power to ever oppose reason. While philosophy and reason are only concerned with knowledge and truth, theology is totally separate, concerned only with obedience and piety. The teachings of the Scriptures, as Spinoza cynically remarks, need not be true, they need only promote pious and obedient acts.[35]

As Edmund Arens has shown, the dichotomy between teaching and action, between doctrinal content and text, between witnessing to the truth and confessing in word and deed, is impossible to maintain once one has taken seriously the constitutive meaning and truth of the communicative praxis of confessing the faith.[36] What is more, there is a failure to be genuinely and fully critical. The modern dichotomy between faith and reason fails to achieve the critical differentiations attained by Thomas Aquinas. What Spinoza evidences is how deeply nominalism has influenced modern dichotomies between intelligence and will, truth and commitment.

The openness of history is not an uncritical openness, a pious wish that has no intelligence. Quite the contrary. What Spinoza, and any exclusive reliance upon the historical-critical methods he pioneered, has done is to truncate the experience of history. To rule out of court the most important aspects of the genuine confession and practice of the Christian faith is not to promote a critical knowledge of history, but rather an ignorant one. The Enlightenment, instead of attending to the genuine witness of the martyrs and saints of the Church, turned rather to the abuses of religion. To define Christianity, or anything, by its abuses is not critical but prejudiced. Imagine if science or art were so judged.

The process of critical history open to the totality of events concretely occurring, as a process from historical experience to historical knowledge,

---

[34]Ibid., 101. Also Yirmiyahu Yovel, *Spinoza and Other Heretics,* Vol. II: The Adventures of Immanence (Princeton: Princeton University Press, 1989).

[35]Ibid., 182–99; cf. 185: "Lastly, it follows that faith does not demand that dogmas should be true as that they should be pious—that is, such as will stir up the heart to obey."

[36]Cf. Edmund Arens, *Bezeugen und Bekennen: Elementare Handlungen des Glaubens* (Düsseldorf: Patmos, 1989) 353–404.

not only deals with the meaning of texts, but also attends to which meanings are true, and what in fact are the realities to which the texts or events refer. As Lonergan points out, a fully critical historical process occurs twice. "In the first instance one is coming to understand one's sources. In the second instance one is using one's understood sources intelligently to come to understand the object to which they are relevant."[37] The first phase of critical history is the very familiar one of identifying authors or historical agents, situating their actions and/or works in time and place, studying their historical contexts and sources, etc. But all of this is only in order to direct attention to what should be the critical historian's main objective, a second phase, aimed at "understanding the process referred to in one's sources."[38]

While a critical historian might not need to know faith, the spiritual life, or the mystery of the Trinity to do textual criticism, establish sources, compare one set of texts with another set of texts (after all, anyone who can read can do that!), it is something else if he or she is going to engage in a history of faith, prayer, or theology as an *intellectus fidei*. If the critical historian has no knowledge of God, no familiarity with faith or prayer, with witness and confessing, then the critical historian is anything but "critical" in the full sense of that word. The so-called critical historian is in fact an ignorant historian when it comes to the second phase of critical history.

Then he or she is like an historian of mathematics who knows little about mathematics. Such a person might well be able to do a smash-up job at comparing various mathematical texts, at dating and placing them more or less precisely, at working out certain social and/or cultural processes that were going on at the time the mathematical texts were being produced, at who used which text to get what advantage in this or that situation, how

---

[37]Lonergan, *Method in Theology* (Toronto: University of Toronto Press, 1992) 189; on objects, also 156–8, 161–2.

[38]As an example, take autobiographies. A critical historian would set about situating Augustine's *Confessions,* Teresa's *Life,* Rousseau's *Confessions* in their very different historical, literary, cultural, contexts, what sources they drew upon, what texts are more reliable, etc. This is fairly standard stuff in historical theology. One can read the results of such critical historical field work in the surveys and articles and books given to graduate students to introduce them to a subject, e.g., Peter Brown's book on Augustine. But can the critical historian make the move to the second phase or instance of critical history when what an Augustine or a Teresa are so obviously discussing is their friendship with the Triune God? What is moving forward in the historical communities of the faithful who down the ages continue to read and meditate upon these works in their contexts of their own deepening friendship with God? Does Peter Brown do the kind of critical history which could make such a second step?

such a text was used in the production of weapons, what the weapons did, etc., Undoubtedly, such a history would be very readable for those who are not interested in knowing the history of mathematics so much as in knowing what else was going on when such and such a mathematics was being done. But no one would claim that such a history would merit the name of a genuinely critical history of mathematics.

I am afraid that there are not many genuinely critical histories of theology done yet. And the sad thing is that what passes for critical histories are usually histories that are critical of theology, that simply assume that what is really real is a secular horizon in which it is at best a private opinion, and at worst a neurotic or psychotic delusion, that an Augustine or a Teresa were caught up in an ever deepening friendship with Father, Son, and Spirit. Why is it that theology and religious studies are so lacking in self-knowledge that they alone, of all the disciplines, now seem so ready to mistake ignorant histories for critical histories? This is hardly a *docta ignorantia!*

I am not stating that one must be moral or holy to write a critical history of morality or of the saints, any more than I am saying that one must be an alcoholic to write a critical history of alcoholism. I am saying one must *know* the realities operative, the processes occurring, in morality, holiness, or alcoholism. Similarly, if one is going to do a critical history of faith, prayer, or theology, one had best know something about the realities of faith, prayer, or theology. Instead, what we have is a widespread conceptualism and what I would call "comparative textology" à la Spinoza. A recognition of the openness of history requires a genuine theology in which faith and reason are neither separated nor confused, but in which they are properly differentiated.

Conclusion: The Redemption of Victims

History is open to the redemptive transformation of the kingdom of God revealed in the life, death, and resurrection of Jesus Christ. The openness of history posited by the theological works of all those who understand the fundamental importance of universal anamnestic solidarity with the victims of history, is an openness which insists upon redemption which only God incarnate in Christ has offered humankind. One has to be fully realistic in the heuristic openness to the totality of all concrete things and events, persons and acts, throughout the whole of history.

This means a concrete heuristic that envisages all the goodness, joy, and justice, as well as all the horror, evil, and injustice that constitutes the ongoing history of the human race. It means recognizing that the innocent victims of injustice cannot receive full justice within the limitations of either life, as a biological span between birth and death, or the limitations of a good life, as the life of excellent cognitive and moral self-constitution by human beings. For neither life nor the good life can raise the dead, bring back the murdered millions whose blood has trenched each page of history. No communities of life or the good life can resurrect the dead victims of the empires of violence, dominative power, and death.[39]

Any fully realistic assessment of the evil in human history, how movements for justice and liberation turn into engines of injustice and oppression, can appreciate Max Horkheimer's comment: "Die großartigste Lehre in beiden Religionen, der jüdischen wie der christlichen, ist . . . die Lehre von der Erbsünde. Sie hat die bisherige Geschichte bestimmt und bestimmt heute für den Denkenden die Welt. Möglich ist sie nur unter der Voraussetzung, daß Gott den Menschen mit einem freien Willen geschaffen hat."[40] The Enlightenment's rejection of theology has meant that the human sciences have studied men and women without the theological categories of sin and grace. Whatever evil humans do is then attributed to their human natures. So violence and war and vice are taken as natural human attributes. Social policies and political regimes are built on such false premises, and so the violence, war, and evil are spread and compounded and intensified by all the modern means of communication and force.

Given sin and the massive injustices in human history, the importance of holiness and the theological virtues cannot be overestimated in the tasks of a new wisdom-oriented enlightenment. The fact that theology has disappeared from the cultural patrimony of our post-Enlightenment intellectual establishment has meant that empirical science is bereft of the wisdom it so desperately needs. For the empirical sciences are charting how human beings behave, how they act. They are ascribing that behavior—no matter how violent and sinful it is—to human nature. On the basis of such studies social policies are formulated, and so the violence and sin become structured into the society and culture.

In such cycles of social and cultural decline the intellectually virtuous tend toward cynicism, while the morally virtuous tend toward stoicism.

---

[39]Cf. M. Lamb, "Christianity within the Political Dialectics of Community and Empire," in N. Biggar, J. Scott, and W. Schweiker, eds., *Cities of Gods: Faith, Politics and Pluralism in Judaism, Christianity and Islam* (New York: Greenwood Press, 1986) 73–100.

[40]Max Horkheimer, *Die Sehnsucht nact dem ganz Anderen* (Hamburg: Furche Verlag, 1970) 64–5.

The intelligent quest for wisdom and science, as well as the moral quest for justice, cannot succumb to cynicism and indifference. Because our kingdom is not of this world, we can dedicate ourselves to the creative and redemptive transformation of this world. Because through faith, hope and love we are in communion with the absolutely transcendent Triune God, we are members of one another in the historically immanent mediations of the missions of the Word and the Spirit to bring about the kingdom of God in our time and culture.

As Sebastian Moore's meditations on desire indicate, all understanding involves a suffering, a *pati,* and it is only when the light of our minds is healed and intensified by the light of faith that we can avoid the temptations to cynicism, skepticism, and despairing nihilism when, from all around us and deep within us, come the cries of the victims.

Only with the strength of the Spirit can the extended passion narratives of all human history narrated in the new covenant be accepted as gospel, as good news of salvation in the glory of the resurrection. Incorporated within the Paschal Victim are all the victims of history, some of whose stories grace us from the opening pages of Genesis to the last pages of Revelation. They teach us a wisdom that is of God, a wisdom of the Blessed "who have come out of great suffering and been washed in the blood of the Lamb. They shall neither hunger nor thirst nor suffer any more, for God shall wipe away every tear from their eyes" (Rev 7:14, 17). If the depth of human suffering is to birth understanding, it is because of the kenosis of the Divine Wisdom who alone can bring good out of evil, grace out of sin, life out of death. Only in the eternal kingdom of God will the empires of history be fully transformed into the justice and agapic love of the Triune Divine Comm-unity.

⟍ 9 ⟋

The Church and Our Desires:
An Inquiry into Ecumenical Criteria

Vernon Gregson

Raising the dynamics of desire into consciousness is one way of naming the task Sebastian Moore has set for himself as his life project. The present study of our desires and the Church takes its inspiration from Sebastian and his mentor and friend, Bernard Lonergan. I recall Father Lonergan on one occasion in Toronto asking me to tell Sebastian, whom he had not seen in a while, "Our friendship is still green." This essay is written with deep gratitude to both of them.

In any attempt at ecumenical dialogue, it soon becomes evident to the participants that the word "Church" is exceedingly ambiguous. Not only does it have different meanings for members of different Christian denominations, it also has different meanings for different individuals within the same denomination. Scriptural, historical, and sociological studies have done and will continue to do much to clarify the matter.

This essay will suggest another, complementary approach. It will explore some of our most basic desires and longings and how in the community that we call Church, we search for their fulfillment. Through a study of the structure and intentionality of some of our deepest desires it will seek to establish a gradually more precise grasp of the nature of the community that the orientation of those desires leads us to pursue and to constitute.

The approach of the paper then will be to articulate and refine the questions to which "Church" is the answer. The value hoped for in so specifying the personal and social questions that are involved in our desire for religious community is that we will be helped in recognizing and appreciating the answers when we find them. Put another way, this essay will contribute to the development of an "ideal type" that may be helpful in identifying the strengths and weaknesses of the concrete historical and contemporary communities that we call "Church." Hence this essay will not study the history of the various meanings of Church, but rather it will try to articulate basic perspectives that may illuminate those historical meanings. It is, then, "an essay in aid of a grammar of 'Church.'"[1]

Such an approach may seem to have its dangers. Is not a study of the orientation of our desires problematic? Are not desires notably fluid and even fickle? Yet, granting that there is no doubt that we do indeed have fleeting desires, we can nonetheless ask whether all our desires, especially our profoundest ones, are really so unsteady. Might not our deepest desires be persistent and trustworthy in their pursuit of their goals?

There are indeed possible pitfalls and dangers to the approach we are taking. It may not be self-evident that our desires are able to bear this type of analysis. If they can, however, immense benefits follow. Should it be the case that our desires have a structure and a clear objective orientation, then we would have access to a base from which to inquire into what we seek from the community we call Church. And, as well, we would have a base for knowing when we have found it.

This essay will suggest precisely that: the needs and desires of our own interiority do give us substantive criteria by which we make our judgments of where the Church is. Who we are, with our needs and desires, determines what we seek and what we recognize to be the healing and beloved community. Discovering what those needs and desires are will be significant for ecumenical dialogue, for dialogue among the world religions, and for dialogue between people of religious and secular consciousness. The issue in each of these dialogues is who we are as human beings and what fulfills the human condition and, insofar as it is broken, what heals it.

Our perspective in forming the ideal type is that of interiority. To some, this might seem a particularly unhelpful perspective to take since a healing community of whatever sort is precisely social and interpersonal. And indeed it is social, but I would suggest that the foundational reality that brings the healing community together and keeps it together (insofar

---

[1]Avery Dulles, *Models of the Church* (New York: Doubleday, 1974); Edward Farley, *Ecclesial Man* (Philadelphia: Fortress Press, 1975); John Gager, *Kingdom and Community* (Englewood Cliffs, N.J.: Prentice Hall, 1975); Hans Küng, *The Church* (New York: Image Books, 1976).

as it is true to its origins) is a shared interior response to the Transcendent, a response mediated both by some event, person, or natural phenomenon, and also mediated by one's own interior desire for God. These two foci seem essential to religious community, but both foci center on the interiority of the believer. This is clearly true of its mediation of the Transcendent through one's longing for union with it, but it is likewise true of the process of the identification and response to the specific mediation of the ultimate. As a matter of fact, it is one's own interiority that recognizes the person or event precisely as symbol of the Transcendent. If the person, event, or natural phenomenon does not elicit from one's interiority the response that one is in the presence of the Transcendent in some way, then the person, event, or natural phenomenon is simply a fact to be acknowledged and does not form the basis of a religious community.

We will take the theologian Bernard Lonergan as tutor for our exploration. His work attempts to articulate the objectivity in the deepest desires of our consciousness. And, further, he develops an anthropology on what he discovers. With his aid we will inquire into how "Church" answers human needs and desires. We will pursue the question, "what are those needs and desires that call for the Church?" The gradually more complete exploration of those needs and desires will, we expect, shed light on our judgments, often spontaneous, of where we find the Church and why we find it there.

We choose Lonergan as our guide not only because of the recognized depth of his analysis but also because the philosophical and theological anthropology that he develops in *Insight: A Study of Human Understanding*[2] and in *Method in Theology*[3] is meant to be verifiable. That is, at each stage Lonergan asks the reader to see if the anthropology he suggests corresponds to the reader's own experience. Through his analysis Lonergan aims at bringing into focus significant structural elements of who we are as humans. Verifiability is unfortunately not a frequent characteristic of much of theology, and the lack of it remains a serious flaw.

Needless to say, in the brief confines of this paper I cannot bring up all the evidence that Lonergan develops for his anthropology in over a thousand carefully crafted pages, but I can bring up some significant elements of his anthropology and give some indication of how they are verifiable. Such an excursus here is necessary since it is essential to establish the basic character and the importance of the desires we are considering.

[2]New York: Philosophical Library, 1958.
[3]New York: Herder & Herder, 1972.

Lonergan begins with a deceptively simple analysis of the processes involved in our knowing and doing. Put succinctly, he suggests that if you reflect on the structure of decisions you have made, you will discover that you engaged in the following sequence of operations: you tried to gather the data pertinent to the decision, you tried to understand that data, you tried to verify your understanding, then you decided how to act on your understanding. These operations followed in spontaneous sequence upon one another; the completion of one operation calls for the beginning of the next. Experiencing any new situation calls for the same four operations. First, we will attend to the data of the new experience. Then we will try to understand the experience. Once we have a preliminary grasp or understanding of the experience, we want to confirm or verify if our understanding is correct or true. Then having confirmed our understanding, we will pose the question of how we should act upon it.

LEVELS OF CONSCIOUSNESS

Deciding	Choosing	How will I act on what I know?
Judging	Knowing	Have I verified my understanding?
Understanding		Do I understand the data?
Experiencing		What are relevant data?

To realize how important it is to fulfill the task or thrust of each of the levels before going on to the next, the reader need only reflect on some occasion when he or she did not gather all the relevant data and yet acted, or was content with the first bright idea and did not understand the issue thoroughly and yet acted, or did not take the time to confirm an understanding and yet decided anyway. The negative consequences of a too hasty move through the four levels, whether the results are disastrous or only embarrassing, show how essential it is for us to achieve the goal of each of the four levels in order to arrive at truth and value.

So basic and necessary are the processes of these four levels of our consciousness, if we are to arrive at what is true and valuable, that we would be right to interpret them to be ethical imperatives derived from the structure of our humanity: be attentive (to experience), be intelligent (in understanding), be reasonable (in judging), be responsible (in deciding and acting). Following these imperatives puts on a solid footing all of our knowing and doing. In fact, without following the dynamism and achieving the goal of each of the levels, we can have no confidence that we have arrived at what is true or have chosen what is valuable.

Those who are not familiar with Lonergan's analysis of the method of our knowing and choosing might be aided to evaluate it better by two experiments. The first is aimed at discovering whether Lonergan has in fact articulated truly basic elements of our cognitional and volitional processes, the second is aimed at discovering whether Lonergan's analysis avoids subjectivism.

The first experiment is to reflect on how one might try to refute Lonergan's position on the essential importance for knowing and living of the four levels of our consciousness. On what grounds might one endeavor to do that? Perhaps by presenting other experience or data. But that would in fact, on the contrary, confirm the importance of the experiential level that he calls attention to. For it is no particular experience that he stands by; rather it is the importance of beginning with data or experience. Perhaps his position can be challenged by showing that he has not understood the data properly. Again, however, that would in fact confirm the necessity of the understanding level that he also calls attention to. For it is not a particular understanding that he calls for; rather, it is the importance of the process of understanding itself. But, if not then by a different understanding, perhaps then by another method of verification than his own. However, again he calls for no particular method of verification, but only for that method appropriate to the question at hand. One has in fact only confirmed the verification level he articulates. If not then by a different method of verification, than perhaps by a different evaluation of the significance of the results. Here too he calls for no particular evaluation of the results, but only that there is such a level and process that follows verification.

In other words, the attempt to refute his analysis would use the very processes he attends to, thus confirming the method he writes of in the very act of trying to refute it.[4] So basic are the levels which he treats of, that attempts to prove his analysis wrong must themselves use the levels.

But it is important to recognize what is confirmed, and what is not, when his method is verified. It is only that he has called attention to fundamental levels of our desire to know the truth and our desire to choose what is really valuable. Other articulations could surely be made of those same levels. And other supplementary levels could be discovered. Certainly, too, refinements in the descriptions of the levels he attends to could be made. Needless to say, his own presentation[5] is itself obviously more detailed and nuanced than I can present here in summary form.

The second experiment is aimed at discovering whether Lonergan's analysis avoids subjectivism. Do the levels of our consciousness really

[4]Lonergan, *Method,* 18–20.
[5]Lonergan, *Insight.*

achieve objectivity? Reflections on your own intellectual and decisional operations are again important here. Call to mind some question you have investigated thoroughly or are in the process of investigating thoroughly. Were you really gathering data or experience you hoped to be relevant to the question at hand, or were you seeking to fabricate evidence for a pre-ordained conclusion? We know almost without fail when we are doing one or the other. And an uneasy conscience is the reward for the latter endeavor. The desire operative in our first, data-gathering level of consciousness gives us unmistakable feedback when we try to use it for merely "subjective" and self-serving purposes. Lonergan suggests then that the first level of our consciousness, rather than being "subjective," is, actually, precisely our capacity to go beyond subjectivism. It is our capacity to transcend ourselves and to arrive at objectivity by the gathering of data truly relevant to the question at hand. The fact that we can err or even sometimes deceive ourselves about whether we have gathered all the relevant data is not really a strong argument against this view, since the recognition of the error or self-deception is also made by the operation of our consciousness itself. The levels of consciousness are self-correcting.

What is true about the objective orientation of the first level is true analogously of each of the other levels. We know when we are really trying to *understand* and when we are being superficial and are trying to contrive an answer. Understanding is our capacity to transcend the merely subjective and to arrive at objectivity. We violate its natural intentionality both at a moral price and at the price finally of not finding what is true. *Judgment,* too, is our capacity to get beyond what is only subjective and to affirm what really is so. We know when we are really working to confirm our understanding and when we are running rough-shod over the evidence. Finally, *deciding* and acting manifest our highest capacity for self-transcendence through our discovery and sometimes our creation of what is really good. We know when we are choosing what is only to our private advantage rather than what is truly valuable.

From this brief presentation of Lonergan's basic analysis and from the two experiments that were suggested, at least the thrust of Lonergan's position should be clear. He aims to articulate basic levels of our knowing and our doing, levels whose orientation is toward objectivity, levels that are not satisfied except with objectivity, levels that are really imperatives of our consciousness.

But what do these matters have to do with "Church"? I would suggest that we are surrounded by and are a part of communities each of which tends to narrow the range of the four levels of our consciousness. We are part of communities that routinely rule some data of our personal or social experience, or data about our world, or data about the transcendent, out of court. We are part of communities that routinely declare certain types of questions or understandings to be irrelevant or useless. We are part of communities that routinely deny or disregard certain types of truths about either the height or depth of the human experience. We are part of communities that routinely undermine or are indifferent to certain types of values that are central to the project of being human. In a word, we need a fuller community that is open to the whole of the human condition, and not only does not itself rule out of court certain data or understandings or truths or values, but which stands as a challenge to all communities that do. That community I suggest is a basic element in what we desire in "Church."

I suggest then as a first criterion that Church is a community where these deep desires, these imperatives of our knowing and of our choosing, this structure of our creativity, are recognized and fostered. And we find Church there, because following these imperatives is our way to become more authentically and completely human. We respond to beauty, truth, and goodness, and we create beauty, truth, and goodness, insofar as we are faithful to the dynamics of our consciousness, which these imperatives express.

On the other hand, when a community we have called Church does not respect and foster these basic imperatives of our humanity, we are deeply saddened and sometimes even led astray. But the deepest part of us knows that the Church is not being authentic to itself when it does that. The Church is not being Church. Insofar as the community we call Church violates these imperatives, or even justifies the violation of them, it fosters not healing, but alienation, and a profound form of alienation, for these violations affect our deepest desires: our way to the true, the good, and the beautiful.[6]

Not that any community we call Church will ever be completely free from failings in this regard, just as we individually will not be free from them. But we are not being true to ourselves when we have these failings, nor is the Church being true to itself. If Lonergan's analysis of the basic structure of our consciousness is correct, then we have already come a long way in understanding our often spontaneous judgments of where the Church is present, and where it is not, where we experience a home, and where we do not. But we have not come far enough. For in addition to the general fostering of attention, intelligence, reasonableness, and responsibility that we expect from the Church, there is a special and more explicit

---

[6]Lonergan, *Method,* 55.

form of these desires that leads us to seek for the Church and to know when we have found it: our desire for God and our desire for communion with those who desire God. Our attentiveness, intelligence, reasonableness, and responsibility extend that far, to a desire to know and to respond to the Transcendent. The ground of the unity that exists among believers is the intensely personal yet shared experience of the longing for the absolute, come alive in us. The communities where that desire has come alive and manifests itself we recognize as the communities that are "the Church."[7]

Just as shared experience, understanding, judgments, and decisions about anything create community among those who share them, whether it be a matter of art or music or baseball or war, so those with the shared experience of a deep longing for God discover communion with those in love with the Transcendent, a communion that crosses the boundaries of all the traditional religions and extends even to those who affirm no formal religion whatsoever. This is our second criterion for "Church." Just as our attentiveness, intelligence, reasonableness, and responsibility recognize when they have attained their goal with regard to our scientific pursuits and to the matters of everyday life, so do they recognize and rejoice when their desire for the Transcendent is on target and they have discovered a community of those who share their desire. Our desire for God then establishes the further base for the community called "the Church" among those who experience it. Why do we find the Church there? It is because our deepest desires have found a home.

But even this analysis of our second criterion of where we find the Church is not yet sufficient. For the Christian, it is the incarnate symbol Jesus Christ who in a special way both awakens the desire for God and confirms the desire he has awakened. He is the real external counterpart of the real internal desire. Both of these foci are important. For any concrete religious community is brought together both by the shared interior response to the Transcendent, of which we have spoken, and by some concrete person or event or natural phenomenon, which mediates the Transcendent.

These two foci seem essential to the full experience and expression of religious community. It is important to note that both foci involve the interiority of the believer. This is obvious with regard to the mediation of the Transcendent through one's own longing for union, but it is likewise true of the identification and response to the specific mediation of the ultimate. For it is one's own interiority that recognizes the person or event as sym-

[7]Ibid., 29.

bol of the Transcendent. In the absence of a profound resonance with one's desire for the Transcendent, the person or event remains merely that and does not become the basis for a religious community. The interior response of the believer is so integral to religious living that where it is respected we know we are in the presence of the community that is rightly called "Church."

But why Jesus Christ? We have been exploring the criteria for Church in relation to the desires and the imperatives of our own interiority. What deep desire of ours does the incarnate symbol of Jesus Christ fulfill, such that we spontaneously recognize that where he is, God is, where he acts, there is the Church. Why this third criterion? Surely our anthropology up to this point has been incomplete. There is, in addition to the desires of which we have spoken, a persistent and profound desire in each of us for healing, a desire to know the presence of God who heals. And like the other desires, it knows when it has been fulfilled, when it has reached its goal. I would suggest, along with Lonergan, that we approach the meaning of Jesus here.

Lonergan asks us to consider four persistent aberrations or biases to which we are all prone. There is the neurotic bias that flees insight into our affects to protect us against repetition of unconscious injury from past trauma. There is the bias of preferring and choosing my own interest, either singly or as a member of a group, over that of others, and the related bias of preferring immediate and short-term solutions to more significant and long-term ones. Lonergan calls these aberrations dramatic bias (bias in the drama of our living), individual bias, group bias, and general bias.[8] The effects of these aberrations can be devastating. They work against the ethical imperatives of our creativity. They lead us to be inattentive, uncomprehending, unreasonable, irresponsible, all in the service of protecting us from pain or of preserving our individual, group, or short-range interests. That is one reason why it is so devastating when the community we call Church sides with inattentiveness, blocks our relevant questions, rules judgments based on data and understanding out of court. When the community we call the Church does that, it sides with precisely those aberrations that we come to the Church to seek healing from.

But how does Jesus heal? He is first of all one like us. His own longing for and rejoicing in God is for us the external counterpart of our own desire for the Transcendent. His intimacy with his Father brings our own desire in his presence to a new level of clarity and freedom and depth. But in

[8]Lonergan, *Insight,* 191–244.

his death and in his rising, our longing for God and Jesus' longing confront the severe challenge of death by crucifixion. Is that longing for God mere illusion? Has it been proven so in the starkest way, with our hope dead on a tree? Or has our hope been confirmed in a way beyond expectation? Has death proven powerless to defeat it? Has the blindness and evil responsible for his death proven powerless to defeat it. Those who find the community of Jesus Christ to be the healing community find it so. We find in God's raising Jesus from the dead the confirmation of our longing and his.[9] And more than that, we discover that the fears which lead us to cling to our neurotic, individual, group, and short-sighted biases begin to be dissolved. For if our longing for God is confirmed in our own experience and in the life, dying, and rising of Jesus, then the anxieties that lead us to cling to ourselves and to our own can begin to recede, as we begin to make our own the expansive vision of God that seems to have animated Jesus' whole experience of life and death.

Meditating on the reality of the cross of Jesus, Lonergan formulates its meaning in this way:

> The Son of God thus became man, suffered, died, and was raised, because the divine wisdom ordained and the divine goodness willed, not to take away the evils of the human race by an exercise of power, but to convert those evils into a certain highest good through the just and mysterious Law of the Cross.[10]

By Jesus' own response to death and to the evils that caused it, and by God's affirmation of Jesus, our deepest fears that our longing for God might be futile, or that the evil we do might separate us from him are addressed and responded to with healing and with compassionate forgiveness.

Where we find the expansiveness of God that Jesus preached and lived, and where we find the healing of our deepest fears, there we discover the Church, the community of Jesus Christ. There we find, too, the liberation to allow our attentiveness, our intelligence, our reasonableness, and our responsibility to have free rein to exercise their creativity, now that the fears that would lead them into myopia have been addressed compassionately

---

[9]For an incisive analysis of redemption from a perspective of interiority, cf. Sebastian Moore, *The Inner Loneliness* (New York: Crossroad, 1982).

[10]Translated from *De Verbo Incarnato* (Rome: Gregorian University Press, 1964) 552, by William P. Loewe, "Toward a Responsible Christian Soteriology," in Matthew L. Lamb, ed., *Creativity and Method: Essays in Honor of Bernard Lonergan* (Milwaukee: Marquette University Press, 1981) 216.

by God. Our deepest desires know when they are fulfilled, our deepest fears know when they are calmed and healed, and our longing for a community where the healing and the fulfillment can be shared and celebrated knows when it has discovered what it has been seeking. The desires and needs of our interiority are our compass to the Church of Jesus Christ. We know where we have found it and why we have found it.

Any substantial community is going to exist over time and will in the course of time develop structures and traditions which will sometimes serve original purposes of the community and sometimes impede them. Our desire for community knows when it is in the presence of authorities and structures that maintain and build up or damage and undermine the purpose of the community. Since the community we call Church responds to such deep and basic desires, the right to judge the extent to which those desires are met belongs as a precious possession of each conscience, as does the corresponding obligation to contribute one's own efforts to build up the community one calls Church.

It is a cause of great sadness that disputes among Christians for centuries have focused to so great an extent on the structure of the Church, which is a subordinate issue, when the most significant goals of the community have so often actually been shared. The desires and longings of which we have written provide the compass to the recognition of grace and truth wherever they are found, and are themselves a manifestation of grace. The healing of the divisions among Christians will enrich all and is incumbent upon all, both the founding churches and those separated from them.

If the analysis presented here is at all adequate, then the Christian Church exists where the following four deep desires are in evidence and are celebrated: the longing for God, the longing for union with those who desire God, the longing for healing of the evil that we suffer and that we do, and the longing for the release of the imperatives of our creativity. And where these elements exist, the community of the Christian Church can be accurately and authentically affirmed, and mutual recognition can be affirmed.

It follows, too, that the ministries of the Church derive their authenticity from the extent to which they help members of the community and others to acknowledge those desires and to live out their implications. It seems obvious that a relationship characteristic of adults, rather than a parental model, would best respect the uniqueness of each adult person's expression of his or her deepest desires.

It would seem that in itself no particular authority structure is preferable to any other, so long as the goals of the community are realized. In historical communities, however, such as the communities that center on Jesus

Christ, the events and structures that have served to build up the community ought to be respected, and continuity with them ought to be sought, but never, of course, at the price of deviating from the goals of the community. To respect what has taken place is not the same as to cling to it.

In this exploration of criteria for "Church," I have urged that our own interiority be looked to as guide. I am not under the illusion that our interiority cannot be mistaken, for surely it can. But we are also capable of recognizing our mistakes and of searching again for what will fulfill our genuine longings. Nor am I under the illusion that our interiority enters fully mature onto the scene. It achieves its original guidance in the family matrix by early training. It is tutored in the home and elsewhere. It is given language and forms in which to express itself. It is also given access to the knowledge and valuations of others, through the myriad forms of belief. Frequently, it is formed by the very traditions that it judges. In fact, traditions often in their wisdom articulate the very criteria under which the traditions themselves are most aptly judged. But finally they must be judged. Our desires know when they have found a home and where it is.

Bernard Lonergan expresses in terms of a two-fold struggle for authenticity the challenge which faces each of us as we come to terms with ourselves and our traditions. I include this lengthy quote because it addresses so strikingly the issues we are exploring.

> So it is that commonly men (sic) have to pay a double price for their personal attainment of authenticity. Not only have they to undo their own lapses from righteousness but more grievously they have to discover what is wrong in the tradition they have inherited and they have to struggle against the massive undertow it sets up. Such resentment against the human condition offers some explanation, perhaps, of the attraction exercised by Rousseau's picture of the noble savage or, again, of the ever recurrent hopes that an earthly paradise would be ushered in by the revolutionary obliteration of the human past. But really the problem is not tradition, but unauthenticity in the formation and transmission of tradition. The cure is not the undoing of tradition but the undoing of its unauthenticity.
>
> The cure is not the undoing of tradition, for that is beyond our power. It is only through socialization, acculturation, education, that we come to know that there is such a thing as tradition, that it has its defects, its dangers, its seductions, that there are evils to be remedied. To learn as much is already to be a product of the tradition, to share its biases, to be marked in a manner that we can change only in the light of what we have learnt and in the directions that such learning opens up. However much we may react, criticize, endeavor to bring about change, the change itself will always be just another state of the tradition, at most a new era, but one whose motives

and whose goals—for all their novelty—will bear the imprint of their past. The issue is not tradition, for as long as men survive, there will be tradition, rich or impoverished, good and evil. The issue is the struggle of authenticity against unauthenticity, and that struggle is part and parcel of the human condition, of our being animals yet equipped to live not just by instinct but principally by the symbols by which we express our self-understanding and our commitments.[11]

Our challenge then is both to overcome our own inauthenticity and to seek to identify and overcome the inauthenticity of the traditions in which we live. No easy task this, and a life-long one as well. But it is a task which the liberation of our own desires requires of us, if those very desires are to find a home.

This study has, we hope, illuminated at least some basic elements of what we desire of the community we call Church. It is not meant to be exclusive. Others might well add other elements and other desires to what they seek from Church. This essay has only sought to identify certain essential rock-bottom dimensions of Church, and to identify them from the perspective of our interiority. In that way it seeks to be "in aid of a grammar of 'Church.'"

Finally, there has been a tension between universality and particularity in what I have presented. The desires are universal, but I have centered on their particular symbolic manifestations in the community called Church. I have centered, therefore, on their realization in the Christian tradition. Obviously, those desires find other homes as well, in other traditions. The encounter among the various homes for our desires is reaching a new level of fruitfulness in our own day. An approach through interiority could be significant for that dialogue. It could make comprehensible the spontaneous respect that one has for the spiritual depth of other traditions, and it would serve to focus dialogue on the shared longings of our humanity and how they are fulfilled.

---

[11]"Religious Experience," in Thomas A. Dunne and Jean-Marc Laporte, eds., *Trinification of the World* (Toronto: Regis College Press, 1978) 77–8.

— 10 —

Stirred Up by Desire:
The Search for an
Incarnational Spirituality

Carla Mae Streeter, O.P.

It has been the ongoing search of Sebastian Moore to free the human heart in its relentless search for the holy. To pursue this search Sebastian has not only shared his work in process through the printed word, he has provided us with an interiority analysis which grounds soteriology in human experience. In so doing, he builds a bridge for the theologian to be able to discuss matters of healing and the integration of the human person with the psychiatrist and the psychologist. He opens the way for an academic ecumenism.

But even more important, Moore invites his theological colleagues to reexamine their own categories, to reshape them as carriers of fuller truth, and so to influence the interconnected web of their own teaching.

The adults who are our students are assuming more and more self-direction in their learning and living. This contemporary phenomenon manifests itself from bouncing aerobic classes, Overeaters Anonymous groups, and crowded New Age weekends, to weekend college, Scripture study, and what some will declare is at the heart of it all: the search for the whole and holy. Theologians ignore this growing phenomenon at their own peril. Students, both traditional and non-traditional come to the theological task with multiple agendas. It is not the role of the theologian to be an academic reed swaying in the cross-currents of these agendas, but unless he or she is very aware of these contextual currents the task of returning from the realm of theory to that of common sense through effective communications in the theological task is short-circuited. Carefully done theoretical work is a ministry: its goal is to challenge what has always gone on in the realm of common sense.

I suggest it is in a three-fold way that Sebastian Moore contributes to this theological task. First, his work is grounded in interiority analysis, which by its very nature—as Lonergan explains—encompasses the realms of theory and common sense and enables us to distinguish and relate them (Lonergan, 1971, 85). This analysis provides the deeper foundation that many of our students are seeking: the link between careful theoretical distinction in theology and their lived lives. Second, because Sebastian's focus is soteriology, it is that area of systematics which has a clearest relation with foundations. Conversion might be described as the vulnerable inner palm of the soteriological hand. By his work, Sebastian has placed that hand on the doorknob of what remains yet to be done: exploring the import of what he has uncovered about the human ego for religious conversion (in addition to its Christian form) and for psychic, moral, and intellectual conversion. Third, because Sebastian's work is grounded in interiority, it has implications for human anthropology. While coming from a distinctly Christian horizon, the work provides grounds for discussion in comparative theology. Its potential here has yet to be explored.

It is with the above context in mind that I state the intent of this essay. There is, I believe, in the writings of Sebastian Moore, a significant contribution to the human search for an incarnational spirituality. Operating from within my own Christian categories, I will suggest that such a spirituality manifests at least three basic principles: incarnateness, sacramentality, and expressed communalness. These three principles effect a healing integration that releases creative operation in the human person. I will examine these three principles, relate them briefly to Sebastian's writings, and project what implications such a distinctly Christian spirituality might have for others in the human family "stirred up by desire."

Incarnational Spirituality

Our first question may be what such a spirituality might be, and then whether we need it. To answer these questions still other questions are uncovered: What is the meaning of spirituality as it is used here? Are there spiritualities that are not properly speaking incarnational? What are the distinguishing characteristics of a spirituality that is incarnational?

To begin, the meaning of the word "spirituality" as used here is quite focused rather than broad.[1] In a recently published work,[2] Daniel Helminiak has focused the term in a workable way for our purposes here. Recognizing that the word spirituality can be an umbrella term for several different meanings, he specifies three that are closely related. The first refers to the human spirit itself as the basis for talk about the spiritual. The second refers to a lived reality, a way of living expressing that source. The third refers to a subject matter, an academic study that treats of the lived reality and its source. It is the second meaning that will be our focus here: spirituality is human living insofar as it is geared toward integration of the intrinsic human dynamism toward authentic self-transcendence, as created by God and reaching fulfillment through the Holy Spirit in Christ. This form as distinctively Christian is not Helminiak's only formulation, but I choose it here because it relates to Sebastian's distinctly Christian focus.

It is not by chance that I begin with these specific categories. In all honesty, it is the only place I can begin. This is not to say my Christian categories are to be imposed on anyone. It is simply to declare that with Panikkar[3] I do not believe *epoche* or the "neutralizing" of one's own categories is possible in entering upon religious dialogue. It puts the theologian in the position that Lonergan points to in the very structure of *Method,* namely, of translating from one's own theological categories back into the world of someone else's common sense understandings. This puts the burden, I believe, where it rightfully belongs. The burden is on ourselves to communicate the message in such a way that the categories of another are respected rather than disdained, and the task is to find a home for the good news in the indigenous categories of a people very different from ourselves.

---

[1] The effort to arrive at a satisfactory definition of what spirituality means is reflected in the writings of both men and women. See Walter Principe, "Toward Defining Spirituality," *Sciences Religieuses/Studies in Religion* 12:2 (1983) 127–41, and Sandra Schneiders, "The Effects of Women's Experience on Their Spirituality," *Spirituality Today* 35:2 (Summer 1983) 100–16; "Scripture and Spirituality," in *Christian Spirituality,* McGinn and Meyendorff, eds. (New York: Crossroad, 1985) 1–20; "Theology and Spirituality: Strangers, Rivals, or Partners?" *Horizons* 13:2 (1986) 253–74; and "Spirituality in the Academy," *Theological Studies* 50 (1989) 676–97. Because neither of these writers is asking the question from the realm of interiority, the operations of the spiritual subject in asking the question do not come under consideration. One is left with choosing a meaning without reference to the authentic operation of the evaluator.

[2] Daniel A. Helminiak, *The Human Core of Spirituality: Mind as Psyche and Spirit* (Albany: State University of New York Press, 1996).

[3] Raimundo Panikkar, in *The Intra-religious Dialogue* (New York: Paulist, 1978) develops the notion of *epoche* more thoroughly.

In this way the term "incarnational" begins to take on meaning beyond the usual Christian connotation of the word. It is with this understanding of the potential broadening of the word, that I press for a spirituality that is incarnational.

But we are getting ahead of the purpose of this essay. Our first task is to press for an authentic incarnational spirituality as understood within our own Christian categories.

The Meaning of "Incarnateness"

For Christians this term has to do with the enfleshment of the divine. Incarnation refers to the fusion of the divine with the human, with matter, in the person of the Word of God. This mystery, known theologically as the hypostatic union, is a distinctive feature of Christian revelation. The incarnation reveals simultaneously something about divine mystery and something about the human. Keeping in mind that it is the human that receives whatever is revealed, the very act of such a union has profound implications. There is obvious desire on the part of the divine to immerse itself in what it has made, or better still, to impress us with the fact that perhaps it has been quite at home there from the beginning. In the Christian tradition there is the clear conviction that neither the divine nor the human is violated in this union. There is neither mixture nor dissolving involved.[4]

What I would like to suggest here is that "incarnateness" might be a philosophical/psychological/physiological category. By this I mean that it can be a term with human meaning in its own right, without directly referring to its basis in Christian religious language. Incarnateness in this sense would mean being at home in one's body, in the flesh. It would mean physiological, psychological integration. It would challenge philosophy to build on the insights of Merleau-Ponty and Karl Stern among others.[5]

To move in this direction requires more than theory. It requires empirical analysis. It is in the interiority analysis of Lonergan that we find the data of consciousness taken seriously and made explicit in the charting of human operations. Here philosophy is in its element, for it is concerned with all that pertains to human processing. Psychology is concerned, for it

---

[4]See J.N.D. Kelly, *Early Christian Doctrines* (New York: Harper & Row, 1958) especially 338–40, for a full treatment of the development of the doctrinal settlement in christology.

[5]See the classic *The Flight from Woman* (New York: Farrar, Straus and Giroux, 1965).

is through human consciousness that psychic strength and illness is discovered and treatment attempted. It pertains to the physiological for the organism is the locus for both psychic and reflective activity, and resonates with this activity for good or ill.

In practical terms this would mean that the integrated human being shows evidence of balanced operation in each of these spheres. The philosopher, psychologist, psychiatrist, and physiologist would bring to the discussion what they would consider human "balance" in their area. It is not hard to see that eventually the sociologist, the political scientist, the ecologist, and the economist would have to be invited into the discussion, for we can no longer afford the mistaken luxury of considering authentic humanness out of context.

This wholistic integrated approach to the human will never begin seriously without the anthropological base that Lonergan maintains interiority analysis provides. If what Lonergan has charted regarding the recurrent pattern of human operation is not adequate, another scheme would have to be invented based on closer scrutiny of the data of consciousness. The importance of this realization is discussed by Sebastian in the final chapter of *Jesus the Liberator of Desire* (Moore, 1989, 119–20).

I would like to push this need further and suggest that the incarnateness I am calling for will require the psychic conversion of which Robert M. Doran writes.[6] Dramatic bias (Lonergan, 1957, 191–203) can so cripple the psyche that the basic images needed for new insights will not even be allowed to arise. I suggest that this psychic censorship can prevent a person from being at home in his or her own flesh. This disincarnateness cripples the intellectual process, for the intelligence cannot operate in a liberated way when under psychic restriction.

---

[6]In consultation with Lonergan before his death, Doran was assured the he "was onto something" in dealing with the censorship that arises from different forms of dramatic bias. Doran is convinced that this censorship aborts the intelligent process at the point of the *image,* thus setting up a selection of only those images that are not painful. This selectivity can result in a denial of much that has to be faced for full integrative growth.

See Robert M. Doran, "Psychic Conversion," *The Thomist* (1977) 200–36; "Subject, Psyche, and Theology's Foundations," *The Journal of Religion* 57:3 (July 1977) 267–87; *Subject and Psyche: Ricoeur, Jung, and the Search for Foundations* (Washington, D.C.: University Press of America, 1977); *Psychic Conversion and Theological Foundations: Toward a Reorientation of the Human Sciences.* American Academy of Religion, Studies in Religion 25, Thomas J. J. Altizer and James O. Duke, eds. (Chico, Calif.: Scholars Press, 1981); "Dramatic Artistry in the Third Stage of Meaning," *Lonergan Workshop II*, Fred Lawrence, ed. (Chico, Calif.: Scholars Press, 1981) 147–200.

Accuracy in the charting of conscious processes is the basis for what Lonergan calls general (theological) categories, those that apply across disciplines because they chart a human process that is common to them all. (*Method,* 285) Neglect of the operations of consciousness in the human subject keeps us adrift in the ambiguous sea of a plurality of theories about the human. The beginning is noting what goes on. Then one is in a position to question how well it is going on in whatever area.

Once we have begun at the beginning, the base in the background of all Sebastian thinks and writes, the Christian is in a position to play a trump card. In the horizon of one who has experienced Christian religious conversion is a figure who captures this authentic integration. There is a concrete person, a lived life that is the paradigm for the authenticity we humanly long for. There is for the Christian familiar with Sebastian's works, a continuity between *The Crucified Is No Stranger* and *Jesus the Liberator of Desire.*

The presence of this figure can be a hazard or a help. If the knowledge one has of Christ Jesus is docetic, this Jesus is no help toward an incarnateness. If one's knowledge is grounded in sound Christian tradition, this Jesus is the key to human authenticity.

How is this so? The traditional doctrine posits that there are two natures or modes of operation in Jesus, the human and the divine. Further, it posits that there is only one person, the eternal Word of God. There is no violation of either of the modes of operation. They do not get "mixed," nor are they "separate." They operate freely, one in deference to the other. What belongs to the realm of one is not imposed on the other. What is human is human, not divine, and what is divine is divine, not human.[7] I am proposing that this concrete mystery is revealing something profound to us about ourselves. Careful consideration brings us to the insight that we might have something here that breaks through the nature-grace impasse, not in a 50-50 resolution, but a 100-100 reality, each working in its own mode of operation.

This, of course, brings up the work currently being attempted on the consciousness of Christ.[8] Of core importance in these efforts is the need to distinguish what *is* from what is *known* or understood. The fact that there

---

[7] See Kelly, *Early Christian Doctrines,* especially the Chalcedon statement on 339.

[8] There are two early attempts at a translation of Lonergan's *De Constitutione Christi Ontologica et Psychologica,* namely that of Brezovec and O'Fallon. Of more interest, however, would be the translation jointly prepared by John Hochban, S.J., and Michael Shields, S.J., and awaiting publication in the *Collected Works* gradually coming out of the University of Toronto Press. This translation is available from the Lonergan Research Institute in Toronto. Of interest also might be Michael Shield's translation of *Pars V, De Redemptione*

is no such thing as "pure nature" is one thing. That that fact is known or understood is another.

In the case of the Incarnate Word this opens up the notion that the human consciousness of Jesus had to come to know what was completely clear to the divine consciousness, yet that divine consciousness never pushed the human process aside, but instead reverenced its unfolding. If this relationship of the divine nature with the human nature in Jesus is a paradigm, then its implications for how divine grace reverences the unfolding of human authenticity from a sin-infested state is startling.

Yet here some major distinctions must be pointed out. Jesus began with a basic human authenticity; we do not. We need to be healed from a degenerate humanness in order that the authentically human can creatively emerge. In us, grace not only effects a relational union, it heals human brokenness so that the human can function properly as it was emotionally, intelligently, and volitionally intended. The implications of this view of the human and its relation to the holy are important when brought to inter-religious dialogue. These implications will be considered later.

In summary, I have called for a broadening of a category typically Christian, that of "incarnateness," to call attention to its philosophical, psychological, and physiological implications.

The Meaning of "Sacramentality"

Once again, at first glance we are referring to a typically Christian category. In Christian terms a sacrament is most properly an external religious ritual that celebrates a hidden sacred reality. The sacrament is said to "effect" what it celebrates, that is, to make the celebrators *become* what they are celebrating. The most familiar context for sacramental meaning is that of the seven sacraments celebrated in the Catholic community. But what if again we plumb the inner core of this reality? Then by sacramentality we might mean the function of something open to the senses pointing to

---

of *De Verbo Incarnato,* also available from the Institute. Both are dated in 1987. Other references dealing with christology that are based on Lonergan's work are: John Ashton, "The Consciousness of Christ," *The Way* 10 (1970) 382–8; Daniel Helminiak's *The Same Jesus: A Contemporary Christology* (Chicago: Loyola University Press, 1986); "Human Solidarity and Collective Union in Christ," *Anglican Theological Review* 70 (1988) 34–59; "Jesus' Humanity and Human Salvation," *Worship* 63 (1989) 429–46; and Roch Kereszty's "Psychological Subject and Consciousness in Christ," *Communio* 11:3 (Fall 1984) 258–77.

something beyond what is accessible to the senses and which cannot be confined to sensible limitation. We would also be speaking of a form of praxis that makes us more and more into what we intend and choose.

In calling for an incarnational spirituality I believe this category, too, must be expanded. Just as incarnateness can be spoken of philosophically, psychologically, and physiologically as an "at homeness" in flesh, so sacramentality must be understood as the celebration of the transforming impact self-transcending humanness can have on another. Certain human activity signs to us an authenticity that is deeply moving. Even in the most dehumanized situation such activity causes a leap of the heart in those not blinded by the situation. The recognition of this sensible experience as a cause of exhilaration has a transformative power to bring about further authentic humanness. What I am calling the sacramental principle here is the activation of what might be a form of moral conversion in another, even one who is considered "irreligious."

In the Flannery O'Connor short story, "A Good Man Is Hard to Find," the escaped convict Misfit experiences a sacramental moment when the old lady he is about to shoot reaches out, touches his face gently, and exclaims, "Why, you look just like my own son!" He recoils and kills her, but as his buddies, who have killed the rest of the southern family, make a remark about the good "fun" they have had that day, Misfit can only mumble that all the "fun" has gone out of it for him. Raw evil has suddenly gone sour in him as a result of the old woman's touch and words. He might try to do business as usual, but he has been changed by her.

To shift slightly to the inner core of what I am designating as the sacramental principle here, it may be helpful to return once again to the religious context that is the source of its meaning. As we have found in the Incarnate Word the paradigm for the principle of incarnateness, so I believe we can find there the key to how sacramentality works.

Sacraments are "givens" in the Catholic community. The word always connotes the ritual. What I am suggesting is that the ritual be regarded as the tip of the sacramental iceberg, the larger portion hidden beneath the direct sensible surface. It is not inaccurate, I think, to begin with the very person of Jesus as a sacramental reality in himself.[9] By this I mean he was an inclusive welcoming person. He was a strengthening person. He was a nurturer of others. He forgave. He healed. He manifested leadership. He was a lover par excellence. All of these are ways of being who he was. He

---

[9]This is the approach taken by Edward Schillebeeckx, O.P., in *Christ the Sacrament of the Encounter with God* (New York: Sheed & Ward, 1963).

acted out of the way he was. What he did prompted change in others. They began to regard themselves differently. The little community of disciples he left behind wanted intently to be "Jesus' People." They wanted to do what he did. Eventually they externally ritualized what he had done. His inclusive welcoming became the "sacrament" of baptism. His strengthening continued in what came to be called confirmation. His nurturing continued in the Eucharist. His forgiving becomes visible in reconciliation. His healing compassion is signed in anointing. The fact that he led and shepherded others was externalized in orders. His unbelievable love is signed to us by faithful married couples.

What is of importance here is to note that a good part of the sacramental reality is not ritualized but is still very real and transformative. It is this grounding in existential living that many of our people have lost. As a result, sacramental ritual is often empty, disconnected from life.

It is my conviction that the expanding of the notion of sacramentality to its core meaning beneath the ritual meaning can be very fruitful to integrate life for those who are not theologically educated. In addition, the impact this notion might have in interreligious dialogue has yet to be explored. It brings with it the challenge to name what is really going on in other traditions as transformative.

The Meaning of "Expressed Communalness"

This third principle of an incarnational spirituality unites two notions: that of visibility, and that of a "we" consciousness in contrast to a "me" consciousness. I am referring to a quality of life that is visibly relational.

It is not difficult to note how expressed communalness flows from being at home in one's own flesh and signing this to others. Being visibly relational follows upon the principles of genuine incarnateness and sacramentality. Without this third principle, both incarnateness and sacramentality might be construed as personal pietism. This third principle leaves no doubt that true human longing is communal and relational. It manifests a two-fold desire: the desire for intimacy with the divine, and the desire for intimacy with other human beings. These are not two distinct directions or communions. The incarnate principle reveals the holy housed in matter. The sacramental principle identifies matter as the locus for transformation. This third principle reveals that the liberation of this longing goes on among *us*. It is something in common, a *common* transformation either entered into or refused.

Nowhere is this unfolded with more delicacy than in the final chapter of Sebastian's *Jesus the Liberator of Desire*. Hidden under the title "A Paradigm Shift in Contemporary Psychology," Sebastian captures what I intend by positing this third principle of an authentic incarnational spirituality, an expressive communalness.

Noting that the baby will cease feeding when its attention is grasped by something colorful, Sebastian turns human self-perception inside out.

> I am not a monad, seeking to keep comfortable and to survive. *I am a relatedness all around, seeking to actualize more and more, to go out more and more, . . .* (118) (Emphasis added.)

Giving credit for this reversal to Lonergan's insights, Sebastian goes on:

> to say that desire is for my relatedness to the world to become actual is to say something new about desire and to say something new about knowing. It is to connect desire with coming-to-know, and it is to connect knowing with desire. (119) . . . the opposition we take for granted between desiring and knowing . . . is false. With this, a flood of dammed-up energy is released. The deep split in our culture between head and heart begins to mend. Knowing is different—it is desire coming to fulfillment. Desire is different—it stretches out to know. (120)

In these few lines the theme that has woven its way through Sebastian's writings swells into a coda.

> I am a total relatedness waiting and wanting to be realized. . . . I am totally connected up without my appreciating all this connectedness. . . . *desire* is for the actualizing of our relatedness. (120)

The book ends with a sonnet which Sebastian suggests is the "etymology of *desiderium:*"

> Desire to know even as I am known:
> That *is* desire, creation coming conscious,
> Amoeba growing out to all, its own,
> The maggot Israel illustrious.
>
> The infant interrupts the flow of warm
> Milk to observe a change in the world scene:
> Eyes opening, lips parted to the charm,
> Islands of ecstasy where we have been.

Desire is to relax into what is,
The unknown knowing one, the dance in three,
Heart of the universe and open kiss
Opens our private worlds so we are we.

Desire indeed is the desire to know,
For we are known, and into this we grow. (121–2)

Sebastian is very clear to note that in this, healing pleasure and desire are not opposed. I suggest he is opening for us a way to begin to understand what really happens in moral conversion. It is the movement from what merely satisfies to what is the long-term good. At first glance this can be understood as opposition. But a closer attentiveness shows this not to be necessarily so.

The healing of bias in us opens us to new value. Liberation brings a new sense of what is worthwhile. We no longer have a "taste" for what satisfied us before. The good now becomes satisfying, the flow of desire now released toward its goal. The long-term good now involves us, not just me. The connections, the relatedness that was hidden now comes into awareness. This is a new positioning, a new and fuller "at homeness." No longer is it just the enfleshment that is my bodiliness, it is a communalness with all that is within my awareness. It is expressive first simply by my way of being. I am "present" in a new way wherever I am. Eventually my speech will happily betray it, and my silence, and my choices.

In these three incarnational principles of incarnateness, sacramentality, and expressive communalness, I suggest we have a glimpse of the fruit of three forms of healing: in psychic conversion the healing of an image-censorship that prevents incarnateness, the effect of personal healing on another in what I have called sacramentality, and a third healing, again personal, that reveals the reality of relatedness and the illusion of isolation.

Admitting this to be so, of what value is it? Is it merely to comfort us in our own Christian camp? Is Sebastian's Jesus, liberator of desire, just our Jesus? Do we clutch him to our breasts and grieve for the rest of the world, or do we have in these three principles of an incarnate spirituality the core of the liberation of desire for *all* peoples?

Stirred Up by Desire: Global Implications

In this final section I would like to bring this reflection on the search for an incarnational spirituality, and Sebastian's contribution to this search, to the threshold of where I think it has to go. We can only stand in the doorway, as it were, but even that, I believe, is filled with promise.

In chapter eleven of *Method,* Bernard Lonergan writes of theological categories that are general and specific. He maintains that the core of both of these types of categories is transcultural (284). I suggest that the work that Sebastian has been about, and the type of depth probing of certain familiar categories from the Christian tradition which we have named "incarnateness," "sacramentality," and "expressive communality," have something to do with making that core systematically explicit.

We enter the company of those who walk in other faith traditions clothed in our own specific Christian theological categories. We can do no other. These categories are the images, symbols, and thought constructs that come from our religious experience of the holy in Christ Jesus. For Christians, God has come to meet us in Christ Jesus. Rather than maintaining that basic fact as an exclusive enclosure, we have need to go to the depths of its core, and ask how the experience of the holy-in-the-human, our distinct experience in Christ Jesus, is common. Thus our push from the more familiar theological terms *incarnate, sacrament,* and *community,* to a more philosophical understanding of these terms anthropologically.

Once we have entered the anthropological realm, we are in company with Sebastian, and we are entering the realm of Lonergan's general theological categories. These are categories that theology shares in common with other disciplines. For Sebastian, this means such realities as intimacy, loneliness, loss, relatedness, ego-centeredness, and insight. These, too, are entered into by the Christian with the concreteness of Christian presuppositions on what the human is. Again, these presuppositions, usually undeclared, cannot be left behind. But core to them are the human operations, revealed through interiority analysis.

We now have two elements of the core: the *special* theological category of the experience of the holy, and the *general* theological category of the human operations. It is this two-dimensioned core that Lonergan maintains is transcultural.

What this implies is that what is true in distinctly Catholic Christian terms just may have meaning transculturally in its core, and this transcultural meaning needs to be teased out. This is just what this brief paper has attempted to begin with the Christian categories of incarnateness, sacramentality, and expressive communalness. Yet it is but a beginning. Perhaps the time has come for a systematic explanation of the Church's constant prayer: "I am the savior of all . . . says the Lord." We can no longer avoid the burning question, "How is this so?"

Conclusion

This essay has attempted to flesh out systematically what Sebastian Moore, the man "stirred up by desire," has been about for some time. It has asserted that Sebastian is onto elements vital to an integrated incarnational spirituality, and has specified three hallmarks of such a spirituality: incarnateness, sacramentality, and expressive communalness. I have suggested that what was attempted here is but an attempt to work with the general and special theological categories that Bernard Lonergan maintains are transcultural at their core, and only at their core, thus protecting the specific cultural differences that form the distinct religious contexts of the peoples of the world. Finally, I have suggested that this approach, which I believe Sebastian exemplifies, opens the way to the inter-religious dialogue which faces the Church in the new millennium. We are fortunate to have his good company.

— 11 —

Surviving Slander with Richard Rolle

Elisabeth Koenig

In *The Crucified Jesus Is No Stranger,* Sebastian Moore poses the question, "How is the crucifixion of Jesus salvific?" Following the method of Bernard Lonergan, his answer depends on ascertaining what the story of Jesus, crucified and risen, means in terms of human self-awareness. Moore's later work, *Jesus the Liberator of Desire,* continues this project with important conclusions both for theology and psychology.[1]

The Crucified Jesus Is No Stranger centers on how the crucifixion of Jesus is "the central drama of man's refusal of his true self." Moore sees in the crucifixion "all the evil in [the believer's] life becoming *explicit* as the wilful destruction of his true self now concrete for him in the man on the cross." It involves a refusal of "some fulness of life to which God is impelling us and which our whole being dreads."

Later, Moore gives as an example from daily life the way the unconscious dynamics of transference and counter-transference contribute to this refusal:

> By "transference" I put my guilt, my self-hatred, into you. Once you pick this up and start reacting, once, that is, you unwittingly let my transference

[1]Sebastian Moore, *The Crucified Jesus Is No Stranger* (Minneapolis: Seabury Press, 1977). The material I quote is on pages x and 26. See also Moore's *Jesus the Liberator of Desire* (New York: Crossroad, 1989). For amplification of Moore's (and others') recourse to psychology for theological understanding, see John McDargh, "Theological Uses of Psychology: Retrospective and Prospective," *Horizons* 12:2 (1985) especially 261–3.

become in you a "counter-transference," you are backing me up in my flight-from-self. This means that reality, your reality, some reality other than myself, is backing me up in my flight-from-self. (The making of you guilty and wretched *is* my flight-from-self in action. It is not merely the consequence of my flight. It *is* it. *You* are where I am running to from myself.)

The fourteenth-century English mystic Richard Rolle comments on a similar dynamic in those frequent passages when he writes of the problem of persecution, slander, and backbiting in his *The Fire of Love*.[2] There are several reasons why I want to consider his life and his writing in the context of a *Festschrift* for Sebastian Moore. Moore's insights into the nature of the flight from the true self are fed, in part, by twentieth-century psychoanalytic theory. Obviously, Rolle had no such theory to guide his perceptions. But his predilection for both solitude and silence made him (sometimes!) a detached observer of human strengths and weaknesses. As he grew in his experience of God's love through a fixed gaze on Jesus Christ, he became increasingly aware of more positive possibilities for human living. In particular, he learned that self-knowledge, which includes humble acceptance of one's sinfulness and weakness, is only possible when one has ceased all gossip, backbiting, and argumentation. Moreover, such self-knowledge is the only occasion for the profoundest realization of God's love.

Why turn to Rolle, a hermit and a mystic, for theological and psychological insight? As we shall see, in his own time his personality was problematic, not only to himself, but also to other people. He was marginal both to his culture and to the Church. But, for a number of reasons, I believe many things beneficial both to human interaction and understanding how God helps Christians can be learned from Rolle and mystics who resemble him.

I think mystics are people who, in the context of their social systems, whether they be families, neighborhoods, towns, or other communities, are unusually sensitive and permeable to the negative affects of the emotional systems of which they are a part. Thus, they are (unconsciously) assigned (by others in the system) the role of psychic bearer of those negative affects.[3] Hence the mystics' preoccupation with purgation and "cleanness."

---

[2]Richard Rolle, *The Fire of Love*, trans. Clifton Wolters (London: Harmondsworth: Penguin, 1972).

[3]My source for systems theory is Murray Bowen, *Family Therapy in Clinical Practice* (New York: Jason Aronson, 1978). For an excellent introduction to and summary of this approach, see Michael Kerr, "Chronic Anxiety and Defining a Self," *Atlantic Monthly* (September 1988) 45–58. And for an intriguing integration of the theory with theological

In a sense, they are "experts" with regard to psychic contamination and its remedies. They have suffered its painful effects, have been driven to seek God and Christ through withdrawal from society and extreme forms of piety, and, consequently, have learned a good deal about what it means to be "made whole" and "clean" in God.

Rolle's profound observations, both of other people and of his own in-most feeling responses to their behavior and to God's love as he discovered it in prayer, can be instructive on several counts. For example, most people these days know about projection and transference, but they do not know how to handle things either when they are caught in the grip of a negative transference they are unconsciously making onto another person, or when they are the object of someone else's projected hate. Richard Rolle, al-though twentieth-century psychoanalytic categories would, of course, be utterly foreign to him, nevertheless seems to have had uncommon insight into what Moore calls the flight from the true self through projection of one's own dark contents onto another. He also found himself undergoing a profound change in affect and orientation through his experience of God in contemplative prayer. Could we go so far as to say that Rolle's compul-sive search and discovery of God as Love had the effect, in the language of psychoanalytic object relations theory, of changing a persecutory inner ob-ject into a good object?[4]

While mindful of the pitfalls of doing psycho-history, I think, never-theless, that there is evidence in Richard Rolle's *The Fire of Love* to suggest that he wrestled with emotional issues stemming from his interaction with others that are similar to those that twentieth-century people (and probably

---

concerns, see Leander S. Harding, Jr., "A Unique and Final Work: The Atonement as a Saving Act of Transformative Obedience," *Journal of Ecumenical Studies*, 24:1 (1987) 80–92.

[4]Object relations theory emphasizes the role played by internalized (or introjected) in-teractions with others, especially early caretakers, as determinative of inner psychodynam-ics and interactions with others later in life, as well. An excellent introduction to the object relations school of analysis is Jay R. Greenberg and Stephen A. Mitchell, *Object Relations in Psychoanalytic Theory* (Cambridge, Mass.: Harvard University Press, 1983). Their chap-ter on the Scottish psychoanalyst W.R.D. Fairbairn (who had some early theological train-ing) is especially suggestive for the concerns of this article. See also John D. Sutherland, *Fairbairn's Journey into the Interior* (London: Free Association Books, 1989). Another source that illuminates some of Rolle's preoccupations is Jeffrey Seinfeld, *The Bad Object: Handling the Negative Therapeutic Reaction in Psychotherapy* (Northvale, N.J.: Jason Aronson, 1990). And, finally, for the use of object relations theory for understanding emo-tional systems, see David E. Scharff and Jill Savege Scharff, *Object Relations Family Therapy* (Northvale, N.J.: Jason Aronson Inc., 1987).

people from all ages) have experienced.[5] Moreover, his highly intentional dedication to prayer enabled him to acquire insight into the nature of life lived in the presence of God's love that is not reserved for mystics alone, but has application to every Christian believer's need for God, especially given the vicissitudes of life in community.

Although Richard Rolle (c. 1300–1349) was popular enough to be considered for sainthood (an Office of lessons and antiphons was written in the 1380s in the unsuccessful effort to have him canonized), not very much is known about his life.[6] We know he was a hermit who frequently changed his abode and that he lived in rural Yorkshire in the early fourteenth century. He had attended Oxford, but he left without earning a degree, and he may have studied at the Sorbonne as well. His popularity persisted after his death (which may have been from the Black Plague). In fact, there was a cult dedicated to Richard Rolle that thrived in the north of England for nearly two hundred years.

Sometimes referred to as "the Father of English Prose," Rolle was the first English mystic to write in English rather than Latin. *The Fire of Love (Incendium Amoris),* the focus of the present study, was, however, written in Latin, as were others of his finest works, including *Melos Amoris, Judica Me Deus,* and *Contra Amatores Mundi.* He wrote out of concern for people to whom he gave spiritual direction. Many of them were women, an interesting fact given that Rolle seems to have had a highly conflicted relationship with women early in life. *The Fire of Love* includes stories of incendiary encounters with three women whom Rolle thinks to have been justified in their attacks on him. Later, his attitude seems to have become one of tender concern.[7]

The occasion for writing *The Fire of Love* was Rolle's experience of being on fire with God's love. He had become so hot that he had to run "his hand over his chest to see if he were actually on fire."[8] The whole book is an explanation and defense of this phenomenon. Rolle's preferred way to pray was "sitting," and he seems to have spent long hours sitting in various

---

[5]An excellent article that treats both inappropriate and appropriate approaches to psychohistory, and makes useful proposals to assure the latter, is Thomas Kohut, "Psychohistory as History," *American Historical Review* 91:2 (1986) 336–54.

[6]Rosamund S. Allen, "Introduction" to *Richard Rolle: The English Writings* (New York: Paulist Press, 1988) 9.

[7]The significance of Rolle's changed attitude toward women is amply discussed in Ann Astell, "Feminine *Figurae* in the Writings of Richard Rolle: A Register of Growth," *Mystics Quarterly* 15:3 (1989) 117–24.

[8]Rolle, *The Fire of Love,* 9.

hermitages and chapels. During these sessions, he would experience not only heat, but also "sweetness" from God and "song." He heard the songs of angels, and, in addition, sang inwardly his own secret songs to Jesus.

Although the book is about the love of God experienced as fire, Rolle makes it clear throughout that his intense and single-minded pursuit of God's love was frequently the occasion for persecution from other people. No doubt, his behavior was often provocative, as he himself indicates on several occasions. Usually, in *The Fire of Love,* he does not reveal the specific details of situations in which people slandered and reviled him. There are no names or places mentioned. But he raises the issue often enough to let the reader know that it was definitely a concern of his and one that compelled him to seek God and to "hold on" to God in prayer.[9] Perhaps we could go so far as to say that persecution was the crucible in which he came to experience that "fire of love."

From the scant details that we have about his life, we know that Rolle did experience uncommon difficulty with other people. Rosamund S. Allen points out that he "could be severe (on himself as much as others) to the point of violence, and this is sometimes apparent in his writing."[10] On his first attempt to become a hermit, he asks his sister to meet him in a woods and bring him two of her tunics, causing her to exclaim that he had gone mad. "There, he . . . vandalized both garments, ripping the sleeves from the gray and the buttons from the white tunic, and . . . then scandalized his sister by dressing up in them, wearing the white next to his skin and the now sleeveless gray tunic over it, completing the ensemble with his father's rain-hood as a cowl."[11]

Rolle also probably disappointed his parents and his patron when he left Oxford without a degree, choosing instead to become a hermit. Later, when his patron, John de Dalton, gave a feast and invited Rolle, the latter could not be found. Eventually, he was located "in a certain 'broken-down old house' or 'room' . . . . he was persuaded to join the feast, ate in silence, tried to retire before the trestle tables on which the meal was served were taken down (a signal for dancing to begin) and was then detained by Dalton and asked details of himself."[12]

---

[9]In medieval mystical literature, this idea of adhering to God in prayer is expressed in a rich and ample vocabulary of technical terms. See Wolfgang Riehle, *The Middle English Mystics* (London: Routledge & Kegan Paul, 1981). His "Middle English Word Index" offers such terms as "adhere," "biholden," "drawen nere," "fastnen," "holden," and "hongen."

[10]Rosamund Allen, "Introduction," 10.

[11]Ibid.

[12]Ibid.

Clearly, Rolle distinguished himself by questioning the faddish preoccupations of his age, including "courtly love, chivalry, and the upward mobility of the developing middle class,"[13] and by his need to be alone. He was especially opposed to the seeking of worldly honor in whatever form it took, whether it were academic prowess, clerical status, opulent clothing, or spiritual heroics.[14] Often he writes of his "many enemies" and of the way in which those who had supported him had now become his greatest opponents.[15] He changes his abode frequently, noting that his way of life made it impossible for him to continue in friendship with people who no longer understood him.

The problem is not just that others judge Rolle harshly and persecute him. Probably more important for a grasp of what his emotional life was like is the fact that he also criticized other people quite vociferously. This is not at all surprising from a psychological point of view, given what we know about patterns of abuse in emotional systems. Some passages from Rolle's texts are among the most hotly misogynist in the Middle Ages (although he later came to love women and to care for them with great dedication). He belittled academic theologians, clerics, and monks, without really having tested for himself the vocation of any of them. Often he seems to be caught in a mechanism of invalidation that causes him to berate others while at the same time being the object of their attempts to discredit his vocation and his lifestyle.

Now I would like to shift focus to the actual text of *The Fire of Love*. What is the God like whom Rolle finds in his long hours of sitting? What effect does Rolle's experience of God's love have on his being the object of slander? What does he learn about people who feel compelled to engage in backbiting? What are the antidotes to it and what offers protection? What in Rolle is transformed through his experience of God's love in prayer, and what does this transformation enable him to see?

The "Prologue" to *The Fire of Love* starts with Rolle's description of his experience of God's love:

---

[13]Ibid., 20.

[14]For a clarifying discussion of how Teresa of Avila distances herself, but also makes use of the attitude toward honor prevalent in sixteenth-century Spain, see Rowan Williams, *Teresa of Avila* (Harrisburg, Penn.: Morehouse Publishing, 1991) especially 18–26, but throughout this magnificent book. The concerns of fourteenth-century England and those of Spain in the sixteenth century differ, of course, but I think there is enough similarity between Rolle's struggles and Teresa's that they can be mutually illuminating.

[15]Allen, "Introduction," 11.

I cannot tell you how surprised I was the first time I felt my heart begin to warm. It was real warmth too, not imaginary, and it felt as if it were actually on fire . . . [it] brought great and unexpected comfort . . . once I realized that it . . . was the gift of my Maker, I was absolutely delighted, and wanted my love to be even greater.[16]

Rolle soon learns that he cannot live heedlessly and still expect this experience to come: "But this eternal and overflowing love does not come when I am relaxing, nor do I feel this spiritual ardour when I am tired out after travelling; nor is it when I am absorbed with worldly interests, or engrossed in never ending arguments . . . ."[17]

At those times, Rolle says, he grows cold. He must make a real effort to stand in his Savior's presence. Only then can he abide in that inner warmth. But what makes it altogether impossible for God's warmth to come is every expression of untruth regarding oneself and every abuse of power. For example, people "who [lord] it over other people" will never become "masters of contemplative love."[18] Nor will those who "dare presume or boast about [their] prowess."[19] What is more, the whole process of being either "belittled" or "praised" by other "men" Rolle labels "madness." Knowledge of oneself as one is before God is the only remedy:

If he has a good look at himself, and takes the trouble to learn what sort of man he is in thought and deed, he will find out soon enough, and discover whether he is deserving of praise or blame. And when he sees that in many things he is blameworthy, and laudable only in few, he is not going lightheartedly to accept the honour and favour which he does not deserve—not unless he is mentally deranged.[20]

In this context begin Rolle's many references to the necessity of humility for there to be any experience of "the sweetness and delight of heaven."[21] For

---

[16]Rolle, *The Fire of Love,* 45.

[17]Ibid., 46.

[18]Ibid., 54.

[19]Ibid., 56.

[20]Ibid., 72.

[21]In this Rolle is, of course, participating in a centuries-long tradition regarding the virtue of humility. See Mary T. Clark, trans., "Confessions," Book 7, Chap. 20, in *Augustine of Hippo: Selected Writings* (New York: Paulist Press, 1984) 77, but other references in the index to humility, as well. Roberta C. Bondi offers a very gentle introduction to the concept in the Fathers in *To Love as God Loves* (Philadelphia: Fortress Press, 1987) Chap. 3. Etienne Gilson discusses humility in *The Christian Philosophy of Thomas Aquinas*

Rolle, it is especially important to maintain an attitude of humility when abuses come: "let him not defend himself when contempt and insults and obloquy are heaped upon him. He must not return an evil word for evil, but accept everything with equanimity: praise and insult alike."[22]

In our time, and certainly in Rolle's own time of knighthood, chivalry, and upward mobility when honor was fiercely defended, such advice sounds like making oneself a rug for everyone to walk on. But I think there is evidence in Rolle's text that he had experienced a deeper psychological and spiritual result (that was not simple repression of anger) from this exercise of humility. He seems to be differentiating himself from entangling arguments, whether they take place between himself and other people, or in his own subjectivity with inner persecutory voices.

For example, in one place Rolle talks about "conceited and touchy people who consider themselves so magnificent as to be beyond any possibility of suffering." He goes on to say, "It is better to avoid them rather than argue with them because they never let go. They defend whatever position they take up, however false or wrong it may be."[23]

By his avoidance of them and his unwillingness to pick up the other end of their tug-of-war rope, Rolle indicates that he has learned the beginning of detachment. Humility, moreover, becomes almost a magic antidote to the onslaughts of envious detractors. In fact, Rolle will go so far as to say that the person "who perseveres in loving God and his neighbour, and yet in his humility and self-knowledge reckons himself to be of no value and inferior to others, will conquer his enemies, have a confident hope in the love of the great Judge, and when he passes from the light of this world be received by angels into eternal joy."[24]

Apparently, for Rolle (and for other people) the practice of humility had the effect of stopping inwardly, at first artificially, but later really, the part of the personality that "splits" off one's own undesirable traits in the projective mechanism that infinitely searches out other people's faults, and grapples with their objections to one, or their failures to understand one's vocation: "Humble men do not look at other people's sins but at their own, nor do they praise their own good deeds but those of others."[25]

(New York: Random House, 1956) 343–4. And Rowan Williams's *Teresa of Avila* offers good insight into this virtue.

[22]Rolle, *The Fire of Love,* 56.

[23]Ibid., 70.

[24]Ibid., 133.

[25]Ibid., 126.

Rolle learned that the consequence of this is that one will be freed from arguments (both those with external detractors and those endless subjective dialogues with inner persecutory voices) to pursue instead one's love for Christ, and that that will have the most wholesome possible effect.

He further seems to acknowledge that persecution may be exactly what is needed if the soul is to become whole in God: "If you yourself are going through persecution or wretchedness or misery, you are experiencing what is exactly right for your present circumstances."[26]

Rolle thinks it inappropriate to hold out for joy at all costs when it is so obvious that Christ and his disciples suffered. He goes on to say that it "will be essential for us to be cleansed by tribulation, sickness, and grief."[27] At another point, Rolle's reaction to persecution is so contrary to expectation that one could imagine him actually pursuing it for the sake of his spiritual growth: "I know this: the more men have been furious with me with their denigrations, the more have I advanced in spiritual growth."[28]

There are many reasons why it is a good thing to learn humility in this life. Rolle disciplined himself to turn to God in prayer, instead of fighting back when people insulted him. What he learned was that "to be despised or to be made a fool of in front of others helps a man rise to the joy of the angels!"[29] For this reason, he counsels people to recognize that, for the sake of their experience of God, "an insult is better than honour, confusion than success, grief than glory." The person who "learns to face all these difficulties with patience will learn humility in this life."

> For before we can arrive at the court of the King . . . we must ourselves be proved here below, whether it is by flattery or detraction, by blandishment or backbiting, by praise or calumny.[30]

In spite of his attempt to lead the hermit's life Rolle is apparently surrounded by people who are far from humble, and their lack of humility clearly has made it very difficult for him to practice humility himself.

---

[26]Ibid., 67.

[27]Ibid.

[28]Ibid., 92. See also Nathan Schwartz-Salant, "Patriarchy in Transformation: Judaic, Christian, and Clinical Perspectives," in Murray Stein and Robert L. Moore, eds., *Jung's Challenge to Contemporary Religion* (Wilmette, Ill.: Chiron Publications, 1987) 41–72. Schwartz-Salant (following M. Eigen) argues that intense persecutory anxieties can be beneficial in the sense that they can have the effect of dissolving psychic containers so that new forms may emerge (42).

[29]Ibid., 69.

[30]Ibid., 70.

Frequently he uses angry, hostile words to characterize those whose motives he doubts or people who have questioned his vocation:

> Shame on [those who are consumed with a desire for knowledge]! An old woman can be more expert in the love of God—and less worldly too—than your theologian with his useless studying. He does it for vanity, to get a reputation, to obtain stipends and official positions. Such a fellow ought to be entitled not "Doctor" but "Fool"![31]

Even today (!) we know academics whose studies probably are ordered more for their own ego-aggrandizement than they are for the advance of knowledge. Were *all* the theologians Rolle met at Oxford (and possibly the Sorbonne) of this type, or is his indignation mixed with anger at himself for failing to complete his studies?

Rolle seems to have engendered tension and anxiety in people wherever he went, because they so often either try to dominate or seduce him with flattery, or belittle him with denigration: "For many of those who used to speak with me were like scorpions: with their head they oozed flattery, and with their tail they struck slanders."[32]

There were other people whose responses to Rolle, apparently, were not so extreme, but he nevertheless felt the need to leave them at the least hint of criticism. He was behaving in the same manner that many other people who carry persecutory inner objects have behaved:

> There are many from whom I have parted, not because they fed me ill or badly, but because our ways of life were not compatible, or for some other adequate reason. Yet I venture to say with blessed Job, "Fools did despise me, and when I parted from them they turned against me." Nevertheless those who said I was not willing to stay in any place where I was not comfortably fed will blush when they see me . . . fasting.[33]

This passage and others like it can give the impression that Rolle indulges himself in his sensitivity, as if, perhaps, to say, "I have special needs because of my great sensitivity"; "I can't be expected to put up with the behaviour/taste/conversation of people like that."[34] An external observer who could not hear the obsessive grind of persecutory inner voices (or take se-

---

[31]Ibid., 61.

[32]Ibid., 72.

[33]Ibid., 78.

[34]Williams, *Teresa of Avila,* 116. Williams argues here that people should not use self-knowledge "as a weapon or defense against others." I would agree, but maintain that people

riously their destructive force) in a person like Rolle might believe that he was self-indulgent. My own tendency is to believe that he is handling his very problematic emotions and other people's very problematic responses to him in the best way he knows.

For example, Rolle indicates that earlier he had tried to tolerate (what we would call) people's projections and manipulations, but what he discovered was that some people are genuinely evil and to spend time with them is to be poisoned:

> And I used to listen to that kind of flattery which all too often can drag the most doughty warriors from their heights down to hell itself. . . . Evil men spoke evil things. . . . Lift the lid of the pan, and there is only stink! Those who speak evil speak out of the abundance of their heart and there lurks the poison of asps![35]

Rolle experienced what all people experience who are consciously differentiating from emotional systems, i.e., that others who are still stuck in the undifferentiated mass of negative emotion strive (unconsciously) to draw the person who is discovering her/his own freedom and creativity back into the morass:

> Sometimes people vilify us because we are too happy. . . . Therefore we have got to be sensible and take special care not to put ourselves into a position where we could unwittingly be a possible cause of evil.[36]

> I myself fled to the wilderness when it proved no longer possible to live harmoniously with men, who, admittedly, were a frequent obstacle to my inner joy. Because I did not do the kind of things they did, they attributed waywardness and bad temper to me. But when I found trouble and heaviness, I called on the name of the Lord.[37]

Rolle had learned that often it is better to withdraw from people who are not interested in spiritual growth, because their only option when confronted with a person who (I would say) is becoming differentiated through a conscious relation to God is to behave destructively:

---

like Rolle, with not only great sensitivity, but also extreme porousness to the toxic affects in emotional systems do have special needs and do need to protect themselves at times.

[35]Rolle, *The Fire of Love,* 92.
[36]Ibid., 120.
[37]Ibid., 128.

> I fancy the reason they grumble and grouse is that they want those who are better than themselves to come down to their level and so conform to their inferiors. These people think they are superior when in fact they are less![38] Humble men do not look at other people's sins but at their own, nor do they praise their own good deeds but those of others.[39]

Although Rolle's observation about these people's motivation is probably correct, his language here belies his own propensity for pride.

Jealousy and envy are particularly problematic emotions for people whose childhood needs to be affirmed, mirrored, and accepted were never met.[40] Rolle seems to be preoccupied with these issues himself, because he so frequently comments on them when he sees them in other people:

> As a matter of fact no one is ever jealous unless he is in truth less than the larger size he thinks himself to be. Such a man will heap insults on people lest they should seem equal to himself. But if anyone is said to be more important, beautiful, or strong, he at once becomes terribly jealous and dejected. But a soul which has been kindled however slightly by the fire of the eternal vision does not look for empty glory and passing praise. It is obvious that men who backbite and are envious of each other do so because they have no love for God—unlike God's elect. Where they are who love God, there too are men as eager for the good of their fellows as they are for themselves. So if you want to love God supremely, learn to abominate all earthly praise. For Christ's sake embrace the contempt of man and his mockery—and brace your mind for the everlasting sequel![41]

This passage not only includes an astute observation of the motivation behind backbiting (jealousy and envy), but it also introduces the discovery that brought continual delight to Rolle, i.e., that the person whose attention is fixed on Christ and his love can be free from both contempt and praise. In fact, the person who knows God's love seems to be able to take into her/himself ("embrace for Christ's sake") the toxic psychic material other people are putting out, neutralize it, and transform it into love. "They may curse, but you bless," Rolle says.[42]

---

[38]Ibid., 141.

[39]Ibid., 126.

[40]The classic source for contemporary understanding of narcissistic personality disorder, and the issues mentioned in this paragraph, is Heinz Kohut, *The Analysis of the Self* (New York: International Universities Press, 1971).

[41]Rolle, *The Fire of Love,* 134.

[42]Ibid., 96.

Rolle's account never gives the impression that this is either easy or automatically continual. "To acquire contemplation means much time and hard work." Moreover, even though the "unspeakable joy" that comes with it makes it much to be desired, "it is not given to anyone, anytime, anyhow."[43] Most important, to all those who would say that Rolle was currying God's favor, attempting to earn love by ascetic discipline, he would respond, "It is not within man's power to achieve it [i.e., contemplation], and however great his efforts they will be inadequate."[44]

Even though Rolle would not classify himself as Pelagian, he has cultivated glimpses of what it would be like ever to live in love rather than hate. To him this has much to do with a certain "stability of mind"[45] that comes to people who have learned to "hold on to God with love."[46] Finally, they are given respite from "hateful confusion" and "stupid thoughts."[47] Ultimately, the contemplative who "holds on to God" in the midst of slanderous assaults will know peace: "The peace known by lovers of Christ comes from their heart being fixed, in longing and in thought, in the love of God; it is a peace that sings and loves and burns and contemplates."[48] This experience frees one not only from suffering the wounds of backbiting, but also from the compulsion to condemn other people for their sins: "The man who lives a holy and righteous life is not going to despise sinners however bad."[49]

Rolle knows that his experience of God's love has brought about a profound transformation in his soul: "My disposition has been changed. Such are my affections now that it is nothing but sin I hate, none but God I fear to offend, nothing but God in which I rejoice."[50] He has discovered love's nature: It is diffusive, unifying, and transforming:

> It is diffusive when it flows out and sheds the rays of its goodness not merely on friends and neighbours, but on enemies and strangers as well. It unites because it makes lovers one in deed and will, and draws into one Christ and every holy soul. He who holds on to God is one in spirit with him, not by nature, but by grace and identity of will. Love has also the power of transforming, for it transforms the lover into his Beloved, and makes him dwell in him.[51]

---

[43]Ibid., 143.
[44]Ibid.
[45]Ibid., 107.
[46]Ibid., 152, and Riehle, *The Middle English Mystics.*
[47]Ibid., 156.
[48]Ibid., 76.
[49]Ibid., 80.
[50]Ibid., 81.
[51]Ibid., 101.

Given what today's analysts of social systems say about the desirability of emotional differentiation for the health of everyone, it is interesting to observe how Rolle's relationships with other people become changed after he has "held on" to God for some time in prayer. He no longer seeks out people to solve his problems: "not only does [he who delights himself in Christ's love] not seek human solace, but [he] even flees from it most strenuously, as if it were smoke hurting his eyes."[52] Although this may sound too "ruggedly-individualist" to contemporary people who are trying to bring about stronger appreciation for life in community,[53] I think Rolle's discovery of wholeness in God is important even given that concern. There is a quality of robust, mature emotionality emerging in Rolle's account of himself that, were it prevalent in communities today, could only encourage everyone's health.

In a poem he inserts toward the end of *The Fire of Love*, Rolle makes the effect of transforming love on the quality of his relationships even more explicit:

> See, my inmost being is in ferment, and the flame of charity has consumed the hateful confusion of my heart, and eliminated the slimy happiness of unclean friendships, and wiped out the stupid thoughts which were so odious when one honestly looked at them. I have genuinely attained a real love. . . .[54]

What has supplanted those unhealthy ways of relating and thinking is Rolle's dedication to study, always in the context of God's grace:

> My worst detractors have been those I once counted my faithful friends. Yet I did not give up the things which helped my soul because of them, but got on with my study, always with the favour of God. I recalled the scripture which said, "They may curse, but you bless." And in the course of time I was granted growth in spiritual joy.[55]

Rolle has learned sufficient detachment from his detractors that he can pursue knowledge of God's love through his study. I like to imagine how the world would be better if everyone had the grace (and leisure) to pursue a God-given interest. Certainly, such internally-referenced activity would

---

[52]Ibid., 131.
[53]Robert Bellah, et al., *Habits of the Heart* (New York: Perennial Library, 1987).
[54]Rolle, *The Fire of Love*, 156.
[55]Ibid., 92.

supplant the need to meddle in other people's lives, and the whole world-system would be better off.

Does the experience of God's love in contemplative prayer transform and neutralize persecutory inner voices? Does it undo the effects of gossip, backbiting, and slander? By the example of Richard Rolle, probably not completely. The emotional tone of *The Fire of Love* remains, at times, a critical one of indignation at the behavior of detractors. But there is also evidence in the text that Richard Rolle has grown considerably. His certain knowledge, gained through arduous hours of sitting in prayer, that he is beloved of God, has drained his enemies' barbs of some of their power.

Most important, Rolle sees that there is another possibility for human living, one that favors the refreshment of God's bracing call to the "slimy happiness" of emotionally-blended friendships. In the end, he has seen that there is a relationship between compulsive slander and the unwilling-ness to tolerate a person who is becoming whole in God. His experience of God's love empowers him to put all flattery and backbiting in perspective. With clearest vision Rolle sees that his freedom to be who he is before God is more important than any "honor" or denigration the world can bestow.

─ 12 ─

AIDS Ministry as a Praxis of Hope

Robert Doran, S.J.

When I was asked to contribute something to this volume honoring my friend and one-time colleague Sebastian Moore, I was a bit at a loss as to precisely what kind of approach to take. Finally, Vernon Gregson asked me to depart from my usual stuffy systematic and methodological style of writing and to engage in some theological reflection on my experience in ministry in Toronto's AIDS community. "Surely," he said, "Sebastian's work can be drawn upon in such theological reflection, and this kind of piece will probably be more appropriate than another of your speculative flights." At the same time that I was attempting to put together something for this volume, I was preparing a presentation as part of a series of public lectures at Regis College in Toronto on "The Reasons for Our Hope." My presentation was to be on hope and AIDS. Perhaps because I was also mulling over a contribution to this volume, I found myself referring to Sebastian's work at both the beginning and the end of my Regis presentation, so that when it was finished I decided simply to edit it and make it my contribution to the present volume. What follows, then, is the substance of a lecture that I delivered at Regis College on AIDS ministry as a praxis of hope.

I will divide my remarks into three parts. I will open with some theological considerations that I think need to be offered from the outset. Then I will present a narrative of some of my experiences during my first three years ministering in the AIDS community in Toronto, a brief history of my involvement. I will conclude with some further theological reflection on those experiences.

I. Two Theological Considerations

My opening theological considerations are twofold. We are talking about hope, about a ministry of hope, and the source of our hope is the resurrection of Jesus from the dead. So I want to speak first about the meaning of resurrection hope in its twofold aspect as (1) hope for the conquering of death, and (2) hope for our lives together here in our communal history. I will speak about both of these aspects of hope as I see them already being embodied in the AIDS community and as I think the ministry of the Church should try to encourage them.

Second, I will present some considerations of sexuality and especially of the Church's pastoral response to persons of homosexual orientation. This latter topic cannot be sidestepped in any discussion of AIDS or of ministry in the AIDS community, especially in a city like Toronto, and I have made the decision to address it as forthrightly and honestly as I can from the outset.

Resurrection Hope

When the first letter of Peter tells us, "Always be ready to give an account to anyone who asks you about the hope that is in you" (3:15), it is clear that the account is to consist largely in an appeal to the resurrection of Jesus from the dead. The same letter says earlier, "By God's great mercy we have been given a new birth unto a living hope through the resurrection of Jesus Christ from the dead" (1:3). The resurrection event is clearly the source of Christian hope, and the hope that it inspires in us is clearly a hope that death is not the final word on our lives, that, as Bernard Lonergan puts it, the grave has ceased to be the limit of human expectation. As Paul writes in 1 Corinthians, "If for this life only we have hoped in Christ, we are of all people most to be pitied" (15:19). And a few verses later he says, "The last enemy to be destroyed is death" (15:26). And again, "When this perishable body puts on imperishability, and this mortal body puts on immortality, then the saying that is written will be fulfilled: 'Death has been swallowed up in victory'" (15:54).

Now clearly, when we are speaking about hope in a community affected by a life-threatening virus, we are speaking in large part about this dimension of hope: that in the resurrection of Jesus death is overcome for all of us. "As all die in Adam, so all will be made alive in Christ" (1 Cor 15:22). In my experience of ministry in the community affected by HIV-infection and AIDS, there are obviously key and poignant moments when this dimension of our hope becomes the central message that people need and want to hear. In our faith, death is not the final word on our lives. Death is a passage to a new and glorious life in which there is no more pain, no more crying, no more grief, for these former things have passed away. This is a dimension of our faith, an essential aspect of Christian hope, and obviously a central feature in any ministry to persons living with HIV-infection and AIDS. This hope is very much alive in some people living with AIDS, and in others there is the cry, "Help me believe that this is true."

This dimension of hope, however, is not the only aspect of hope present in this community, nor is it the only aspect of hope that someone ministering in this community needs to foster and is called upon to encourage. There are other dimensions of hope that either live in the community or at times need to be stirred into flame. This should not be surprising within a Christian and biblical framework, since the Scriptures, when speaking of the resurrection as source of our hope beyond death, always go on to speak about the implications of such hope for our lives in this world.

Most notable among the other dimensions of hope present in the AIDS community, of course, are the aspects of hope surrounding the medical realities of AIDS: the hope that sooner rather than later the scientists at work trying to develop vaccines and other medications will be successful, the hope that for a given individual the condition of being HIV-positive will be a chronic manageable disease, and so on. These hopes are realistically grounded in many instances, and they are part of the positive and courageous outlook that a person living with HIV and AIDS needs to take on his or her life.

But there is also another hope that is more comprehensive of the ultimate meaning of AIDS, and that includes many features in its embrace. It is the hope of a community that has been profoundly affected by the presence in its midst of a life-threatening virus. It is the hope of a community that has been profoundly affected also by enormous loss and grief. It is the hope of a community that has powerfully united to meet the reality of AIDS. It is the hope that this complex community experience will make a difference in history, that it will change the way people live, that it will not simply be forgotten when AIDS is over, that it will be remembered, that the love AIDS called forth will be forever celebrated, that the community affected by AIDS will be changed for the better by the indelible memory of the way it rose to the occasion in love and service, and that the rest of the world will adopt a new attitude towards this community.

I would like to try to articulate something of what is moving in the AIDS community that gives substance and ground to this hope, and I would like briefly to attempt to relate this hope to the resurrection of Jesus from the dead.

I will draw on two contemporary authors who, at least in some of their work, have been preoccupied with the question, What is the meaning of the resurrection of Jesus from the dead, what is its meaning for our communal lives here in history? For Rosemary Haughton in *The Passionate God,* the answer to this question has something to do with the passionate bodily exchange of human love as the analogue and indeed the locus of God's passionate love for us. She writes at the beginning of this extraordinary book that something happened to *bodies* when Jesus rose from the dead, and the entire book is an attempt to understand just what *did* happen to bodies when Jesus rose from the dead. Her answer has something to do with the release of the body as the carrier of the passionate exchange not only of human love but also of the love between God and us.

Sebastian Moore finds the answer to the question, What is the meaning of the resurrection of Jesus from the dead?, lies paradigmatically in the experience of the disciples being unconditionally loved even though they ran away from God's embodied passion for them in Jesus. In that experience of being unconditionally loved they found themselves released into the new creation that is a new way of being embodied lovers in this world. So too for us: the meaning of the resurrection of Jesus from the dead, its meaning for our lives together in this world, is God's unconditional love for us even in the face of our denial of God's embodied passionate love for us.

If these answers are saying something about the meaning of the resurrection—the release of the body as carrier of human and divine love, and the power of unconditional love even in the face of human denial and betrayal—then I have to say that nowhere in my fifty-plus years of life and more than twenty-two years of ordained ministry have I found the resurrection meaning more fully embodied than in the community affected by AIDS that I am privileged to be a part of. This community is owning the release of the body as a carrier of love, and it is owning the power of unconditional love, in ways that, I dare say, constitute something new in history. If I am right, the power of the resurrection is breaking through in this community, and it is breaking through for all of us. The experience of this community *will* make a difference, and the difference will be experienced by anyone who takes time to savor the reality and become part of it.

Thus, while AIDS calls forth in many the question and the response of hope in the sense of risen life beyond death, this hope is intimately connected, I think, with convictions that something is emerging in the experience of this community that is very important for the human future.

New connections are being forged, new relationships are being born, new ways of being in the world and new ways of loving are being tested and found to work. There is a hope experienced by many living with HIV and AIDS, then, that, no matter what happens to them, it will have a meaning for others, that they will leave a legacy, that it will not be in vain, especially for their own community. There is a hope, too, that the lesbian and gay community will be renewed as it comes to acknowledge the power and the wonder of its response to AIDS. There is a hope that the unconditional love often found in this community's response to AIDS will last after AIDS is over, that the community will be forever different and forever better because of the memory both of those who have died of the complications of AIDS and of those who cared for them. And, finally, there is a hope that, because of AIDS and because of the enormous self-sacrifice that it has called forth in the lesbian and gay community, the rest of society, including the churches and the synagogues, will finally come to acknowledge not only that they have been wrong in their judgments of this community, and violent in their attitudes toward this community, but also that this community is, to use a current Canadian buzzword, a distinct society with its own gifts, its own spiritual and cultural resources, and its own grace that permeates the way people live, the way they interact, and the way they love.

The Church's Pastoral Response to Homosexual Persons

This brings me to the second opening set of theological considerations, that having to do with sexuality and the Church's pastoral response to persons of homosexual orientation.

There will be a peculiar emotional valence for some readers to almost everything I say in this paper. It will be different for different people. I dare say that it is already being experienced. And it has to do, not so much with AIDS as with sexuality. It is important, I think, to acknowledge this from the outset, and I ask my readers to process it as they proceed with the paper.

First, however, let me clarify the facts. AIDS is not a gay disease. Worldwide it affects heterosexual people in far greater numbers than it does homosexual people. The World Health Organization recently stated that seventy-five percent of those living with HIV-infection and AIDS around the world are heterosexual. The incidence of heterosexual people contracting HIV-infection in Canada and the United States is rising, though, some say, not as dramatically as had been predicted.

Nonetheless, in North America until recently, AIDS affected predominantly gay men, and this is still very much the case in Toronto. In Toronto, too, it is the gay and lesbian community alone that has mobilized to provide grassroots services to those living with or affected by AIDS. And so my reflections will necessarily be given from this perspective. My presence in the AIDS community in Toronto is, more specifically, a presence in the gay community, a community that, among other things, is suffering from the effects of AIDS. My reflections are given from this experience.

Ironically, and tragically, AIDS is making possible a presence of ministry in the wider gay and lesbian community that would have been far more difficult for at least Catholics to sustain were it not for AIDS. I find it tragic but true that it had to take a life-threatening virus before a priest could move publicly and openly in the gay community. On the other hand, this may also be one of the sources of hope surrounding AIDS, for no one can move in this community and experience its response to AIDS without realizing, if you did not know it earlier, that our Church's teaching about and response to homosexual persons is not only pastorally insensitive and inadequate; it is also erroneous and at times violent. One cannot spend time in this community without recognizing that the grace of God is powerfully active here, especially but not only as this community comes to terms with AIDS. There is a love operative in the gay community that is a function of God's grace, and this love is intimately connected with sexuality, yes, with the way people make love. This is something that the official teaching of our Church has not to date been able to acknowledge. But Rosemary Haughton put it succinctly in *The Passionate God:* "many homosexual relationships exhibit a fidelity and tenderness whose holiness is evident."

Rosemary Haughton wrote this in a book published in 1982, before AIDS was the issue it is today. The force of her statement is exponentially magnified in the context of AIDS. The stories of fidelity and tenderness that can be found in every apartment building in the Church-Wellesley area of Toronto, as in every neighborhood affected by AIDS, should be shouted from the mountaintops for all the world to hear. Yes, there is here a way of life and of loving whose holiness is evident.

Now I ask you simply to imagine what the infamous Letter to the Bishops of the Catholic Church on the Pastoral Care of Homosexual Persons issued by the Congregation for the Doctrine of the Faith on (of all days) Halloween of 1986—maybe God *does* have a sense of humor!—might have been like if it had begun with such an affirmation? "Many homosexual relationships exhibit a fidelity and tenderness whose holiness is evident." In fact, the Letter never mentions fidelity and tenderness, to say nothing of exhorting the bishops to encourage the development and exercise of such virtues. Nor does it acknowledge the heroic charity witnessed in the gay community's response to AIDS, nor the suffering of families, lovers, and friends affected by a loved one's contraction of the AIDS virus. Nor does it ask the forgiveness of gay and lesbian people for the violence perpetrated upon them because of centuries of homophobic church teaching. In fact, in section 10, in language reminiscent of anti-Semitic pronouncements on the part of Nazi leaders in the 1930s, it subtly condones continued violence: ". . . when civil legislation is introduced to protect behavior to which no one has any conceivable right, neither the Church nor society at large [note the 'two perfect societies' conception of history] should be surprised when other distorted notions and practices gain ground, and irrational and violent reactions increase." And Pilate washed his hands and said, "I am innocent of this man's blood; see to it yourselves."

Now I am not attempting here to offer an alternative ethical position on homosexual love. That is not the purpose of this paper, nor is it the essence of my ministry to persons living with AIDS. I am calling attention to the problem of the Church's pastoral response to homosexual persons, and I am doing so because the perception of the Church in the community affected by AIDS is one of the most difficult obstacles to effective ministry. The Letter that I have just mentioned fails to consider in any adequate fashion *any* of the most important aspects in the pastoral care of homosexual persons: fidelity, tenderness, AIDS, violence against homosexual persons, etc. It is a wonder to me at times that some people still want the ministry of the Church, and it is a source of great admiration to me that some of the people I have met have been given the grace to forgive the Church.

II. A Personal Narrative

During the summer of 1988 I began to experience a quiet, peaceful, but relentless attraction to involvement in the AIDS community in Toronto. Over the course of the summer I tested this attraction according to the various Ignatian counsels regarding discernment and election, and I ended the summer with the conviction that I was indeed to get involved in this community.

It was important to me that I find the right way into involvement. For me personally—and I think this is true generally—I could not get involved in AIDS ministry in any other way than from the grassroots, participating in the lives of persons living with AIDS, first as a friend and then as a member of their community, known and loved as one of them. I could not come parachuting in from above, particularly as some representative of the

Church, all of a sudden appearing on the scene equipped with the ministerial resources of a church that was perceived as having rejected those to whom I was attempting to be present.

Furthermore, it was important to me that my involvement be at least loosely affiliated with the local AIDS organizations, and that it not be some kind of parallel institutional involvement. Rather, if some kind of parallel institutional presence were to be developed, it had to be from the base of contacts that I might be able to establish through the local AIDS organizations. And so I had to wait for the proper opportunity, and be ready to seize it when it came.

The opportunity arrived when I attended a weekend retreat conducted by Bill McNichols, a Jesuit who at that time had been ministering for several years to persons living with AIDS in New York. The retreat was entitled "Jesus as a Person with AIDS." Bill employed the simple but highly effective technique of the traditional Catholic devotion of the Stations of the Cross, placing in the person of Jesus a man who had received the diagnosis of being HIV-positive. At each step of the man's journey with HIV an identification was made with one of the moments along the way of the cross, and a fifteenth station was added, marking this man's entrance into God's glory in the life of the resurrection. The retreat was attended by some persons living with HIV and AIDS, and one of the people whom I met at the retreat shortly thereafter suggested that I start attending a weekly Healing Circle sponsored on Sunday evenings by the AIDS Committee of Toronto.

The Healing Circle meets each Sunday evening at 7 P.M. It employs techniques of relaxation exercises, guided meditation, and holistic health practices, and includes a period of "check-in" or sharing, where each person has the opportunity to share as little or as much as he or she wishes about just how life has been going for them. For quite some time the Healing Circle was the only event of a spiritual nature in Toronto designed specifically for persons with HIV and AIDS. It has been the seed ground of many other projects. Some persons attend almost every week, while others come more sporadically. I began attending in May of 1989, and I have been going almost every week since. Almost all of my initial contacts in the AIDS community came through participation in the Healing Circle, and many of these contacts remain at least indirectly a function of this participation. In keeping with my own desires as to how I wanted to get involved, I did not initially identify myself as a priest, nor did I indicate that I was HIV-negative. I was simply Bob. My friend, of course knew that I was a priest and that I was HIV-negative, and I was not trying to hide anything; I just wanted the ministerial part of my identity to become known only as people came to know me as a human being and a friend.

In October of 1989 I was approached by one of the coordinators of the Healing Circle, who was at that time also an AIDS support counselor at the AIDS Committee of Toronto, and asked if I would help him form a Spiritual Support Team as a new service sponsored by the AIDS Committee of Toronto. It was his perception that there were surfacing among some of the clientele at this organization some spiritual needs that could not be met by the regular AIDS Support counselors. The Spiritual Support Team was to be a multi-faith team of resource persons from different spiritual traditions who would be available to be called upon when such needs were expressed. He and I assembled a group of persons from Buddhist, Jewish, and various Christian backgrounds, and we began to meet as a group in the spring of 1990 and to hammer out a mission statement. In its first two years the team assembled a list of spiritual counselors from the different traditions which is made available to the staff, volunteers, and clients of the AIDS Committee of Toronto. Having chaired this team for two years, for reasons of time I decided that in general this would be the only committee that I would allow myself to get involved in. I had been involved in several other committees over the past couple of years, but I made the decision that my AIDS energies have to be saved for individuals affected by the virus and for occasional talks in which I can be a spokesperson, as minister and theologian, for the community affected by AIDS.

During the summer of 1989 I asked the Jesuit provincial to allow me to move out of the community into my own apartment, at least partly for the sake of being more available to persons living with AIDS or affected by HIV and AIDS. This discussion with Bill Addley, then provincial, was probably the best conversation that I have ever had with a Jesuit superior— not only because he gave me what I wanted, but also because it was conducted in an atmosphere of trust, of discernment of my path. It served to cement the Province's trust in what I was trying to do. At that time, too, Bill agreed to a modest monthly budget for AIDS-related expenses. During that summer I found an apartment in the center of the AIDS-affected community and in close proximity to the major local AIDS organizations. I have used this space as a place to conduct meetings and to host persons living with or affected by AIDS.

The next step in the story is the launching of a monthly healing service for the HIV-affected community. The service is conducted at Our Lady of Lourdes Church in Toronto. In the summer of 1990 it was called to my attention by a friend that Bill McNichols had for several years been conducting a regular eucharistic service for persons living with AIDS and their friends and families, a service that included the sacrament of the anointing of the sick. The moment I heard this I knew, without further questions, that we were going to do this in Toronto. I began to talk with people about the idea and to gather a team of persons who would assist me in getting this liturgy started. In September of 1990 I invited about twelve people to my apartment, and we quickly organized our resources, so that we began the service only three weeks later, at the beginning of AIDS Awareness Week in October. The collaboration has been quite wonderful: musicians, publicity, people to take responsibility for a reception after each service, and so on. The service is held on the third Saturday of each month. It has been well received by a number of people in the community and attendance is gradually growing, so that we are now gathering about twice as many people each month as we did at the beginning. We are quite open about our belief that there is a healing power to the sacrament of anointing, while being careful not to encourage any feeling of false hope. Unquestionably there is, for some, spiritual and emotional healing taking place. Any physical healing, which could run all the way from slowing down the progression of the virus to seroconversion, will, I believe, always remain hidden from us.

Over the course of the past two years I have been asked to speak at several functions. I once represented the AIDS Committee of Toronto in speaking to the Unitarian Congregation in Toronto. In June of 1990 I was resident theologian at the U.S. National Catholic AIDS Conference at Notre Dame, where my job was to give one of two closing talks, summing up the proceedings of the Conference and reflecting theologically on what had transpired. Subsequently I have spoken at a Theology and AIDS Conference held in Toronto, and also addressed the chaplains' session at the meeting of the Ontario Hospital Association. I was also asked to speak to the Jesuit novices at Guelph on AIDS ministry as an aspect of the Society of Jesus' mission of faith and social justice.

But through all of this the major amount of my time has been spent with persons—time as a friend, time as a priest, whatever kind of time people asked for and needed. I have had the privilege of being asked to conduct a number of funeral and memorial services, and these have affected me profoundly.

III. Theological Reflection

I will conclude with a brief theological reflection on the following points: (1) inculturation, (2) holistic health and spirituality, (3) spirituality and religion, (4) love and the formation of a new community, (5) the notion of legacy, (6) anger-grief-burnout, (7) intimacy, and finally (8) a return full circle to the notion of unconditional love.

Inculturation

Theoretically I could perhaps have gotten involved in AIDS ministry in other ways, as a function of some organized church outreach. But I am happy that I took the approach I did: meeting people simply as Bob, forming friendships, becoming an integral member of the HIV-affected community, and working as much as possible in tandem with local AIDS organizations. This has enabled me and those with whom I work to have a grassroots base for our own distinct contributions, such as the healing service at Our Lady of Lourdes Church. Even if one comes into this kind of ministry from some organized church outreach, one has to establish grassroots contact and relationships with local AIDS organizations, or one will be totally ineffective. My first advice to anyone getting involved in some kind of ministry in the AIDS community is: Move at the grassroots level in the community, let people come to know you, and to love you, and to challenge you to let go of the pretensions and hypocrisies and fears and cowardice that any of us coming from an organized religious affiliation will have.

Holistic Health and Spirituality

One advantage of taking this approach is that I have gained the realization that pastoral care or spiritual support is but one part of a holistic approach to the health and well-being of persons living with HIV and AIDS, and that it must be integrated with other dimensions. In Toronto at least, persons living with AIDS have many resources available, if they choose to utilize them: excellent AIDS counselors, knowledgeable doctors, support groups, courses on holistic approaches to health, courses on meditation, financial and legal assistance, spiritual support. The AIDS Committee of Toronto promotes a program that is tailored to each person, including physical, emotional, mental, and spiritual aspects. All of these must be addressed in an integrated fashion, and anyone engaged primarily in one of these has to be aware of the other areas and resources that exist to meet them.

Spirituality and Religion

The term "spirituality" is used quite freely in the AIDS community, and frequently it is contrasted with "religion." The attitude prevalent

among many in the HIV-affected community can be summed up in the
expression "Religion, No; Spirituality, Yes." The term "religion" here refers
to organized institutional expressions of almost whatever denomination. It
is a term that has a quite negative connotation in the community. But the
terms "spiritual" and "spirituality" reflect, in part at least, a hunger for an
interior life, a striving to develop such a life, a recognition of a need and
desire for such a new way of living. What does the term mean concretely
in the AIDS community? The Hassle Free Clinic in Toronto, which has
been providing anonymous testing for HIV for some time, conducts a
group of what they call Body-positive support groups, and they include
under the spiritual aspects of a holistic approach the following questions:

- Do I take an active role in my own healing?
- What is my attitude towards my life: positive, negative, apathetic?
- What is my attitude toward my own death?
- Do I have a hopeful, courageous outlook?
- How do I cope with life's uncertainties and ambiguities?
- Do I forgive all people in my life, regardless of perceived hurts?
- How much time do I spend in solitude, and is it quality time?
- Am I satisfied with the level of meaning and direction in my life?
- Do I enjoy inner peace?
- Do I have a feeling of inner strength?
- Do I really accept and love myself?
- Do I know from experience that I am loved unconditionally from
  the deepest power of the universe?

Spiritual counseling, as part of a larger program tailored to each person, involves at least these matters and usually more, depending on the
background and desires of the person. Persons diagnosed as HIV-positive
are almost forced to face some or all of these issues. And the first issue is
the key to the others: Do I take an active role in my own healing? Many
tend simply to give up, to regard themselves as under a death sentence; and
nothing else will ensue until that attitude is transcended.

Gays and lesbians will often find that the spiritualities inherited from
their religious backgrounds are part of the problem that needs to be healed.
I continue to find this especially with dying patients. They have difficulty
accepting the fact that God loves them unconditionally, just as they are,
and they cannot acknowledge the goodness and grace that have frequently
been part of their love lives. Religion has introduced destructive, unhealthy
patterns of relating to themselves, to others, to society, to family, to God.

It has induced self hatred, toxic shame, paralyzing fear, unnecessary and unhealthy guilt. These tapes inscribed by legalistic and life-denying ideologies have set up systems of feelings, images, beliefs, and judgments that, along with the body, need to be healed. In fact, many are convinced that such oppression is even partly responsible for the contraction of HIV by some persons. Spiritual healing depends primarily on the profound experience, almost always mediated by human love, that I am radically and unconditionally loved by God, loved just as I am, including my sexual being, and that nothing can separate me from that love, no matter what happens. HIV-affected persons who are finding spiritual healing are coming to such affirmations, and as they do so they are realizing that the messages they had introjected from the churches were simply erroneous.

Love and the Formation of a New Community

The central spiritual reality finding articulation in the AIDS community, however, is love. A mystery of deep spiritual significance is being played out in this community. It goes something like this. First, in my experience there has been no other group of people where self-sacrificing, unconditional love plays such a prominent role in establishing the mood and atmosphere of life; and I am convinced that wherever this kind of love is present the God in whom I believe is present and active. Second, God's love and grace are here manifest precisely where the dominant mentalities in religion and culture would tend to deny God's presence. I believe persons living with AIDS and HIV are among today's suffering servants of God in the sense of the servant in Deutero-Isaiah, mediating in their love, patience, courage, and pain, the birth of a new community in history, a community that cuts across the divisions of race, gender, class, and sexual orientation. We are seeing again what Jesus spoke of when he said that the stone rejected by the builders has become the cornerstone of a new temple, a new community. We are also seeing again what Jesus spoke of when he said that the persons rejected, marginalized, ostracized by the religious and cultural authorities of his own time were closer to the reign of God than were these authorities themselves. The theological mystery of AIDS lives on some such level as this, and anyone working in this community will be experiencing something of a share in this mystery.

I am more impressed with persons living with AIDS who have come to forgive the Church or who are trying to forgive the Church than I am with anything the churches have done to seek reconciliation with persons living with AIDS. We in the churches have to learn from the HIV/AIDS community what it is to love; only when we have done this will we be provided with anything worth while to offer in this community.

The Notion of Legacy

I believe that persons living with AIDS and dying of the complications of AIDS will leave, through others, a legacy to the rest of their community. Let me give you two examples, where I experienced that the legacy was to be communicated to others through me.

Howard was a man whom I met through a mutual friend. I spoke with him a number of times during the last year of his life, was invited to his apartment once for dinner, was given a lawn chair that he insisted I use on my balcony, and was asked by him to minister to him in his last days and conduct his memorial service.

Howard was admitted to St. Michael's Hospital in Toronto about three weeks before he died. I visited him there five times in these three weeks. On the first three occasions he was wrestling with an overwhelming fear and panic about what he knew was coming. I could manage only to calm him down a bit, but the fear and panic would always return. Between the third and fourth times that I visited him, something had occurred—I do not know and never will know just what it was. It was something that enabled him to transcend his fear and panic definitively. And on the final occasion, which I am convinced in retrospect Howard knew would be the last time we would talk, just as I was leaving his room for the last time, Howard spoke to me words that he wanted me to pass onto others living with AIDS. He said, "Tell them there is nothing to be afraid of." This was Howard's legacy, something very similar to Jesus' words to the disciples on the night before his own death, "Do not let your hearts be troubled." It was a legacy that was to be passed on to others living with AIDS, and to be passed on through me, a legacy to others who would be facing the same things that Howard had faced and conquered.

Robert is another example. I was asked to visit Robert in December of 1990, when he was still living at home. We worked out a pattern of regular visits during which Robert would receive Communion. I continued to visit him, with the help of another friend, several times a week right up to his death at Casey House, an AIDS hospice, in August of 1991. When I was writing the homily for his memorial service I was given the insight that Robert was a man who many years earlier had been enabled by God to forgive the Church the hurt it had done to him as a gay man. Robert forgave the Church, and decided he would not deprive himself of the resources of

Church life that were important to him, especially the Eucharist. Before he became too sick, Robert went to Mass every day; and after he became sick he continued to receive Communion every day. In all the time that I knew him—and I came to know him very well—I never heard a bitter word from him about the Church. His legacy, again to be passed on to others, was about forgiveness of the hurts that are done to us, and the freedom to make up our own minds about our relationship to God, no matter what the life-denying messages of the Church may unfortunately be telling us.

Anger–Grief–Burnout

This brings me to my own *anger*. I need to learn from people like Robert how to forgive dimensions of the Church that anger me. I need help from others to deal with my own anger, and I do not hesitate to admit this. But I also know what it is that angers me. I want to see my Church respond humanely and humbly, aware of the profound hurt that it has caused and is causing, and of the deep mistakes that it has made. I accuse the Church of a silent conspiracy with death in the face of the AIDS crisis, and I will not be satisfied until this has changed. But I must learn from people like Robert to forgive the Church's continuing silent conspiracy with death, even as I try to do what I can to awaken Church people, including leaders, to social responsibility and to the courage to admit the Church's mistakes.

One of the overwhelming phenomena encountered in this ministry is the presence of what has come to be called cumulative *grief*. In a recent personal exercise, one of the counselors at the AIDS Committee of Toronto sat down and wrote out the names of those whom he knew who had died of the complications of AIDS, ranging from very close and intimate friends to acquaintances whom he knew at least well enough to stop and talk with them on the street. His list came to over 175 names. He then asked a bereavement group of some thirty-five people to engage in the same exercise, and they found that among them they were grieving over five thousand deaths.

Such grief is too much for the human spirit to bear. It is similar to the phenomenon of the Holocaust, and the community affected by it will take as long as the Jewish people are taking to deal with their grief, anger, and sorrow.

All of this raises the issue of *burnout*. I need to continue to learn to put boundaries on what I am able to do. Many of us in the so-called helping professions have boundary problems. We tend to be co-dependent people, at least to a certain extent. Some of us get involved in the helping professions partly out of a sense of expiation or of guilt. Many gay people engage in AIDS services out of what has come to be called survivors' guilt. All of this has to be negotiated over and over again if one is to sustain work in this ministry. Otherwise, one will simply be driven by compulsions and obsessions and will burn out very quickly.

Along these lines I have found it helpful that I am not engaged in this work on a full-time basis. It has been important that I have something else, even something that at times is, frankly, boring—something that does not involve me constantly at the depths that are affected by issues of sexuality and mortality.

Intimacy

I cannot end a presentation on hope by talking of anger, grief, and burnout. So let me add a word about intimacy and unconditional love, thus coming full circle on my earlier reflections drawing on Rosemary Haughton and Sebastian Moore.

Anyone in this work will be challenged to grow in his or her capacity for intimacy, if only because the AIDS community in general is working so hard at encouraging in people the capacity for responsible but also playful intimacy. Somehow we are all learning how to love in new ways. The gay community has always been involved in exploring the creative possibilities of intimacy and love in ways unknown to others, and today that is happening with a renewed seriousness, sense of responsibility, and dedication. Those engaged in AIDS ministry will be invited into explorations of intimacy, and while these may be at times challenging and demanding, ultimately they will also be life-giving and exhilarating. For, as Rosemary Haughton saw so clearly in *The Passionate God,* it is the bodily exchange of human love that is the medium of God's passionate love for us.

Unconditional Love

And finally, we return to Sebastian Moore's insight into the unconditional love that is the meaning of the resurrection for our communal lives together in this world. In my other incarnation, as a systematic theologian, I gave a seminar at the Lonergan Research Institute in which I argued that the created reality that a metaphysical theology called sanctifying grace or a created communication of the divine nature is available to us in consciousness, precisely in the experience of being unconditionally loved, and of being invited to love in return. Not everybody at that seminar agreed with me, but I am ready to stand by that affirmation. I am ready also to admit where I learned it: from my friends who are living with AIDS. I learned it from the AIDS community in Toronto; from the lovers who show the fidelity and tenderness that makes their relationships holy. A man living with AIDS, who came to talk with me about once a month, was just about ready to leave my office one day when another question occurred to him. He looked me in the eye, and asked, "Just what the hell is the state of grace?" All I could say is that he had been talking about it for the past hour, because he had been telling me how his experience convinced him that, no matter what cultural and religious institutions had communicated to him, he was radically and unconditionally loved by God. I said, "If that isn't what it is, then I don't know what is."

— 13 —

The Gospels as Revelation and Transformation: A Tribute to Sebastian Moore

David Tracy

Pleas to reunite theology and spirituality have rarely been stronger. Far more rare, however, has been the reality of theology and spirituality united in *oeuvre* and person. Those of us who have had the grace to know Sebastian Moore and his work over the years can bear witness to his unique ability to produce contemporary spiritual theology.[1] As contemporary, his work has developed Bernard Lonergan's notion of the modern turn to the realm of interiority more creatively than any other theologian. In spirituality, Sebastian Moore has united some of the genius of his Benedictine traditions to some of the best modern transpersonal psychology. In theology, he has brilliantly rethought the Pauline soteriology of the cross-resurrection into new and persuasive mystical-prophetic ways.[2]

Like many of his friends and admirers, I consider myself blessed to know and read Sebastian Moore. Is any theologian better at rethinking the

---

[1] See especially Sebastian Moore, *The Crucified Jesus Is No Stranger* (New York: Seabury, 1980); *The Fire and the Rose Are One* (New York: Seabury, 1980); *Let This Mind Be in You* (New York: Harper & Row, 1985); *Jesus the Liberator of Desire* (New York: Crossroad, 1989).

[2] For some fine studies of Moore's work, see William Loewe, "Encountering the Crucified God: The Soteriology of Sebastian Moore," *Horizons* 9 (1982) 216–36, and Stephen J. Duffy, Elisabeth Koenig, and William Loewe, "Review Symposium," *Horizons* 18 (1991) 93–129.

reality of human desire? Is there anyone more daring or fruitful in relating a contemporary Christian transforming experience of Jesus Christ with speculations on the original disciples? There is a wholeness in Sebastian Moore's texts that merits my admiration and often my envy for his unique range and genius at truly spiritual theology. As a partial contribution and tribute to this signal theologian of the disclosive and transformative power of the gospels, I offer this hermeneutical study of the importance of the rediscovery of narrative in Christian theology.

I. Revelation: Word as Logos and Kerygma

The recent rediscovery of the central role of written narrative in Christian revelation provides a welcome occasion to return to modern discussions of revelation, Word, and written text. The explicitly Christian dialectic of Word and written text provides a distinct understanding of divine revelation.[3]

In Christian theology, the doctrine or symbol of revelation may be understood as the event of divine self-manifestation in the Word, Jesus Christ, as testified to or witnessed to in the written words of Scripture. Every element in this descriptive definition of revelation has occasioned controversy in Christian hermeneutics. Every element needs clarification if one is to understand the relationships of Word, written text, and revelation in Christian self-understanding. Before concentrating on the new developments on the role of the passion narratives for understanding Christian revelation, it is first necessary to clarify the principal terms in the definition of Christian revelation in order to reach a first approximation of the character of the central dialectic of Christianity on Word and written text.

To return, therefore, to the proposed definition: (Christian) revelation is the event of divine self-manifestation in the Word, Jesus Christ, as testified to or witnessed to in the written words of Scripture.

To clarify the principal elements in this definition is to recall some of the central debates of contemporary Christian theology.

1) Event. "Event" language in contemporary theology indicates the gratuitous or gracious character of divine revelation. The very fact that God

---

[3]See especially Hans Frei, *The Eclipse of Biblical Narrative: A Study in Eighteenth and Nineteenth Century Hermeneutics* (New Haven: Yale University Press, 1974); Paul Ricoeur, *Time and Narrative,* 3 vols. (Chicago: University of Chicago Press, 1984–88). An alternative version of this essay will be published in a volume on *Hermeneutics and Writing in Italy,* edited by Marco Olivetti.

reveals Godself is grace, event, happening. Theologically, revelation is never a human achievement, work, or necessity; revelation must be understood as event, happening, gratuity, grace. Hermeneutically, the category "event" *(Ereignis)* is applicable even to word as Word-event *(Sprach-Ereignis)* as a happening of language itself and, therefore, as not under the control of the modern subject.

2) "The event of divine self-manifestation." The language of divine self-manifestation indicates, theologically, that revelation is not construed primarily (as in the older manual scholastic traditions) as propositional truths that otherwise would be unknown (i.e., supernatural or revealed truths). Rather, in modern theologies, revelation is construed primarily on an interpersonal or encounter model as an event of divine self-manifestation to humanity. This interpersonal model of revelation further assumes that some person-like characteristics (namely, intelligence and love) must be employed to understand the reality of God as God manifests God's self as Wisdom and Love. The dangers of anthropomorphism here are real but finally unavoidable (as Buber insisted in his critique of Spinoza and in his insistence on the biblical God as "Thou"). Indeed, despite some strong qualifications on the use of personal language for God, all modern theologians who employ the category of revelation as divine self-manifestation also must at some time use (biblical) personal language and thereby interpersonal models for God as Wisdom and Love.

Hermeneutically, this use of the category "manifestation" also is indicative of the hermeneutical notion of truth as primordially an event of manifestation (or disclosure-concealment).[4] The subjective correlate to the objectivity of manifestation is recognition. In a similar manner, the theological counterpart to the event-gift-grace of revelation as divine self-manifestation is the gift, grace, happening (but never work) of faith as re-orientation of trust in and loyalty to the God disclosing Godself in the Word, Jesus Christ.

3) "Event of divine self-manifestation in the Word, Jesus Christ." The decisive event of God's self-manifestation is, as Karl Barth insisted, not merely an event but a person, i.e., the person of Jesus of Nazareth proclaimed and manifested as the Christ and thereby as the decisive Word-

---

[4]For a survey here, see James J. De Censo, *Hermeneutics and the Disclosure of Truth: A Study in the Work of Heidegger, Gadamer, and Ricoeur* (Charlottesville: University Press of Virginia, 1990). In theology, see Werner G. Jeanrond, *Theological Hermeneutics: Development and Significance* (New York: Crossroad, 1991); Claude Geffré, *The Risk of Interpretation*, trans. David Smith (New York: Paulist, 1987); Klaus Berger, *Exegese und Philosophie. Stuttgarter Bibelstudien* 123/124 (Stuttgart: Katholisches Bibelwerk, 1984).

event of divine self-manifestation. Here one cannot find a strict hermeneutical correlate. One can, however, find analogous ways of hermeneutically clarifying the nature of Word as Divine Self-Expression. In traditional
Christian theism, the ultimate understanding of the Word is the Second
Person of the Trinity. In my judgment, any fully Christian theological
understanding of God would need that further trinitarian clarification in
order to understand both the intrinsically relational character of the doctrine or symbol of revelation, and the intrinsically relational (i.e., explicitly
trinitarian) reality of the Christian understanding of God.

For present purposes these further important questions on the trinitarian nature of God as clarified by the Christian understanding of revelation in the Word Jesus Christ need not be pressed. Rather there is a prior
need to clarify how the Word enters the Christian understanding of revelation as an entirely dialectical reality that determines the Christian understanding of Word.

The dialectic of the Word in Christian theological self-understanding
begins with the hermeneutical insight that Word is both Logos and
Kerygma.[5] Hermeneutically, Word is, therefore, both disclosure-manifes-
tation (Word as Logos) and proclamation-disruption (Word as Kerygma).
In history of religion terms, Logos becomes "religion as manifestation," especially the manifestation of primordial correspondences occurring
throughout all reality. The archaic, meditative, and mystical traditions analyzed by Mircea Eliade and others are the clearest illustrations of these
"Logos" traditions, just as sacrament, nature, creation, cosmos, and analogical correspondences are the clearest Christian analogies of Word as
Logos manifesting all reality (God-cosmos-history-self) as a vast system of
disclosive and participating analogical correspondences. The reality of the
participating symbol (sacrament) is crucial for Word as Logos.

In history of religion terms, Word as Kerygma or proclamation also
becomes Word as interruption, disruption, i.e., Word as distancing from a
sense of manifestory participation. Where Word as Logos discloses a vast
system of participatory and analogical correspondences, Word as proclamation both discloses and conceals itself as proclamatory interruption of
all senses of continuity, participation, and rootedness (all now labelled "pa-

---

[5]See Paul Ricoeur, "Manifestation and Proclamation," *The Journal of the Blaisdell
Institute* 12 (Winter 1978), and "Toward a Hermeneutic of the Idea of Revelation," *Harvard
Theological Review* 70 (1977) 1–37; and David Tracy, *The Analogical Imagination* (New
York: Crossroad, 1981) 193–229. Note also Sebastian Moore's brilliant review of Paul and
Matthew for his mystical-prophetic theology of cross-resurrection and discipleship.

ganism"). When Johann Baptist Metz (here, following Walter Benjamin) describes religion with the one word, "interruption," he well describes this classical trajectory of the prophetic, apocalyptic, proclamatory Word in Judaism and Christianity.

In Christian theology the dialectic of Word as disclosive Logos and Word as interruptive Kerygma can be found in all the classic dichotomies become dialectical antinomies of Christian theological self-understanding. Consider the contrast between logos christologies, beginning with the disclosive manifestory Gospel of John, and apocalyptic christologies like Mark's, or proclamatory and disruptive christologies of the Cross like Paul's christology of Christ crucified. Or consider the contrast in Christian theologies between the comprehensible-incomprehensible Logos traditions' understanding of God in Aquinas and Rahner, and the hidden-revealed proclamatory God of Luther and Calvin. Recall Tillich's formulation of the dialectic of Protestant principle (word as disruptive, critical, suspicious proclamation) and Catholic substance (word as participatory logos). Or recall, in conceptual terms, the differences between the analogical languages of classical Orthodox, Anglican, and Catholic theologies and the negative dialectical thought of classical Protestant theologies.

Even in terms of the symbols of incarnation-cross-resurrection, Word as Logos instinctively appeals to the symbol of incarnation, whereas Word as Kerygma instinctively appeals to cross. Both find the need for one another in their distinct appeals to the symbol of resurrection to complete the dialectic of Christian symbols. Only the fuller symbol system of incarnation-cross-resurrection clarifies the dialectic of Jesus the Christ as the Word, i.e., as both Logos and Kerygma, both John's word of Glory and Paul's crucified Christ, both Mark's word of the cross and Luke's word of resurrection-ascension.

It would be possible to clarify further the Christian understanding of Word through a fuller exposition of one or another of the classical dialectics noted above (incarnation-cross; sacrament-word; cosmos-history; symbol-allegory; icon-idol; analogy-dialectic; comprehensible-incomprehensible God or hidden-revealed God; creation-redemption; nature-grace or grace-sin; love-justice; participation-distance; continuity-discontinuity; continuity-interruption). Pervading all these dialectics, however, is the originating Christian dialectic of revelation as Word: Jesus the Christ as Word—Word as Logos and Word as proclamation. It also would be possible to see this same dialectic continued in the two distinct readings of the tradition: either the prophetic-apocalyptic reading of the Word-as-proclamation tradition beginning with Mark and Paul, or the meditative tradition that yields wisdom, mystical, and archaic (cosmic) readings of Word as disclosive Logos beginning with John.

As anyone familiar with the history of Christian theological reflection can readily see, all these formulations of the Christian dialectic of Word have been tried and reformulated over and over again in the history of Christian reflection. Each of them has yielded genuine fruit. However, too many of those theological formulations of the dialectic of the Christian revelation as Word have ignored the fact that Jesus Christ as Word is both disclosive Logos and disruptive proclamation of God and humanity, of cosmos and history. Word, therefore, manifests both nearness and distance, both participation and interruption.

To ignore this dual function of Jesus as the Christ is to ignore the fact that the Word, Jesus Christ, is testified to and indeed rendered in written words, i.e., in Scripture. This singular fact of revelation as written Scripture cannot be hermeneutically and theologically irrelevant. The fuller Christian description of revelation, in the event of divine self-manifestation in the Word, Jesus the Christ, is testified to and witnessed to in the written words of the Scriptures. Here writing as such enters into Christian self-understanding of revelation as Word. Christianity must affirm its self-understanding in its scriptural-biblical base and in its Jewish, not Greek, roots. Christian theology, moreover, must leave behind both naive and gnostic notions of the Letter and the Spirit in order to understand the place of written Scripture in Christian self-understanding. Only by a focus on Scripture as written word may any adequate hermeneutics of the Christian understanding of revelation through Word in writing occur.

II. Scripture: Rendering the Revelation Present Through Writing

The written books collectively named the Bible may be viewed in various ways: as literature, as a resource for history, as a religious classic, or as sacred texts. For Christianity, however, the New Testament and the Christian Old Testament is Scripture:[6] the written original witness to revelation. The decisive revelation for the Christian occurs in the event and person of Jesus Christ as true Word of God.

[6]For an expansion and documentation of my position in this section, see my essay "On Reading the Scriptures Theologically," in Bruce D. Marshall, ed., *Theology and Dialogue: Essays in Conversation with George Lindbeck* (Notre Dame: University of Notre Dame Press, 1990) 35–69.

The Word, Jesus Christ, is affirmed as present to the community and the individual Christian in two principal forms: word (proclamation) and sacrament (those disclosive signs that render present what they signify). Even the common confession of the principal Christian churches—"We believe *in* Jesus Christ *with* the apostles"—is dependent on this notion of the Word's presence to the community. The rule for the *lex credendi* is the *lex orandi*. The present worshipping community renders present the same Jesus Christ in word and sacrament to all Christian believers. The Scripture remains the authoritative *normans non normata*. The written texts called Scripture assure that the Christ of the present Christian community is the same Christ witnessed to and testified to by the apostolic witnesses as the decisive self-manifestation of God and humanity. Neither "Scripture alone" nor "Scripture and tradition" clarify this important hermeneutical role of Scripture for the Christian. Rather, one may speak of Scripture-in-tradition, i.e., the rendering present in word and sacrament of the Word witnessed to in the Scriptures as decisively present in Jesus Christ.

The recent recovery of the import of the genre "gospel" as a proclamatory narrative can clarify this peculiar, indeed unique, role of written narrative and confessional scriptural texts for Christian self-understanding. If gospel is both proclamation and narrative, gospel is both a proclamatory confession of faith and a disclosive narration of the reality of that confessed faith by and for the worshipping community of Christians then and now. *Lex credendi* is based on the presence of the Word as Logos and Kerygma to the worshipping community *(lex orandi)*. Both are held together, I suggest, by what may be named the peculiar role of narrative writing as rendering present what is absent in the *lex narrandi* of the passion narrative. But this is, perhaps, to move too rapidly. There is need first to pay attention to the common confession of the Christian community in order to note how that common confession demands a common ecclesial written narrative.

There remains, in all Christian discourse, a need to see what is common in order to clarify the nature of the differences. The main Christian confession can be stated abstractly, as follows: "We believe *in* Jesus the Christ *with* the apostles." To state the confession as a thus abstracted common confession is helpful. For thus stated it clarifies both what Christians are and are not claiming. What they are claiming may be interpreted as follows: how Christians understand all reality—God, cosmos, history, self—they understand primarily by their affirmation of Jesus Christ as Logos and Kerygma: the decisive manifestation of who God is and who human beings are empowered and commanded to become. By believing *in* this singular Jesus of Nazareth as the Christ and therefore as Word, Christians construe all reality anew in that light: who God is, how nature and history are ultimately to be understood, and who the self is. To eliminate any element of this central confession is to change (sometimes radically, sometimes subtly) the Christian understanding of reality. For example, the Christian confession is not "We believe in Christ," so that the Sophia-Logos tradition, unrelated to the ministry, teaching, death, and resurrection of this Jesus of Nazareth, confessed to be the Christ, can suffice. Alternatively, the confession also is not "We believe in Jesus," so that a Jesusology or an alternative portrait of Jesus (e.g., the various quests for the "historical Jesus") can replace the ecclesial Christian confession "We believe in Jesus Christ."

Moreover, the preposition "with" in the phrase *"with* the apostles" cannot be allowed to be replaced by the preposition "in." Then, in effect, the tradition or doctrine of church or apostolic office or apostolic text would replace Jesus Christ as that divine reality *in* which the Christian ultimately believes. To state it clearly, the contemporary Christian believes *in* Jesus Christ *with* the apostles. Aside from the intense inner-Christian debates on what this crucial phrase, "with the apostles," means more exactly, this much is shared by Christians: the New Testament texts of the early apostolic communities' testimonies to Jesus as the Christ are the authoritative written texts. As authoritative, those texts are the principal means by which the contemporary Christian's faith in the presence of Jesus Christ as Word is tested for its fundamental fidelity to the originating Christian witness to Jesus Christ. Indeed, it may be linguistically preferable to call the New Testament the "apostolic writings" in order to highlight that the entire New Testament is a text of witness to the presence of Jesus Christ as Word, both Kerygma and Logos.

However, to affirm the major role of these texts is also to acknowledge a new Christian hermeneutical question: where within the pluralism of texts and genres of the New Testament may one find the central Christian construal of the Word, this Jesus as the Christ (and thereby the Christian construal of God, self, history, and nature)? Even the confession "We believe in Jesus Christ with the apostles" is stated, after all, in the genre of confession. The confession as such is abstracted from the diversity of New Testament christologies of Word in order to affirm the fundamental unity amidst diversity. The confession, in sum, is a legitimate abstraction from the New Testament even if it is not an explicitly New Testament confession itself. Nor, for that matter, is confession the principal New Testament genre. Here the rediscovery of narrative in contemporary Christian thought shows its true promise.

The major genre for the original communities' self-interpretation is gospel—that peculiar, perhaps unique, genre that unites Word as proclamation and disclosive Word rendered present through written narrative. Amidst the diversity of narratives in the four Gospels and elsewhere in the New Testament, moreover, the passion narratives are the principal narratives by which the Christian community first rendered in written form its understanding of who this singular Jesus of Nazareth, proclaimed to be the Christ, is.

It is undoubtedly an exaggeration (but a useful one) to say with Martin Kähler that the four Gospels are four passion narratives with extended and different introductions. The reason this statement is an exaggeration is that the different "introductions" are described more accurately as different renderings of the Word present in and through the common narrative. There is, to be sure, a notable difference between the genre of apocalyptic drama employed by Mark, the genre of realistic, history-like narrative employed by Luke, and the genre of narrative meditation employed by John.[7] As hermeneutics clarifies, those genres are not merely taxonomic of meaning but rather they are productive of meaning. They provide distinct renderings of the common passion narrative. Nonetheless, the reason why Kähler's famous statement is still a useful exaggeration should be noted: the passion narratives and their relatively history-like realistic character— despite their otherwise important differences—are the central Christian narratives for rendering present Jesus Christ as Word. If one wants to know who Jesus Christ is for Christians, the passion narratives are the primary place to search. There one finds in realistic and history-like fashion the central Christian construal of who this Jesus confessed to be the Christ is, and even why Jesus and he alone is thus construed. The *lex credendi* of Jesus Christ as Word is grounded in the *lex orandi:* both are rendered present then and now in the *lex narrandi* of the passion narratives, in the Jesus disclosed and proclaimed as the Christ, the Word, in and through the passion narrative.

It is not an overstatement to say that the common confession logically leads to the passion narratives. The genre of confession affirms, in properly abstract terms, what only the genre of narrative shows: how the Word is rendered present in the ministry and message, the cross and resurrection of this Jesus of Nazareth who is the Christ, the Word of God. The passion narrative shows how and why the Christian community "believes *in* Jesus Christ *with* the apostles." Only these narratives can adequately show and

---

[7]See Norman Perrin, *The New Testament: An Introduction* (New York: Harcourt, Brace, Jovanovich, 1974); idem., *Jesus and the Language of the Kingdom* (Philadelphia: Fortress, 1978).

not merely state (confess) the identity of this Jesus Christ, present to the Christian community in word and sacrament. Only these narratives can show who he really is, as present to the Christian community.

Without the new emphasis on the passion narratives for justifying who Jesus is for the Christian community, revelation can subtly become in modern theology the event of divine self-manifestation as general revelation or transcendental revelation, weakening considerably the specifically Christian content of revelation. The latter may be described as the Christ-event, even the Word-event. However, without the specificity provided by the written passion narratives, it is difficult to see how revelation is the revelation of Jesus the Christ as Word. Even the common confession, although affirmed, becomes in effect, "We believe in Christ" without the plain, ecclesial sense of the written passion narratives.

The passion narrative provides the plain, ecclesial sense with its realism and its history-like character to specify and clarify the event of divine self-manifestation as the event and person of *Jesus* Christ as Word. To offer the Word without the written narrative is to affirm an increasingly de-specified, generic (or, at best, generically Christian) Word. Hans Frei's recovery of the written passion narrative (and, through that narrative, the other narratives of the ministry of this Jesus and the other genres of both Testaments) is the recovery of the ecclesial, plain sense of the Scripture as the written witness to the Word.

The principal but not sole meaning of plain sense is the "obvious or direct sense of the text for the Christian community."[8] The secondary meaning of plain sense (related to, indeed dependent on, the first) clarifies, through a modest use of literary critical methods, how to read the passion narratives as "history-like," realistic narratives. In one reading, the identity of Jesus as the Christ and through that identity (and thereby presence), the further identities of both God and the Christian (both individually and communally) are rendered through close attention to the narrative interactions of an unsubstitutable character (Jesus) and the highly specific circumstances of all the events constituting the gospel accounts of the passion and resurrection. These narrative interactions allow for an identity-clarification of the agent's (Jesus) intentions and actions and, through that narrative identification, a manifestation of the agent as present to the Christian community as Jesus Christ.[9]

[8]See Kathryn E. Tanner, "Theology and the Plain Sense," in Garrett Green, ed., *Scriptural Authority and Narrative Interpretation* (Philadelphia: Fortress, 1987).

[9]Hans Frei, *The Identity of Jesus Christ: The Hermeneutical Bases of Dogmatic Theology* (Philadelphia: Fortress, 1975).

The plain sense of these narratives, with or without the aid of literary criticism on the specific narrative interactions of character and circumstance in the passion narratives, has traditionally been, is, and should be both realistic and history-like. In sum, the obvious and direct sense of the common passion narratives (i.e., the first meaning of plain sense—their sense for the Christian community who affirms them as Scripture—) is history-like and realistic. It is difficult to exaggerate the importance of this narrative insight for Christian theology. Even those, like myself, who have found little theological fruit in "quests for the historical Jesus," much less in further debates on textual inerrancy, interpretive infallibility, or unbroken and unambiguous tradition, nevertheless have often been hampered by a relative inability (before the new work in narrative) to show how the realistic and history-like character of these narratives is the plain sense of the Christian community.

The passion narrative shows us how and why the Christian community "believes *in* Jesus Christ *with* the apostles." Who Jesus Christ is when Christians confess that Jesus Christ is present to them ("we believe *in* Jesus Christ"): this they discover fully only through the narrative rendering of the passion accounts. For Christians, that narrative rendering also accords with the common confession ("we believe with the apostles"). Both the common confession and the common narrative cohere in affirming that plain sense. But only the narrative can show, and not merely state (confess), who this Jesus Christ, present to us in word and sacrament, really is for the Christian.

There is little doubt that, among the Gospels, the Gospel of Luke (more exactly, Luke-Acts) best fits the history-like, realistic reading of the new emphasis on the plain sense of the passion narratives.[10] This is both Luke's singular advantage as well as disadvantage. The advantage is obvious: Luke assures the realism and history-like, continuous character of the gospel narrative. The disadvantage is equally obvious: in what way can Luke's common realistic narrative clarify how the cross, suffering, and negativity are understood adequately (Word as Kerygma) or how the narrative also is disclosive of all reality embracing the correspondences of the Word as Logos to all reality (including the cosmos). Luke grounds the gospel's realism and, as some Lukan scholars now insist, also employs a notion of necessity to clarify and deepen that realism. At the same time, one begins to realize the importance of four (or, with Paul, five?) gospel renderings of the common confession and common narrative. One turns, in sum, to how

---

[10]Hans Frei is persuasive on this point.

Word as disruptive, disorienting *Kerygma* and Word as disclosive, manifestory *Logos* is rendered present in the written narratives of the other
gospels as disruptive Word (*Kerygma*) and disclosive Word *(Logos)*.

III. Word Rendered Present in Written Texts: The Gospels

From the new perspectives of narrative theologies, the written texts of
the four Gospels can be interpreted as rendering present through written
form the reality of the Christ as none other than this Jesus of Nazareth.
Jesus is the one whose identity and presence as the Christ is found through
observing the narrative interaction of his character and the ever-changing
situation in the details of the gospel narratives. There is, however, a further
clue to the Gospels that the new narrativists seem to have missed: the two
very different yet finally complementary ways in which Jesus Christ as
Word of God is rendered present in the two very different kinds of narrative texts and gospels.

Theologians and philosophers are tempted to move immediately to
the contrast on the nature of Jesus Christ as Word in the second-order
theological languages for Word in John (Word as Logos of glory) and Paul
(Word as proclamation of the crucified Christ). There are good reasons to
continue to affirm these contrasting theological languages for Jesus Christ
as Word. However, to clarify how written texts can render present these two
classically different languages for the Word, one must pay attention not
only to the second-order language of John and Paul, but first and primarily
to the first-order narrative language of the Gospels, including John's Gospel.

To clarify the relationship of Christ and Jesus, theologies of the Word
can be understood as grounded in the written words on the ministry, message, and passion-resurrection of Jesus of Nazareth. For the Christian, the
Word lives not merely as the Christ of God but as the Christ rendered present in this Jesus as he is found in the written narrative texts of the gospel.
The tragic texture of those gospel texts can, of course, be maintained in the
dialectical language and theological concepts of Paul. But that tragic texture is rendered present primordially in and through the gospel narrations
of Jesus of Nazareth, the Christ, the Word of God.

The new narrative theologies are correct, I believe, to emphasize (with
Hans Frei) the Lukan narratives as the first narratives to reflect upon
hermeneutically. The first meaning of the plain sense of the Gospels affirmed by the Christian tradition, as we noted above, is its ecclesial character as realistic and history-like. Clearly Luke is the most realistic and

history-like of all the Gospels. Moreover, the further narrative sense of those terms is best noted (among the Gospels) in the detailed, realistic interactions of Luke's very clear, consistent, hero-like portrait of Jesus and the comprehending disciples as Luke's narrative of necessity moves inexorably forward with singular temporal and spatial continuity. Recall, for example, the role of geography in Luke, as the narrative of the gospel leads to Jerusalem and the narrative of Acts to Rome.

I suspect that the realism and history-like character of the Christian gospel still is best embedded in the Christian ecclesial consciousness in a basically Lukan form. Surely the reality of the Church as the continuation of the history narrated in Luke's Gospel is a feature of both the ecclesial meaning of the plain sense of Luke and of the narrative rendering of that plain sense in the Acts of the Apostles. Perhaps we can say that among all the Gospels, Luke best discloses the basic realism of the Word as the Word of God (for Luke, principally as Spirit). Luke renders that Word in realistic and history-like form in his two narratives on the ministry and message, the cross, resurrection, ascension, Pentecost, the missionary journeys of the disciples, and the emerging Church.

The principal Word that Luke-Acts discloses is a realistic word: The Word, the Spirit of Christ, is disclosed in the clarity of the message (e.g., on justice for the poor) of Luke's heroic Jesus as well as in the continuities of Jesus' ministry, fate, and resurrection, as even these acts of God yield to the teleological continuities of the emergent Christian Church. Luke's narratives, analogous to the Yahwist narratives of the Old Testament, establish such continuities for understanding history itself. His narratives accomplish this by allowing the Word as Spirit to disclose a continuous history in Jesus and in the Church. Salvation-history (Cullmann) still finds its clearest expression in Luke.

In that sense, Luke's narrative rendering of the Word as history-like and realistic does match the reality of rendering the identity and thereby presence of Jesus as the Christ through the interaction of Jesus' relatively clear heroic character and the relatively continuous circumstances of Jesus' hero-like actions and sufferings. All this is surely in Luke-Acts, the primordial foundation document for a Christian realistic and history-like self-understanding. But there are aspects of the Word missing from Luke-Acts: first, the tragic sense of reality manifested in the totally innocent suffering (the cross) of Jesus as well as the disruptive, non-continuous character of history; second, the expression of the relationships of these realistic, history-like disclosures of continuity not only in history but in nature, the cosmos, indeed, in all reality. For these other renderings of the

Word in written text one must leave the realistic, history-like Luke and move toward the Word as disruptive proclamation in the apocalyptic narrative of Mark, to the tragic-wisdom narrative of Matthew, and to the dialectical language of Paul. One also must move toward the Word as disclosure of all reality as interrelated through the Word as Logos in John's Gospel and the First Letter of John.

Apocalyptic is the principal context and genre for the intertestamental period.[11] Apocalyptic is also the principal genre for understanding the rendering of the Word in the earliest gospel, the Gospel of Mark. Indeed, it is striking how proclamatory-as-kerygmatic, how interruptive-as-apocalyptic, Mark's Gospel narrative actually is. This kerygmatic Word is shown not just in the great interruption of the so-called little apocalypse of Mark 13, nor only in the strange non-closure of the gospel. The Word as proclamation also is shown in the narrative contrast of the non-comprehending disciples with the comprehending demons, the mad, and the marginal, as well as in the purely eschatological, not heroic, portrait of Mark's apocalyptic Jesus. In Mark's reading of the gospel narrative, the continuities of Luke yield to the disruptive non-continuities of an apocalyptic version of history. Here the Word is rendered with all the power and disruption of the Word as apocalyptic kerygma. In Mark the cross, not the resurrection, is central. The disturbed and disturbing interactions of Mark's apocalyptic Jesus with his confused and finally terrified disciples unite with the tragic undertones of the whole gospel to produce a classic narrative that renders in writing the Word as disruptive Kerygma.

This same Markan note of Word as Kerygma continues, in different ways, in the discourses and narratives of Matthew and the dialectical language of Paul. Indeed, Mark and Paul unite in their emphasis upon the cross as the heart of the matter: the cross, which, in Mark, teaches the disruptive and unwelcome truth of the Word as apocalyptic interruption when even Jesus, the eschatological prophet, cries out from the cross, "My God, my God, why have you forsaken me?"; the cross, which surely determines the heart of Paul's vision of the Crucified One; the cross, which encourages, in its cruciform vision, Paul's development of a relentlessly dialectical language ("and so much more," "and not yet," "Jesus Christ and him crucified") to render into theological-conceptual language the paradoxes to all thought of the concept of Word as disorienting proclamation.

---

[11]See John Collins, *Apocalyptic as Genre* (Missoula: Semeia-Scholars Press, 1978); Ernst Käsemann, "The Beginnings of Christian Theology" and "On the Subject of Primitive Christian Apocalyptic," in *Essays on New Testament Themes* (London: SCM Press, 1968).

Matthew, the most Jewish of the Gospels, takes many curious turns. Matthew understands Word as Logos, i.e., disclosure of Wisdom in the prominence accorded the great Matthean discourses and through the narrative of Jesus as a new Moses, providing a new Torah for the new covenanted community. At the same time, however, Matthew understands Word as interruptive proclamation of the Cross in the tragic inexorability that pervades the whole gospel. Notice in the narrative of Matthew how each of the succeeding discourses becomes more and more troubled, less and less confident, as they narratively parallel the non-comprehension and non-acceptance by others of the Wisdom of earlier discourses. The tragic inexorability takes hold of the whole Matthean narrative, as it moves relentlessly to the great Discourse of Judgment in Matthew 25 and the final tragic vision of the passion narrative. The Gospel of Matthew, in fact, may be read as the great mixed-discourse narrative of the New Testament: his Jesus as the Christ is rendered present as both the new Wisdom or Logos of the great discourses and as the prophet who speaks a kerygmatic word.

The unique mixture of discourse and narrative in Matthew's Gospel can be viewed as a kind of transitional text between the Word as Kerygma and the Word as Logos. The Word as Logos, however, finds its classic portrayal in the Gospel of John. In keeping with John's vision of Jesus Christ as Logos, this gospel insists on producing a meditative narrative that forces the careful reader to meditate while narrating and to narrate while meditating. It is not only the role of the great Prologue on the Logos nor only the insistence on Visible Form throughout the fourth gospel that determines John's unique rendering present of the Word as Logos: the whole world is disclosed as visible form and sacrament through Logos. Rather John's choice of his written form—a meditative narrative—bears a resemblance, as Amos Wilder observes, to an oratorio like Handel's Messiah more than it does to a realistic narrative like Luke or an apocalyptic, if not modernist, narrative like Mark, or the discourse narrative of tragic wisdom of Matthew.[12]

In John, the meditative vision of the Word as Logos provides theology with an analogical language of the all-embracing disclosive resemblances of God-cosmos-history in and through the visible form of the Logos. Where Paul moves instinctively to dialectical language in order to reveal the hidden-revealed God proclaimed in the cross of Christ crucified, John finds even the Cross as the lifting up disclosive of all reality as graced, and sacramental,

---

[12]Amos Wilder, *The Language of the Gospel: Early Christian Rhetoric* (New York: Harper & Row, 1964) 120.

through the comprehensible-incomprehensible sign of glory. John's rendering of the Word as Logos through his Book of Signs and his Book of Glory, as Simone Weil saw, unites in a new form the realities of necessity and freedom, disclosed in moments of tragic beauty. Moreover, John opens up his gospel narratives to two readings more difficult to find in the kerygmatic renderings: first, a reading of the archaic realities manifested in the signs (the cross is both historical crucifixion and cosmic tree) and, secondly, the mystical readings suggested by the meditative narrative (the visible form of the Logos manifests the possibilities of image mysticism, love mysticism, and trinitarian mysticism, just as the pervasive irony of John discloses the possibilities of more apophatic readings).

Clearly, there is much more work to be done on each of these great written "renderings present" of Jesus Christ as Word of disorienting Kerygma and of disclosive Logos. Perhaps enough has been said, however, to suggest why and how writing is necessary to understand Christian revelation. The texts of the gospel are not only texts of testimony to a Word outside the text, but testimony to a Word rendered present in and through those peculiar texts named Scripture, especially the narrative texts. Christianity, too, is finally a religion of the book: Spirit is rendered present in and through letter; Christ as Word is rendered Jesus in and through the written gospel narratives. As Sebastian Moore has taught us all: Jesus Christ as Word both confronts us in our arrested and self-deluding desires and liberates us to the self-affirming desire for God disclosed in the Word, Logos and Kerygma.

14

The Bedded Axle-Tree

Dom Sebastian Moore, O.S.B.

> *Garlic and sapphires in the mud*
> *Clot the bedded axle-tree.*
> *The trilling wire in the blood*
> *Sings below inveterate scars*
> *Appeasing long forgotten wars.*
> *The dance along the artery*
> *The circulation of the lymph*
> *Are figured in the drift of stars*
> *Ascend to summer in the tree*
> *We move above the moving tree*
> *In light upon the figured leaf*
> *And hear upon the sodden floor*
> *Below, the boarhound and the boar*
> *Pursue their pattern as before*
> *But reconciled among the stars.*
>
> —T. S. Eliot, *Burnt Norton*

I want to look at a problem, the recognition of which will, I suspect, take us into the heart of our time. It concerns male sexuality. And of course, being a follower of Lonergan, I have to say that this means my sexuality.

The existence, and the inequity, of a male-dominated society has been recognized for a long time. What is now required is that we discover why men tend to form such a society. Madonna Kolbenschlag, in her fine book

Lost in the Land of Oz (San Francisco, 1988) puts her finger on the sore spot: the necessity, in man, to deny the proto-femininity that all humans share. (Walter Ong looks at this from a much more literary point of view; see his *Fighting for Life: Contest, Sexuality, and Consciousness* [Ithica, 1981].) Implied in Kolbenschlag's book, which is addressed to women, is the need for men to recover from the inherited ravages of the fight with their proto-femininity, in other words, to be liberated from the felt need to dominate. In *Iron John: A Book about Men* (New York, 1992) Robert Bly has addressed the problem of male identity from the male point of view, but his "wild man," successfully distinguished by him from both the macho and the wimp "in touch with his femininity," is articulated with a "mythy mind" such as Wallace Stephens predicates of Jove. Here, as in the crucial matter of the resurrection, a major obstacle to understanding is using the language of myth and thinking one is explaining. If you think you are explaining when in fact you are mything, you are mything the point!

More is needed. The quest for the dynamic of male identity is still blocked. I have recently run into two books that, for me at least, have an "Open Sesame!" feel about them. They are by Jungians. *Phallos,* by Eugene Monick, and *The Phallic Quest,* by James Wyly (Santa Rosa/Toronto, 1995). One can hardly read them on the plane, because of the illustrations, to which I shall return.

Where to start? About fifteen years ago, Fellini made a film of "Satyricon," a fable by Petronius (second century C.E.). The protagonist, Encolpius (which means "the crotch," as Ganymede means "happy genitals"—these people certainly were in the raw!), finds himself impotent, and searches everywhere for a cure. In the course of the search, he becomes a very inflated, grandiose character. Eventually he is cured, *not* by the god phallos who has got "split off" from his personality, but by "other gods" who administer the cure via humiliation. These are the main features of the story, fastened upon by James Wyly: the initial loss of phallic power, the split-off character of phallos who can only taunt the victim with his impotence but cannot heal him, the consequent displacement of phallic energy into grandiosity, hubris, inflation, the recovery of potency through humiliation under the power of "other gods."

Let us take this story as providing, in its main outline, a structure for understanding the dynamic of male sexuality. But the structure is incomplete. Why is sexual potency lost in the first place? Our authors suggest an answer to this question that is the theme of this paper. There is a stage in the development of the male psyche when the man has discovered his sexual potency but is still, emotionally, subject to the mother. He may be sexually active, but within her parameters. Erich Neumann, in *The Origin and History of Consciousness* (Princeton, 1954), describes Attis and the other youthful heroes of that culture, as "obliging boys." They "service" the Great Mother. Monick makes the intriguing suggestion that this is why the statuary of the period has the male beautifully formed but with a very small penis, while there are statues of Priapus that tell another story. His member is gargantuan—these are the illustrations I referred to. What common sense calls dirty pictures, Jung calls warnings from the unconscious!

For what is happening is that the god phallos—identical with the Hindu Shiva, the oldest of the gods—finds himself restricted by the controlling mother, and rebels against this by "splitting-off" into the unconscious, whence he wreaks havoc on the mother-constricted male. And the main thesis of my authors is that the male psyche in our western culture has not advanced beyond a relationship to woman that is shaped by the relationship of the young man to the mother.

Obviously, individual men outgrow this filial stance. But we are talking about a maturing process that needs to happen on a universal scale, where inertia is the rule. There is, after all, a dramatic disparity between the way a man relates to his spouse and the way, among men, he talks about women. The thesis is, that so long as the latter way of thinking remains immature, any advances made in the former are fragile, certainly are not strong enough to set the pace. The culture, its assumptions, society's laws, the whole vast web of interconnected understandings that make a society, still represent, as women know very well, an idea of the status of woman that is not that of equal partner with man. What I am suggesting is that this by now established subjugation of woman can be, and has to be, seen as the fixation of man in a state previous to equality with woman, the state, that is, of son subject to the mother, which assuredly is the opposite of the superior state but which, precisely through being in the inferior position, feels compelled to capture the superior position. The point is that equality is an emotional achievement. Apart from such emotional maturity, it is a question of one or the other getting on top, in other words, of Hegel's master-slave dialectic.

What has happened so far in our Western culture is that man, sensing the overwhelming "natural" supremacy of woman as mother, but unable to grow beyond this into a partnership relationship with her, has developed a *cultural* preeminence to offset this *natural* inferiority. Thus, another way of saying what needs to happen is for man to discover in himself a natural capacity to level up with woman, as opposed to a cultural power to counteract her natural supremacy.

In terms of symbolism, this would mean a profound change in the significance of phallos. Phallos in our culture means male sexual energy prevented from growth by emotional fixation on the mother and so exiled from the male psyche to find expression in symbols of domination and grandiosity, spires, obelisks, and the rest, to say nothing of nuclear missiles. The real question is, what is the emotional quality of the skyward thrust of phallos when this is integrated into a regenerate male psyche that has—to revert to Satyricon—rediscovered its potency, through humiliation, as oriented to a spouse-spouse, not a son-mother, relationship? It certainly doesn't go limp! But it is quite differently erect. Somehow it takes its place as yang in the primordial pattern of yin/yang. I remember, for instance, how during a very bad bout of mental sickness and lassitude, I found myself becoming newly aware of the beautiful structured power in trees. I remember, too, the earliest dream Jung could recall: "It was a huge thing, reaching almost to the ceiling. But it was of a curious composition: it was made of skin and naked flesh, and on top there was something like a rounded head with no face and no hair. On the very top of the head was a single eye, gazing motionlessly upwards." Then he heard his mother saying, "That is the man-eater!" (*Memories, Dreams and Reflections* [ET New York, 1963] 26–7). As I read this, it occurs to me how awkward it feels, in mixed, that is to say in human, company, to expose the male awe at phallos. But until we do so, we shall remain rapists at heart. It is the never-admitted male cult of this god that has displaced itself into all the assumptions of a male-controlled world. We have to come clean. There is a proto-masculinity that would mesh into our proto-femininity instead of fighting it and creating the world of culture over against that of nature. What on earth am I talking about? I am talking on the borders of two realms, the physical and the symbolic—just like Christianity does or tries to, but I'm coming to that.

The pattern, to reiterate, is: mother-domination; split-off of the phallos involving male inflation, the now anarchic phallos instilling a sense of limitless grandiosity; the crucial fact that phallos thus exiled can only disturb and destroy, cannot heal; the necessity for humiliation under the control of "other gods"—as we should say, a "higher power"; the final reintegration of phallos, now the organ not of domination but of union.

It is not difficult to trace this pattern, or at least fragments of it, in modern literature. It is surely the organizing principle of Eliot's poem "The Waste Land." Significantly, it is only latterly that I have seen, behind vague images of "fertility ritual," the far more powerful image of the sexually wounded Fisher King replicated in a barren land abounding in phallic imagery all trivial and sterile, and in the end the voice of the thunder, the humbling from a mysterious other source, bringing rain.

The most dramatic example, to which Wyly devotes a whole chapter, is Thomas Mann's *Death in Venice*. Here is the description of the central character, Aschenbach.

> Aschenbach's whole soul, from the very beginning, was bent on fame—and thus, while not precisely precocious, yet thanks to the unmistakable trenchancy of his personal accent he was early ripe and ready for a career. Almost before he was out of high school he had a name. Ten years later he had learned to sit at his desk and sustain and live up to his growing reputation, to write gracious and pregnant phrases in letters that must needs be brief, for many claims press upon the solid and successful man. At forty, worn down by the strains and stresses of his actual task, he had to deal with a daily post heavy with tributes from his own and foreign countries.
>
> Remote on the one hand from the banal, on the other from the eccentric, his genius was calculated to win at once the adhesion of the general public and the admiration, both sympathetic and stimulating, of the connoisseur. From childhood up he was pushed on every side to achievement, and achievement of no ordinary kind; and so his young days never knew the sweet idleness and blithe *laissez aller* that belong to youth. A nice observer once said of him in company—it was at the time when he fell ill in Vienna in his thirty-fifth year: "You see, Aschenbach has always lived like this"— here the speaker closed the fingers of his left hand to a fist—"never like this"—and he let his open hand hang relaxed from the back of his chair. It was apt. And this attitude was the more morally valiant in that Aschenbach was not by nature robust—he was only called to the constant tension of his career, not actually born to it (*Death in Venice* [ET New York, 1965] 9).

This is a marvelous description, in Mann's nearly overblown prose, of the inflated ego; and no ordinary ego, rather the whole modern early-displacement ("he has always lived like this") of phallic energy into, not mere power but aesthetic control of a worldwide audience. But now crisis is round the corner, presaged by depression in which he takes a holiday in Venice. There he sees the boy Tadzio, and is shaken to the core. He responds to the crisis by arrogantly trying to absorb the god who now is troubling him into the ironclad strategy of his inflated, logos-crafting ego.

> He would write, and moreover he would write in Tadzio's presence. This lad should be in a sense his model, his style should follow the lines of the figure that seemed to him divine; he would match up this beauty into the realms of the mind, as once the eagle bore the Trojan shepherd aloft. Never

had the pride of the word been so sweet to him, never had he known so well that Eros is in the word, as in those perilous and precious hours when he sat at his rude table, within the shade of his awning, his idol full in his view and the music of his voice in his ears, and fashioned his little essays after the model Tadzio's beauty set: that page and a half of choicest prose, so chaste, so lofty, so poignant with feeling, which would shortly be the wonder and admiration of the multitude (*Death in Venice*, 29).

This is a ghastly mistake, but it is typical of modern man. Thus slighted beyond endurance, the god deploys all his anarchic force in the form of a dream, Mann's account of which has to be quoted in full.

That night he had a fearful dream—if dream be the right word for a mental and physical experience which did indeed befall him in deep sleep, as a thing quite apart and real to his senses, yet without his seeing himself as present in it. Rather its theatre seemed to be his own soul, and the events burst in from the outside, violently overcoming the profound resistance of his spirit; passed him through and left him, left the whole cultural structure of a lifetime trampled on, ravaged, and destroyed.

The beginning was fear; fear and desire, with a shuddering curiosity. Night reigned, and his senses were on the alert; he heard loud, confused noises from far away, clamor and hubbub. There was a rattling, a crashing, a low dull thunder; shrill halloos and a kind of howl with a long-drawn u-sound at the end. And with all these, dominating them all, lute-notes of the cruelest sweetness, deep and cooing, keeping shamelessly on until the listener felt his very entrails bewitched. He heard a voice, naming, though darkly, that which was to come: "The stranger god!" A glow lighted up the surrounding mist and by it he recognized a mountain scene like that about his country home. From the wooded heights, from among the tree-trunks and crumbling moss-covered rocks, a troop came tumbling and raging down, a whirling rout of men and animals, and overflowed the hillside with flames and human forms, with clamour and the reeling dance. The females stumbled over the long, hairy pelts that dangled from their girdles; with heads flung back they uttered loud hoarse cries and shook their tambourines high in the air; brandished naked daggers or torches vomiting trails of sparks. They shrieked, holding their breasts in both hands; coiling snakes with quivering tongues they clutched about their waists. Horned and hairy males, girt about the loins with hides, drooped heads and lifted arms and thighs in unison, as they beat on brazen vessels that gave out droning thunder, or thumped madly on drums. There were troops of beardless youths armed with garlanded staves; these ran after goats and thrust their staves against the creature's flanks, then clung to the plunging horns and let themselves be borne off with triumphant shouts. And one and all the mad

rout yelled that cry, composed of soft consonants with a long-drawn u-
sound at the end, so sweet and wild it was together, and like nothing ever
heard before! It would ring through the air like the bellow of a challenging
stag, and be given back many-tongued; or they would use it to goad each
other on to dance with wild excess of tossing limbs—they never let it die.
But the deep, beguiling notes of the flute wove in and out and over all.
Beguiling too it was to him who struggled in the grip of these sights and
sounds, shamelessly awaiting the coming feast and the uttermost surrender.
He trembled, he shrank, his will was steadfast to preserve and uphold his
own god against this stranger who was sworn enemy to dignity and self-
control. But the mountain wall took up the noise and howling and gave it
back manifold; it rose high, swelled to a madness that carried him away. His
senses reeled in the steam of panting bodies, the acrid stench from the goats,
the odour as of stagnant waters—and another, too familiar smell—of
wounds, uncleanness, and disease. His heart throbbed to the drums, his
brain reeled, a blind rage seized him, a whirling lust, he craved with all his
soul to join the ring that formed about the obscene symbol of the godhead,
which they were unveiling and elevating, monstrous and wooden, while
from full throats they yelled their rallying cry. Foam dripped from their lips,
they drove each other on with lewd gesturings and beckoning hands. They
laughed, they howled, they thrust their pointed staves into each other's flesh
and licked the blood as it ran down. But now the dreamer was in them and
of them, the stranger god was his own. Yes, it was he who was flinging himself upon the animals, who bit and tore and swallowed smoking gobbets of
flesh—while on the trampled moss there now began the rites in honour of
the god, an orgy of promiscuous embraces—and in his very soul he tasted
the bestial degradation of his fall (*Death in Venice,* 66–8).

Before this frightful onslaught of the oldest of the gods, Aschenbach
capitulates. Far from surrendering to a higher power, he lets himself be de-
graded into a cosmeticized travesty of youth, allowing the Venetian barber
to turn him into a dandy. Finally he succumbs to the city's plague, contemplating his idol striding out into the lagoon. A curious touch, added by
Visconti in the film, has Tadzio eventually turn round and beckon his wor-
shipper to follow him out into the void.

Besides the evidence of literature, there is the evidence of life itself. The
gay community knows the nightly hunt for phallic meaning, when the
bars close and there is a feverish search for a partner for the night. People
remark on the frenetic nature of this behavior, for which promiscuity is not
an accurate term. It surely makes more sense as the blind attempt to come
to terms with a driving god, than as ordinary lust on a large scale—this is
an area where, as with the supernatural, common sense is a disaster. And

the very term homosexuality is becoming threadbare. In Lonergan's terms, it is description posing as explanation, which always lands you in trouble. Surely we have a more generic concept of the sexual dynamic in the mother-based exile of the phallic, the attempt to come to terms with which has as subsets the inflated lust for power in straight men and the more overt phallic quest in gay men. In the end, as we shall see, there is no "coming to terms" with this god. There is only the grace of feeling myself as gift, in which the god is transformed into spiritual energy.

The burden of *Death in Venice* is that modern man has no way to salvation such as is dramatized in ancient tales like "Satyricon." We are learning that this is not true. We are discovering again their "other gods" in the form of the "higher power," whose agent is, as theirs was, humiliation. Bill Wilson, the founder of Alcoholics Anonymous, spelled out and put into practice the insight of Jung, that addiction, of which the most potent form is the thraldom of the split-off phallos, cannot be healed from that quarter except insofar as from that quarter comes the bottoming-out demanding surrender to the higher power.

Thus if we put together the plight of modern man, manifest in "The Waste Land," and *Death in Venice,* and played out in contemporary society straight and gay, with the working of the Twelve Steps Program, we have the complete pattern, all its stages present. The extraordinarily wide applicability of the TSP shows that the Spirit is active in helping us to negotiate spiritual disintegration, which I am exploring in terms of male sexuality—in terms, that is, of the shape of our society, of its acceptance of the competitive as normative, of its tolerance of war, of its subjugation to what Paul calls the reign of death.

Now we must ask how Christianity has fared in all this. First, let us reflect on the Catholic priesthood in light of the pattern I have tried to discern. Second, and connected with our first consideration, the doctrine of the Virgin Birth and the role of the image of Jesus and Mary, Son and Mother. Finally, I come to Christianity's unchanging, never adequately understood, source of human transformation, the risen Jesus.

The celibate priesthood is extraordinarily symptomatic of the arrested condition of the Western male. We are the sons of Mother Church, our phallic energy exiled in obedience to her command. Our history shows, especially in the higher echelons of the priesthood, the resultant transformation of phallic energy into dominative power. And now our order is manifesting, to an embarrassing degree, the symptoms of denial, of resistance to the change which is being demanded of Western man generally. As we have spearheaded the earlier, and now unraveling phase of patriarchy, might we not be called on to play a creative role in the next phase? Certainly the "humiliation" stage is massively upon us, as dioceses are bankrupting themselves with lawsuits over our sexual irregularities. And at the other end, Rome is now overtly misogynistic, as the recent affair over the Czech priests shows. As someone put it to me recently, if you manage to follow the bouncing ball in the current Roman response to these men, you will see that it is woman.

It surely is helpful to locate these bizarre manifestations within a larger and deeper pattern, that suggested by the still arrested condition of the Western male.

Now for my reflections on the Virgin Birth of Christ. At first blush, this appears as the ultimate revelatory backing for the Mother-Son, domination-reverse-domination relationship. But when we look more closely into the doctrine, this changes dramatically. The Virgin Birth redeems the mother from the fate that is hers in a religion that has not seen beyond the cosmos, in other words, paganism: to be subject to man for her status as mother; to dominate man as son; to suffer the reversal of this domination as man, still the son emotionally, and *because* still the son emotionally, has to reverse this domination in nature to fashion a domination by the male through all the organs of culture. The Virgin Mother is subject to God alone. As a result she does not have to make that *first* reversal of domination by her man and dominate the Son, with whom, on the contrary, she is participant in the mystery of redemption, in which there is no Lordship, only participation. But throughout the Christian ages that have preceded us, the image of the Mother and the Son has been pulled into the overpowering magnetic field of the culture and reshaped after its pattern of domination and its reversal, the Mother dominating the Son as mother, the Son dominating the Mother as Lord. Domination-reversal has travestied the original revelatory pattern. It is this reshaped Mother-Son image that has displaced the spousal image that the story of the Fall, as interpreted by Phyllis Trible, offers as the divine paradigm for man and woman.

The reintegration of phallos humbled and restored to his partnership role, can look to the very beginning, where is revealed the status of man and woman in the perspective of the transcendent God. Mary is indeed a second Eve, for Eve in her turn is subject only to God—it is only by a gross but understandable mistranslation that she is seen as "coming out of the man." What God brings her out of is not a man, but an "earthling," sexually undifferentiated until God makes two of it, and then he cries out, in words suggestive of the Song of Songs, "behold bone of my bone, flesh of my flesh!" The pattern is God-dependent and spousal. It *falls* into the

God-independent dependency-and-its-reversal pattern, with which we are tragically familiar.

This is the point at which I find it appropriate to insert the account of a devastating experience I have had through reading Stephen Mitchell's *The Gospel According to Jesus* (New York, 1991). Let me start with the following words of Kierkegaard, quoted by Mitchell.

> We say that she was highly honoured among women. . . . It is true that Mary conceived the child in a miraculous fashion, but she nevertheless did it "after the manner of women" (Genesis 18:1), and pregnancy is a time of anxiety, distress, and paradox. It is true that the angel was a ministering spirit, but he wasn't a meddler: he did not appear to the other girls in Israel and say, "Don't despise Mary; the extraordinary is happening to her." The angel appeared only to Mary, and no one could understand her. Has any woman been as humiliated as Mary was, and isn't it true here also that the one whom God blesses he curses in the same breath? This is the Spirit's view of Mary, and she is not—it is revolting that I have to say this, but it is even more revolting that people have inanely and sanctimoniously depicted her this way—she is not a lady lounging in her gorgeous robes and playing with an infant god *(Fear and Trembling)*.

Matthew's account of the birth of Jesus is clearly answering the charge that Jesus was illegitimate, a charge that arose naturally from the fact that he was born too soon after Mary and Joseph came together. Matthew's explanation, of course, is that Jesus was conceived miraculously, but Mitchell does not accept this explanation, and sees Mary simply as an unwed mother. This is how the neighbors must have seen her. This is the situation that she and Jesus had to live with, and in those days this was a very tough thing to have to live with. Mitchell sees the relations between Jesus and his mother in this way, and finds as an important ingredient in Jesus' life the slowly reached forgiveness of his mother, an interpretation offensive to Catholic piety but inescapable if one rejects Matthew's miraculous explanation of the birth of Jesus. And even if one accepts this explanation, there were still the taunts of the neighbors and the inevitable tension introduced by these into the family itself.

The effect of my exposure to this natural interpretation of the birth of Jesus by a brilliantly persuasive writer proved to be devastating. I lay awake all night, not even dozing, while a voice in my head kept saying, over and over again, "She's nothing but a whore, and the Church has made her into the Madonna, it's all a huge fake!" I felt my faith draining away. But I remembered St. Ignatius's axiom that fear does not come from the good

Spirit, and I was full of fear, so I knew where the voice was not coming from.

The next day was awful, living physically on "reserve tanks" after a sleepless night, and with my mind in a complete turmoil.

The following night I slept deeply without dreams, and I woke up to a wonderful peace, a sense of total resolution. I knew this was of God, coming from a deeper level of myself than I was familiar with, at which the intellectual and the affective were fused. I could not put what I then understood into words, but some things became crystal clear, the chief one being that in the infinite mind concepts like legitimate and illegitimate do not exist. I think God gave me a glimpse of this mind, in which our petty social categories are nothing. He let his own Son be begotten out of wedlock to free us from our categories and tell us who we truly are, his own sons and daughters.

But we have ignored this, ignored the embarrassment Mary was put in by God. We have prettified the story, just as though Gabriel *had* gone around to all the other girls in the neighborhood telling them about Mary. We have lost touch with the woman who *inwardly* makes a surrender to God terrifying in its totality, and *outwardly* is exposed to the gossip of neighbors. In her stead, we have a dignified lady holding a ladylike conversation with a visiting angel.

The story of the Annunciation is exquisitely beautiful. And it is a story, coming out of a people who explained things by telling stories. What the story is explaining is the faith of the community in Jesus, shown to them as Son of God raised from the dead. It takes us back to his mystery where it begins as the Son of God in the womb of a consenting Mother. But what that consent was, how it shaped itself, what form it took in her ongoing life, this we cannot know. We only know that it cannot have been a sedate dialogue with a visiting angel. In collapsing the deep consent into the dialogue, we have disguised its terror and brought the mystery down to the level of Santa Claus.

We need to restore the mystery in all its starkness. The Word is made flesh. The flesh is the Mother's. The Mother is willing. That says it all.

It has taken an author who does not believe in the incarnation to force me to discover in myself, in the terror of a sleepless night filled with horrid voices, something of the fusion of the infinite with the finite condition, something of its huge silence, something of God's refusal to be put into our neat parcels of being. For I have to tell you that God did not deny the voice that said, "Mary is a whore!" He swallowed that voice in a vast silence whose only word is, "My ways are not your ways."

Of course my experience is a clear case of what Freud calls reaction formation, the way in which a situation too dreadful will reverse itself in the psyche to produce happiness. The notion, however, of reaction formation as a radical explanation depends on the assumption that ultimately reality is grim and sad, reaction formation a denial mechanism. This is the assumption under which Freud, and all modernity, works. Once it is denied, and joy reaffirmed as the most real, then reaction formation can be seen as mediating this reality in dire circumstances. The supreme instance of this is, of course, when he who "is joy for all ages" comes into his own among his own in the Upper Room, dissolving the reign of death. As Dan Maguire put it, "the primacy of joy is a minority report, filed by Christians and children."

Alas, we have preferred "our ways." We have substituted "the lady in her gorgeous robes playing with an infant god" for the awful mystery of Nazareth. The worst consequence of this is that when someone senses that this picture of Mary is legendary, senses the fairy-tale quality of the Christmas story, the person thinks she is losing the faith. In reality, this could be the *beginning* of faith, the possibility of tasting the real mystery of God in the flesh, as I think I did that night. Insofar as the Church has tied the mystery up in the legend, people feel that in seeing past the legend they are losing the faith. To greet the infant Jesus, we have made ourselves infantile. I once heard a young Jesuit saying in a sermon, "God said to Mary, 'I want to be one of you. How about it!'" I knew this was all wrong. He was so obviously pleased with himself. God comes down to the level of the flesh, not to the level of our cute little fantasies.

Piety has found in Mary seven sorrows. Seven is a perfect number, but there is an eighth, and it underlies and pervades them all: the suffering, at the world's hands, of the woman passive to God and not to man. The Word is made flesh. The flesh is the Mother's. The Mother is willing. That says it all. I am sure you will have realized that I have transplanted this experience, with the Christmas sermon it created, into my text, with results less than elegant. But there is surely a fit. I mean, there is a close connection, if not identity, between the cultural refashioning of the original Jesus-Mary image into the reverse-domination pattern, and the prettifying of the nativity story. What both add up to is a model of mother and son that says to women, "You are virgins, until you are mothers," and to men, "You are sons not spouses." The spousal image, the whole mediation of the Song of Songs, is excluded.

We cannot begin to deal with the question of whether the Virgin Birth is to be taken "literally" until we have recovered its spiritual significance from what two millennia of sexually immature Christian humanity have made of it: a mother-son pattern from which phallos is banished and therefore still "outstanding" (if the pun may be allowed!) that has so powerfully reinforced the split image of Christian man, sexually dominating and spiritually sexless, of Christian woman as virgin and mother but never as spouse.

Finally, I am beginning to recognize the perspective in which the transformation of male sexuality has to be seen, the perspective of gift or grace.

Everyone's life is a journey. Northrop Fry has been able to find only three images of our life that are common to all cultures and all times: of marriage as union with the Godhead, of the shared meal as divine participation, and of life as a journey. The journey is most poorly understood as linear. It is most truly understood as a progressive centering, a growing toward the light, a becoming light. By far the most quoted lines in modern poetry are those of Eliot: "And the end of all our exploring/Will be to arrive where we started/And know the place for the first time."

The center is where I come to know, in every fiber of my being, that I am gift. If I am a gift, there is a giver. And if I *am* the gift, there is no me to whom the gift is made. The giver, then, gives not "to me" but "to be," gives to be to that which is not, and thus is being-itself, in respect of which I am not. To be nothing before God is the ecstasy of the creature, as Eckhart makes clear—or obscure. Catherine of Siena hears in prayer, "I am who is, you are who is not."

Toward this supreme truth of myself as gifted I am drawn as to a magnetic center. But the center has a power to draw that far exceeds all philosophical understanding, and that overcomes the huge resistance and systemic bias that we call sin. Here the sense of being nothing but gift, of not being anything for the giver to give to, of not having this solid substantive self that resists description as givenness-to-nothing, here at the center is the mystery that is Jesus, God's gift not to God but to us.

This emptiness of self finds expression in a willed death by violence that in any other than a divine person would be suicidal. He could die for others only because he lived not for himself but for the all-encompassing mystery. He empties himself because he is radically empty of self. This perfection of death as love and of love as death is the vibrant heart of all existence, and we feel its attraction in the words of Paul: "For the love of Christ overwhelms us when we consider that if one man died for all, then all have died; his purpose in dying for all was that those who live should live not any more for themselves, but for him who died and was raised to life" (2 Cor 5:14-15). In this saying of Paul we have Jesus the liberator of desire. For what is implied is, that we do not *want* to live for ourselves, but without Jesus we find we have to.

Jesus became this center for desire, became all of himself, once he had died: for then he could make himself known fully to his own. The presence that comes upon those in the Upper Room is neither of the dead nor of the living, but of him who liberates our desire from these categories. This is how the tradition knows, from the beginning, that he descended into the realm of the dead to embrace this in the sweep of his new life. In the new age of Christ, there is no more living and dead, as there is no more male and female, Jew and Gentile, slave and free. His God, who is "not of the dead but of the living," is now ours.

It is of the first importance, for the whole work of transformation to which we are called in our time, to hold firmly in focus the presence of the risen Jesus, for it is in this presence that we come to know ourselves as gift, and it is only in so knowing ourselves that we can have that fullness of self-love that liberates phallos from the *libido dominandi*. The conclusion that powerfully emerges from the work of Pheme Perkins on the resurrection (*Resurrection: New Testament Witness and Contemporary Reflection*, Garden City, 1984) is that the heart of the resurrection faith is a new presence of Jesus to the community. Faith knows the risen Jesus as its source: so it knows that it is not the source of the risenness of Jesus. To opt for the latter view is to have a different concept of faith from the Catholic, a concept that is really hope in disguise, a faith of which hope is the center. I know that my Redeemer liveth. I do not hope that my Redeemer liveth. To explain the difference between the two positions, however, is, according to Rowan Williams, the most difficult task in resurrection theology (*Resurrection: Interpeting the Easter Gospel*, New York, 1984). And the most necessary: faith, at its birthplace, seeking understanding.

Finally, to claim for Jesus the uniqueness, in all times and places, that Christianity must claim for him, and to mean by this claim anything short of what he reveals of himself in dissolving the reign of death, to make it refer to him as otherwise known, for instance as teacher, as exemplar, is to make of Christianity a monstrous dwarfing of the ineffable to our pathetic human measure. Christianity will outgrow this harmful and cruel imposition on other faiths, only when it rediscovers the risen presence in its midst, and behaves accordingly.

Here in conclusion are two didactic sonnets.

> Mother and Son, the languor of the west,
> Reduce man to the hero pleasing her

Never to give her of his truly best
But hold it high, the lonely conqueror.

The Virgin Mother we have paganized
Into the goddess of divided man,
Forgotten her first freedom that, God-sized,
Engages her in God's salvific plan

That, older than the oldest of the gods,
Espouses him so man may at last grow
To phallic fullness that is not at odds
With the first giftedness he comes to know.

The axle-tree long bedded in neglect
Shall find its bed of love and recollect.

* * * * *

This giver gives not to me but to be:
Conversely, then, to be is to receive.
Can the self given make response in me?
This too is gift, given us to believe

And know in deed: the one we crucified
Afterwards came among us, and we were
Taken through the opening in his side
Where death dissolves in light its opener.

The story has bewitched me for too long
For me not to be sure it is my own.
But can I let it reach into my wrong
Done me and by me leaving me alone?

Can I connect, calling for total loss,
The folly of myself and of the cross?

Select Bibliography of
Dom Sebastian Moore, O.S.B.

Books

Before the Deluge. With Anselm Hurt. Westminster: Newman Press, 1968.

The Crucified Jesus Is No Stranger. New York: Seabury Press, 1977.

The Dreamer Not the Dream. With Kevin Maguire. London: Darton, Longman and Todd; Glen Rock: Newman Press, 1970.

The Experience of Prayer. With Kevin Maguire. London: Darton, Longman and Todd, 1969.

The Fire and the Rose Are One. New York: Seabury Press, 1980.

God Is a New Language. London: Darton, Longman and Todd; Westminster: Newman Press, 1967.

The Inner Loneliness. New York: Crossroad, 1982.

Jesus the Liberator of Desire. New York: Crossroad, 1989.

Let This Mind Be in You: The Quest for Identity through Oedipus to Christ. Minneapolis: Winston Press, 1985.

No Exit. London: Darton, Longman and Todd; Glen Rock: Newman Press, 1968.

Articles

"The Affirmation of Order: Therapy for Modernity in Bernard Lonergan's Analysis of Judgment," *Lonergan Workshop,* vol. 8 (1990) 109–33.

"Analogy and the Free Mind," *Downside Review* 76 (1958) 1–28.

"Analogy: A Retraction and a Challenge," *Downside Review* 76 (1958) 125–48.

"Analogy and Karl Barth," *Downside Review* 71 (1952–53) 175–80.

"Author's Response," in "Review Symposium: Three Perspectives" (on *Jesus the Liberator of Desire*, with Stephen J. Duffy, Elisabeth Koenig, and William P. Loewe), *Horizons* 18 (1991) 123–9.

"Bishops' Dilemma: The Cruel Irony of Deterrence," *Commonweal* (September 24, 1982) 484–5.

"A Catholic Neurosis?" *The Clergy Review* 46 (1961) 641–7.

"Christ Today," *Catholic World* 206 (1967) 109–10.

"Christian Self-Discovery," *Lonergan Workshop,* vol. 1 (1978) 187–221.

"The Communication of a Dangerous Memory," in *Communicating a Dangerous Memory: Soundings in Political Theology. Supplementary Issue of the Lonergan Workshop Journal Volume 6* (1987) 55–61.

"The Communication of a Dangerous Memory," in Timothy P. Fallon and Philip Boo Riley, eds. *Religion and Culture: Essays in Honor of Bernard Lonergan, S.J.* (Albany: State University of New York Press, 1987) 237–41.

"Consciousness," *Downside Review* 75 (1957) 305–24.

"Crisis over Contraception," *The Tablet* 243 (7 October 1989) 1146–8.

"Critical and Symbolic Realism: Lonergan and Coleridge," *Lonergan Workshop*, vol. 12 (1996) 147–78.

"Death as the Delimiting of Desire: A Key Concept in Soteriology," in Stephen Kepnes and David Tracy, eds. *The Challenge of Psychology to Faith* (Edinburgh: T & T Clark; New York: Seabury, 1982) 51–6.

"The Discovery of Metaphysics—One Man's War," in *Spirit as Inquiry: Lonergan Festschrift* (Chicago: Saint Xavier College, 1964) 120–4.

"The Easter Egg," *New Blackfriars* 48 (1967) 517–20.

"An Empty Tomb Revisited," *Downside Review* 99 (1981) 239–47.

"Experiencing the Resurrection," *Commonweal* 109 (January 29, 1982) 47–9.

"F. R. Leavis: A Memoir," *Method: Journal of Lonergan Studies* 1 (1983) 214–22.

"For a Soteriology of the Existential Subject," in Matthew L. Lamb, ed. *Creativity and Method: Essays in Honor of Bernard Lonergan, S.J.* (Milwaukee, Wisc.: Marquette University Press, 1981) 229–47.

"For Bernard Lonergan," in F. E. Crowe and R. M. Doran, eds. *Compass: A Jesuit Journal: Special Issue* (March 1985) 9.

"Foreword" to *Lonergan, Spirituality, and the Meeting of Religions,* by Vernon Gregson (Lanham, N.Y.: University Press of America, 1985).

"The Forming and Transforming of Ego: An Explanatory Psychology of Soteriology," *Lonergan Workshop,* vol. 8 (1980) 165–89.

"God Suffered," *Downside Review* 77 (1958–59) 122–40.

"*Hamlet* and the Affective Roots of Decision," *Lonergan Workshop,* vol. 7 (1988) 179–202.

"In Water and in Blood," *Lonergan Workshop,* vol. 11 (1995) 91–104.

"The 'Infallible' Temptation," *Commonweal* (October 10, 1986) 525–7.

"The Instruction of Adults," *Downside Review* 74 (1956) 157–64.

"Jesus the Liberator of Desire: Reclaiming Ancient Images," *Cross Currents* 40 (1990) 477–98.

"Jesus the Liberator of Desire: Reclaiming Ancient Images," *Downside Review* 108 (1990) 1–19.

"The Language of Love," *Lonergan Workshop,* vol. 3 (1982) 83–105.

Letter, "Moore's Defense," *Crisis* 8/7 (July–August 1990) 10–1.

Letter, "A Stand on Contraception," *The Tablet* 243 (8 April 1989) 393.

Letter, "The Teaching on Contraception," *The Tablet* 243 (1 July 1989) 755.

Letter, "The Teaching on Contraception," *The Tablet* 243 (29 July 1989) 867–8. Answer to July 15 letter of John Finnis.

Letter, "The Teaching on Contraception," *The Tablet* 243 (9 September 1989) 1027.

"Life, Death, and Resurrection: Notes Toward a Theology of Redemption," *The Clergy Review* 48 (1963) 203–16.

"The Logic of Unity," *The Tablet* (24 May 1958) 489–90.

"The Mass as an Offering: A Note," *Downside Review* 70 (1951–52) 130–3.

"The New Life," in *Lonergan Workshop,* vol. 5 (1985) 145–62.

"The New Life," *The Way* 24 (1984) 42–52.

"Night Thoughts of a Christian," *Downside Review* 102 (1984) 235–42.

"On Quenching the Spirit," *Downside Review* 74 (1956) 1–7.

"Original Sin, Sex, Resurrection, and Trinity," *Lonergan Workshop,* vol. 4 (1983) 85–98.

"Out of This World," *The Clergy Review* 50 (1965) 579–86.

"Persons and Metaphysic," *New Blackfriars* 49 (1968) 233–6.

"Philosophical Insight," *The Month* 22 (1959) 102–7.

"Ratzinger's 'Nature' Isn't Natural: Aquinas, Contraception, and Statistics," *Commonweal* 117 (January 26, 1990) 49–52.

"Realism or Empiricism?" *The Clergy Review* 46 (1961) 98–103.

"Reflections on Death," *Downside Review* 70 (1951–52) 373–83.

"Reflections on Death—II," *Downside Review* 71 (1952–53) 14–24.

"Reflections on the Thought of Sartre," *Downside Review* 72 (1953–54) 146–52.

"The Resurrection: A Confusing Paradigm Shift," *Downside Review* 98 (1980) 257–66.

"Rhythm and Psalmody," *Clergy Review* 30 (1945) 72–7.

"The Search for the Beginning," in S. Sykes, ed. *Christ, Faith and History* (London: Cambridge University Press, 1972) 79–94.

"The Secular Implications of Liturgy," in Nicholas Lash, ed. *The Christian Priesthood* (London: Darton, Longman and Todd, 1970).

"Self-Love: The Challenge to Theology," *Compass: A Jesuit Journal* 8/4 (September 1990) 32–5.

"Sex, God, and the Church," in Mary Anne Huddleston, ed. *Celibate Loving: Encounters in Three Dimensions* (Ramsey/New York: Paulist Press, 1984).

"Some Principles for an Adequate Theism," *Downside Review* 95 (1977) 201–12.

"Spirituality and the Primacy of the Dramatic Pattern of Living," *Lonergan Workshop*, vol. 10 (1994) 279–96.

"The Theology of the Mass and the Liturgical Datum," *Downside Review* 69 (1950–51) 31–44.

"Towards a Eucharistic Definition of Sacrifice," *Downside Review* 69 (1950–51) 428–39.

"The Word of God: Kerygma and Theorem, A Note," *The Heythrop Journal* 5 (1964) 268–75.

Index of Names